THE JOURNAL OF ESTHER EDWARDS BURR

The Journal of Esther Edwards Burr
1754–1757

Edited, with an Introduction, by
Carol F. Karlsen and Laurie Crumpacker

YALE UNIVERSITY PRESS
NEW HAVEN AND LONDON

Designed by Nancy Ovedovitz and set in Garamond No. 3 type by Eastern Typesetting Company. Printed in the United States of America by Edwards Brothers Inc., Ann Arbor, Michigan.

Library of Congress Cataloging in Publication Data

Burr, Esther Edwards.
  The journal of Esther Edwards Burr, 1754–1757.
  Includes bibliographical references and index.
  1. Burr, Esther Edwards. 2. Wives—United States—Biography. 3. Burr family. 4. Women—United States—History—18th century. I. Karlsen, Carol F., 1940–   . II. Crumpacker, Laurie, 1941–   . III. Title.
E302.6.B93A4   1984   973.2'6'0924   [B] 83-16958
ISBN 0-300-02900-4

Grateful acknowledgment is made to the following institutions for permission to publish documents in their manuscript collections:

Yale University Library, for the Journal of Mrs. Esther Burr addressed to Miss Sarah Prince of Boston, October 1754–September 1757, in the Beinecke Rare Book and Manuscript Library; and for one letter in the Burr Family Papers, Sterling Memorial Library.

Franklin Trask Library, Andover Newton Theological School, for nine letters.

Department of Rare Books and Manuscripts, Boston Public Library, by courtesy of the Trustees, for one letter and an excerpt from the journal of Sarah Prince Gill.

Congregational Library of the American Congregational Association, Boston, for one letter.

Princeton University Library, for one letter in the Aaron Burr Collection.

10   9   8   7   6   5   4   3   2   1

CONTENTS

PREFACE

This book has been a long time coming. Nearly a decade has passed since the day we met at an impromptu women's caucus at an American Studies conference and discovered our mutual interest in the obscure letter-journal of Esther Edwards Burr. We were both just beginning course work toward our Ph.D.s, and the idea of publishing the journal was barely thinkable. Completion of our individual seminar papers on the journal seemed task enough at hand. But over the next couple of years, a growing friendship and working relationship emerged from our common interest in "Esther"—and in the eighteenth-century evangelical sisterhood of which she was a part. When the subject of editing the journal did come up, it was never a question of who would do it, only how the effort would be shared. Thus it has remained.

Without the help and encouragement of numerous other people, however, this book would still be a long way off. We would like here to thank them all, and to acknowledge by name those to whom we are most indebted.

To Kathryn Kish Sklar we owe our appreciation of her enthusiastic support of this project, almost from its inception. Jeanne Boydston and Nancy F. Cott, equally convinced of the value of Esther Burr's journal for students of women's history, nudged us along when we seemed to bog down and took the time to read and critique our introduction. Edmund S. Morgan and Norman Pettit, our advisors in graduate school, not only read patiently more than one draft of our interpretive essays but, along with David D. Hall, provided invaluable advice on editing the journal. At crucial stages of our work, and in numerous ways, Anne T. Margolis, Christine Stansell, and Cecelia Tichi also offered their encouragement and criticism.

At the time when the original ideas for the introduction were taking shape, we were each members of a women's history study group, one in Boston, one in New Haven. Our friends there read and commented on our work as it developed. For both their support and their insights, we are grateful to Judith Babbitts, the late Hannah Bewick, Claudia Bushman, Anne Farnam, Miriam Hansen, Barbara Hobson, Nikki Irvine, Eugenia Kaledin, Polly Kaufman, Louise Knauer, Elaine Lawless, Susan Porter, Betty Reinhardt, Louise Stevenson, Donna Vanderheiden, Candice Waid, and Susan Walton. We also wish to thank Anne Boylan, Linda Henry, Alice S. Rossi, and Carroll Smith-Rosenberg for their comments on early drafts of our work and Philip Greven, Mary Beth Norton, and Patricia J. Tracy for their interest and assistance during later stages.

Several other persons and institutions offered special assistance for which we are grateful. Though they may have forgotten by now, James Axtell and Carolyn Forrey first let us know of the journal's existence. Yale University granted us permission to publish it, and Marjorie Wynne at the Beinecke Rare Book and Manuscript Library kindly made the arrangements and aided us in several other particulars. Other members of the Beinecke and Sterling Memorial Library staffs, Dianna Yount at Andover Newton Theological School, and the librarians at Princeton were all enormously helpful. At Princeton, James McLachlan generously allowed us to read his then-unpublished *Princetonians, 1748–1768,* which greatly facilitated our identification of persons mentioned in the journal. Ruth Hirsch of Simmons College and Nancy Jones took on the onerous task of typing the final manuscript. Laura Spencer, Keith Edwards, and Gerry Pearlberg, students at Bard College, and Kristin Peterson helped with many of the last details.

Finally, for believing in the importance of both our work and Esther's, our deepest appreciation goes to our respective families—Stephen, Flint, and Clyde Crumpacker, Elena and Flint Taylor; and Kirsten and Todd Harvey, Brooke Karlsen, Manuel Ayala, and Jeanne Boydston.

NOTE TO THE READER

The original copy of Esther Burr's letter-journal, held in Beinecke Rare Book and Manuscript Library at Yale University, is identified and described as "The Journal of Mrs. Esther Burr addressed to Miss Sarah Prince of Boston, October 1754–September 1757." Its 354 pages are published here in their complete form for the first time.[1]

In preparing the text for publication, we have maintained the author's own style. The schooling she received as a girl was unusual for her time and reflected her family's social and economic position; yet it was not comparable to that given the boys in the Edwards and Burr families. The letters follow the erratic habits of spelling, punctuation, and capitalization that were common among the women in her family. In order to allow for gender and class comparisons, we have modernized only to clarify material that would otherwise be obscure or ambiguous.

With a few exceptions, the author's spelling has been preserved as it appears in the manuscript. When the meaning of a word is unclear, we have retained it as written, followed by the correct spelling in italics within a square bracket. Subsequent usages of the same word have been silently corrected, as have spelling errors that appear to be "slips of the pen." Capitalization remains as written, except that we have capitalized the first letter of a sentence following

---

1. Although at the turn of this century, District of Columbia clergyman and Howard University president Jeremiah E. Rankin published a "ladies' gift book" entitled *Esther Burr's Journal,* readers should be aware that this journal is not Esther Burr's own. Rankin apparently had access to the original manuscript, for he quoted directly from it in the final pages of his volume. But the woman he portrayed is largely a creation of his imagination. We suspect that he did not publish the real journal because it did not present the model of uncomplaining piety and devotion to husband and family that he desired for Victorian women. Copies of Rankin's book are rare, but a second-edition volume (Washington, D.C.: Howard University Print, 1902) can be found in Sterling Library, Yale University.

a period. The letters *s* and *j,* uniformly capitalized in colonial writings, have been lowered. However, the words *sister* and *son* have not been altered, as Burr normally capitalized the words *brother* and *daughter.*

Punctuation has also been preserved. We have provided additional periods and commas only when the sense would otherwise be lost. Burr often separated her thoughts with dots and dashes. These have been retained, except that dots have been reduced to three (four at the end of a sentence). We have eliminated her superfluous dashes, those accompanying other punctuation or used decoratively at the end of a line. Where Burr underlined her words, they appear here in italics.

In general, abbreviations and contractions have been kept in their original form except when their meaning is unclear. Other exceptions are *&, &c, yt,* and *ye,* which have been regularized to *and, etc., that,* and *the.* Names and places in abbreviated form have also been expanded. For instance, E———n appears here as Elizabeth Town, retaining her normal spelling. Raised letters have been lowered and apostrophes and quotation marks raised. While the date, place, salutation, and complimentary closing remain as the author wrote them, for ease of reference we have added the day, month, and year at the beginning of each entry.

Where ambiguous, spelling, punctuation, capitalization, and abbreviations have been presented in their modern form.

Marginalia have been incorporated into the body of the text within parentheses. If the author's intention is unclear, we have added the material where it logically belongs. If the passage does not fit easily into the text, we have added it at the end of the journal entry or subjoined it in a note. Burr's pagination is at times confusing and repetitious; therefore, we have eliminated her individual page numbers. She also numbered the letters in a series, as they were usually hand-carried to Boston at irregular intervals. These packet numbers have been retained and appear at the beginning of each series.

Textual problems have been treated as follows: (1) Mutilated or illegible words are indicated by three dots within square brackets (or four dots at the end of a sentence). If the words are conjecturable, we have inserted them in square brackets. If we are unsure of our conjecture, we have followed the bracketed words with a question mark. (2) Deleted material appears as dots within angle brackets. (3) Words that Burr apparently left out but that are necessary for clarity we have added in italics and placed in square brackets, as we have all other editorial insertions and emendations.

One final note on persons mentioned in the journal. It has been relatively easy to identify most of the men who appear, since they were often college graduates and/or prominent figures of their time. The women, on the other hand, who were denied access to colleges and have usually been recognized in historical records only as men's wives and mothers, are difficult to discuss in any but familial terms, if at all. To avoid perpetuating this bias but at the same time to facilitate research in either men's or women's history, whenever possible we have described these people in terms of their relationship to the author and with biographical information common to women and men alike (such as place of residence, family origin, etc.). When known, men's occupations are usually recorded, but for the sake of balance and brevity, we have focused on the period the journal covers, leaving largely unnoted the extensive political work many of these men later engaged in as either patriots or loyalists.

Each identification is followed by a reference or two, which should be read simply as a starting point for future research. Because wives and husbands are often discussed separately in the journal, we have identified both the first time one of them appears, referring the reader to that note when Burr mentions the other. If no footnote follows someone's name, we have not found any information on that person.

ABBREVIATIONS

AND	Manuscript Collections, Franklin Trask Library, Andover Newton Theological School, Newton Centre, Massachusetts.
BPL	Manuscript Collections, Boston Public Library, Boston, Massachusetts.
DAB	*Dictionary of American Biography,* by Allen Johnson and Dumas Malone (New York: Charles Scribner's Sons, 1928–).
Dexter	*Biographical Sketches of the Graduates of Yale College . . . ,* by Franklin Bowditch Dexter (New York and New Haven: Henry Holt and Co., 1885–1912).
DNB	*Dictionary of National Biography,* by Leslie Stephen and Sidney Lee (London: Oxford University Press, 1885–).
Edwards Genealogy	*Timothy and Rhoda Ogden Edwards . . . A Genealogy,* compiled by William H. Edwards (Cincinnati: Robert Clarke, 1903).
McLachlan	*Princetonians, 1748–1768: A Biographical Dictionary,* by James McLachlan (Princeton: Princeton University Press, 1976).
NEHGR	*New England Historical and Genealogical Register* (Boston: Samuel G. Drake and the New England Historic Genealogical Society, 1847–).
OED	*The Oxford English Dictionary: A New English Dictionary on Historical Principles* (Oxford: Clarendon Press, 1888–).
Princeton	Manuscript Collections, Princeton University Library, Princeton, New Jersey.

Sibley

Biographical Sketches of the Graduates of Harvard University . . . , by John Langdon Sibley (Cambridge: Charles William Sever, 1873–85), continued as *Sibley's Harvard Graduates . . . Biographical Sketches of Those Who Attended Harvard College . . . ,* by Clifford Kenyon Shipton (Cambridge and Boston: Massachusetts Historical Society, 1933–).

Webster

A History of the Presbyterian Church in America . . . , by Richard Webster (Philadelphia: Joseph M. Wilson, 1857).

Wheeler

The Ogden Family in America . . . , compiled by William Ogden Wheeler (Philadelphia: J. B. Lippincott, 1907).

Yale

Manuscript Collections, Sterling Memorial Library, Yale University, New Haven, Connecticut.

PART I

Introduction

In October 1754, Esther Burr began to keep an almost daily record of her thoughts and activities, a practice she continued for nearly three years. This was no ordinary diary; nor was it meant solely for her own eyes. She wrote the journal as a series of letters, which she gathered up every few weeks and sent off in packets to Boston to Sarah Prince, her closest friend. Sarah Prince kept a comparable journal for Esther Burr.

Like so many women's writings, Sarah Prince's half of this correspondence has not survived, but fortunately Esther Burr's journal has.[1] We know relatively little about colonial women's day-to-day experiences, and even less about their perceptions of themselves and the world in which they lived.[2] Unusually detailed and intimate, Esther Burr's journal offers twentieth-century readers a rare glimpse into both the public and private life of an articulate and spirited eighteenth-century woman.

1. Sarah Prince (1728–71), after 1759 Sarah Prince Gill, did leave a journal of meditations dated October 23, 1743–March 17, 1745 and January 1, 1756–June 17, 1764. This manuscript is in the Rare Book and Manuscript Collection of Boston Public Library. An excerpt from this journal is included in the present volume, and a transcript of the complete document, edited by Rebecca Husman, is available in Kellogg Library, Bard College.

2. Until quite recently, scholarship on colonial women and family life has tended to stress unique economic and social opportunities afforded white women by the conditions of early settlement—sometimes directly contrasting the "favorable" position of these women with that of their European foremothers and/or their nineteenth- and twentieth-century descendants. This interpretation, based on such pioneer studies as Alice Morse Earle, *Colonial Dames and Good Wives* (Boston and New York: Houghton Mifflin, 1895), and Elisabeth Anthony Dexter, *Colonial Women of Affairs: A Study of Women in Business and the Professions in America before 1776* (Boston and New York: Houghton Mifflin, 1924), is apparent in most monographs that touch on women in the colonial period. Focusing on either parts or the whole of this view, new studies have raised serious questions about its validity. For the best sustained critique, see the works of Mary Beth Norton, especially "The Myth of the Golden Age," in Carol Ruth Berkin and Mary Beth Norton, eds., *Women of America: A History* (Boston: Houghton Mifflin, 1979), pp. 37–47, and *Liberty's Daughters: The Revolutionary Experience of American Women, 1750–1800* (Boston: Little, Brown, 1980). Another excellent reinterpretation is Laurel Thatcher Ulrich, *Good Wives: Image and Reality in the Lives of Women in*

Recent colonial studies have drawn attention to variations in the experience of women from different class, racial, regional, and religious backgrounds and have begun to account for significant changes over generations and over the course of individual life cycles.[3] To suggest, therefore, that Esther Burr's journal reveals something about colonial women is not to say that her life was in any way typical. Most significantly, Burr was born into one of New England's elite families, and she married into another—a class background that set her apart from most women. At a time when few females were able

---

Northern New England, 1650–1750 (New York: Alfred A. Knopf, 1982). Other revisions can be found in Alexander Keyssar, "Widowhood in Eighteenth-Century Massachusetts: A Problem in the History of the Family," *Perspectives in American History* 8 (1974): 83–119; Nancy F. Cott, "Divorce and the Changing Status of Women in Eighteenth-Century Massachusetts," *William and Mary Quarterly,* 3d ser., 33 (1976): 586–614; Mary Maples Dunn, "Saints and Sisters: Congregational and Quaker Women in the Early Colonial Period," *American Quarterly* 30 (Winter 1978): 582–601; Lyle Koehler, *A Search for Power: The "Weaker Sex" in Seventeenth-Century New England* (Urbana, Ill.: University of Illinois Press, 1980); and Carol F. Karlsen, *The Devil in the Shape of a Woman: Witchcraft in Seventeenth-Century New England* (New York: W. W. Norton, forthcoming).

3. See, for example, Norton, *Liberty's Daughters,* esp. pp. 4–39, and "A Cherished Spirit of Independence: The Life of an Eighteenth-Century Boston Businesswoman," in Berkin and Norton, *Women of America,* pp. 48–67; Ulrich, *Good Wives,* pp. 13–34, 68–86, 226–35; Julie A. Matthaei, *An Economic History of Women in America: Women's Work, the Sexual Division of Labor, and the Development of Capitalism* (New York: Schocken Books, 1982), pp. 28–97; Russell R. Menard, "The Maryland Slave Population, 1658–1730: A Demographic Profile of Blacks in Four Counties," *William and Mary Quarterly,* 3d ser., 32 (January 1975): 29–54; Douglas Lamar Jones, "The Strolling Poor: Transiency in Eighteenth-Century Massachusetts," *Journal of Social History* (Spring 1975): 28–54; Lois Green Carr and Lorena S. Walsh, "The Planter's Wife: The Experience of White Women in Seventeenth-Century Maryland," in Nancy F. Cott and Elizabeth H. Pleck, eds., *A Heritage of Her Own: Toward a New Social History of American Women* (New York: Simon and Schuster, 1979), pp. 25–57; Robert V. Wells, *Revolutions in Americans' Lives: A Demographic Perspective on the History of Americans, Their Families, and Their Society* (Westport, Conn.: Greenwood Press, 1982), pp. 3–88; Daniel Scott Smith and Michael S. Hindus, "Premarital Pregnancy in America 1640–1971: An Overview and Interpretation," *Journal of Interdisciplinary History* 4 (Spring 1975): 537–70; and Ann D. Gordon and Mari Jo Buhle, "Sex and Class in Colonial and Nineteenth-Century America," in Berenice A. Carroll, ed., *Liberating Women's History: Theoretical and Critical Essays* (Urbana, Ill.: University of Illinois Press, 1976), pp. 278–300.

to acquire more than rudimentary skills in reading and writing, she received an education in her home which rivaled that of the majority of colonial men.[4] Because of her privileged background she had not only the ability but also the time to write. The careful preservation of her journal for more than two hundred years further attests to the unusual status of the Edwards and Burr families.

In spite of her unusual position, however, Burr shared with other northern colonial women of her time a set of historical circumstances of critical importance to her sex. The eighteenth century witnessed rapid growth of commercial centers, increasingly unequal distribution of wealth, rising populations of Afro-American slaves and ethnically and religiously diverse immigrant groups, successive migrations west, north, and southward into sparsely settled regions, clashes of religious denominations and of cultural values, growth of higher educational institutions as training centers for the professions—all of which contributed to the distinct texture of eighteenth-century life. The impact of such developments on women's social and economic roles was enormous, particularly as the northern colonies began the transition from a domestic to a market economy and as the religious values that had played a determining role in shaping colonial institutions were challenged by the mores of the marketplace. Although these changes were not fully apparent until the advent of large-scale manufacturing in the early nineteenth century, for Esther Burr, as for a significant number of other women coming of age in the mid-eighteenth century, they were already palpable.[5]

4. For estimates of female literacy based on signatures on wills, see Kenneth A. Lockridge, *Literacy in Colonial New England: An Inquiry into the Social Context of Literacy in the Early Modern West* (New York: W. W. Norton, 1974), pp. 4, 39–42, 52–58.

5. Although the sources referred to above in note 3 often touch on the effect of these broad changes on women's lives, few studies are careful to distinguish periods within the larger colonial era. For works that do make these distinctions and specifically address the early and mid-eighteenth century, see especially Wells, *Revolutions in Americans' Lives,* pp. 3–88; Mary Beth Norton's forthcoming article in *American Historical Review,* tentatively entitled "The Evolution of Women's Experience in Early America"; and Jeanne Boydston's forthcoming dissertation, tentatively entitled "Home and Work: The Industrialization of Housework in the United States" (Yale University).

Thus, while Esther Burr's journal remains distinctly the record of one woman's response to the events of her time, the ways in which she came to terms with these conditions were not unique. For this reason the journal also illuminates for us some of the larger contours of American women's history.

The Valley Years

Esther Edwards Burr was born in Northampton, Massachusetts, February 13, 1732, the third of Jonathan and Sarah Pierpont Edwards's eleven children. Her father, regarded by scholars today as the most important American theologian of the eighteenth century, was then minister of Northampton's Congregational church and a leader and principal defender of the series of religious revivals known as the Great Awakening.[6] Trained for the ministry at Yale, he was one of a long family line of prominent Calvinists. His grandfather, Solomon Stoddard, was known as the "Pope" of the Connecticut Valley, so influential was his church leadership in the late seventeenth and early eighteenth centuries; and his grandmother, Esther Warham Mather Stoddard, led women's prayer groups throughout her long life. Rumored to have been even more forceful and learned than her husband, Esther Stoddard's example had a particularly powerful influence on three generations of Edwards women.

Though a less familiar historical figure than her husband Jonathan, Sarah Pierpont Edwards is also well known to students of colonial religion. At the height of the Great Awakening in 1742, Sarah Edwards underwent a mystical religious experience, the nature of which she carefully recorded at her husband's request. A year later, in a major defense of the Awakening, Jonathan published a close

6. For an overview of the Great Awakening in New England, see Sydney E. Ahlstrom, *A Religious History of the American People* (New Haven: Yale University Press, 1972), pp. 280–94. A more detailed account of the New England revivals can be found in Edwin S. Gaustad, *The Great Awakening in New England* (New York: Harpers, 1957). On Jonathan Edwards's life and work, see Ola Elizabeth Winslow, *Jonathan Edwards, 1703–1758* (New York: Macmillan Co., 1940), and Perry Miller, *Jonathan Edwards* (New York: William Sloan, 1949). For a fine study of Edwards and his community, see Patricia J. Tracy, *Jonathan Edwards, Pastor: Religion and Society in Eighteenth-Century Northampton* (New York: Hill and Wang, 1979).

account of her experience, presenting it as a model of conversion and encouraging other Christians to emulate it.[7] Like Jonathan, Sarah was descended from a family of religious leaders. Her great-grandfather, first-generation Puritan minister Thomas Hooker, had begun the settlement of Connecticut; and her father, James Pierpont, was pastor of New Haven's First Church and a founder of Yale. From her youth, Sarah was reported to have been unusually pious and well-versed in religious matters.[8]

The Edwardses' marriage was, in the words of Jonathan Edwards, an "uncommon union,"[9] and the intimate environment in which Esther grew up was described by family friends in glowing terms. Samuel Hopkins, Jonathan's biographer and a frequent visitor to the Northampton parsonage, said of Jonathan and Sarah's relationship that "no person of discerning could be conversant in the family without observing and admiring the great harmony, and mutual love and esteem that subsisted between them."[10] Their affection and regard for one another apparently carried over to their relationships with their children. Despite the birth of a child nearly every two years and the presence of a succession of live-in ministerial students, there seems to have been little observable family discord. Joseph Emerson, one of Esther's early suitors, remarked that the Edwardses were "the most agreeable Family I was ever acquainted with."[11]

Of Esther during her Northampton years we know very little.

7. Sarah Edwards's version of her religious experience is in Sereno E. Dwight, *The Life of President Edwards* (New York: G. & C. & H. Carvill, 1830), pp. 171–86. Jonathan Edwards's version is in C. C. Goen, ed., *The Great Awakening*, vol. 4 of *Works* (New Haven: Yale University Press, 1972), pp. 331–47; Jonathan's original title was *Some Thoughts Concerning the Present Revival of Religion in New England* (Boston, 1743).

8. See Jonathan Edwards, "Sarah Pierrepont," in Clarence H. Faust and Thomas H. Johnson, eds., *Jonathan Edwards: Representative Selections*, rev. ed. (New York: Hill and Wang, 1962), p. 56.

9. William Shippen to Sarah Edwards, March 22, 1758 (AND). In this letter Dr. Shippen, who attended Jonathan Edwards's final illness, reported this description of their marriage as some of Edwards's final words.

10. Samuel Hopkins, *The Life and Character of the Late Reverend, Learned and Pious Mr. Jonathan Edwards* (Edinburgh: Alexander Jardine, 1799), p. 112.

11. Samuel A. Green, ed., *Diary Kept by the Reverend Joseph Emerson of Pepperell, Mass., August 1, 1748–April 9, 1749* (Cambridge, Mass.: John Wilson & Son, 1911), p. 8.

Samuel Hopkins remembered her as having "a lively, sprightly imagination, a quick and penetrating thought [and] . . . a peculiar smartness in her make and temper. . . . She knew how to be pleasant and facetious," he added, "without trespassing on the bonds of gravity, or strict and serious religion."[12] Lucy Edwards, who was not quite so taken with her sister's charm, once commented that "she never could bear pestering very well."[13] Both descriptions reveal something about Esther's temperament, but only Hopkins's tells us anything about her early religious influences. Under the guidance of her parents, Esther grew up with the strong spiritual commitment characteristic of conscientious Puritans. It is thus to her family's involvement in the religious revivals of the 1730s and 1740s that we must turn first if we are to understand the concerns of her adult life.

Esther's childhood years corresponded almost exactly with the first Great Awakening in New England. It was her father who inaugurated the revivals in 1734, after he noticed a spirit of unrest among Northampton's young people and directed their energies toward the salvation of their souls. During the next several months, he declared three hundred townspeople "savingly wrought upon,"[14] and religious stirrings were felt in a number of other Connecticut Valley towns. Although the euphoria subsided rather abruptly in the spring of 1735, news of people turning to God in other colonies kept alive hopes that the long-lamented declension of colonial piety had finally been checked.[15] The Awakening was, in fact, barely under way.

In 1740, when Esther was eight, the "divine fire" was dramatically rekindled by "Grand Itinerant" George Whitefield during his whirlwind tour of New England.[16] Both the crowds he drew and the

12. Hopkins, *Edwards,* p. 104.
13. Lucy Edwards to Mary Dwight, August 20, 1754 (AND); below, p. 289.
14. Goen, *Great Awakening,* p. 147.
15. For more on "declension," see David D. Hall, *The Faithful Shepherd: A History of the New England Ministry in the Seventeenth Century* (Chapel Hill: University of North Carolina Press, 1972), pp. 227–48, and Robert G. Pope, "New England versus the New England Mind: The Myth of Declension," in Alden T. Vaughan and Francis J. Bremer, eds., *Puritan New England: Essays on Religion, Society, and Culture* (New York: St. Martin's Press, 1977), pp. 314–25.
16. Goen, *Great Awakening,* pp. 48–50.

tremendous outpouring of religious feeling he evoked were unprecedented. As soon as Whitefield had moved on into the middle and southern colonies, he was followed by Gilbert Tennent, James Davenport, and other itinerants who stoked the revival fires to a roaring blaze. Before the Awakening subsided in 1743, thousands of people had undergone the intensely emotional conversion experiences Esther's father had been fostering for nearly a decade. Among the "awakened" was Esther's mother who, though she had been converted as a child, experienced several further conversion-like experiences between 1734 and 1742.

Thus, during the crucial years of Esther's development, her parents (and the other adults around her) were continually preoccupied with this "remarkable pouring out of the Spirit," the revivals in New England.[17] At the dinner table Esther listened to innumerable discussions of how best to further God's work and to silence the Awakening's detractors. In the meetinghouse as well as at home she witnessed her mother and dozens of other people alternating between elation and despair over the state of their souls. She learned at a young age the necessity of continual struggle against sinfulness within. In this way she developed what was to be a lifelong conviction that the only true religion was indeed heartfelt, nothing short of a total and joyous submission to the will of God.[18]

17. Ibid., p. 154.

18. Esther's father, Jonathan Edwards, preached the desirability of "heartfelt" or emotional religion throughout his career. See especially his *A Treatise Concerning Religious Affections*, in John E. Smith, ed., *Religious Affections*, vol. 2 of *Works* (New Haven: Yale University Press, 1959), pp. 96–118. For studies of the effects of evangelical religion on colonial men and women, see Philip Greven, *The Protestant Temperament: Patterns of Child-Rearing, Religious Experience, and the Self in Early America* (New York: Alfred A. Knopf, 1977), pp. 21–148, and Barbara L. Epstein, *The Politics of Domesticity: Women, Evangelism, and Temperance in Nineteenth-Century America* (Middletown, Conn.: Wesleyan University Press, 1981), pp. 11–44. Further examination of the Awakening's influence on a New England minister and his community can be found in Christopher M. Jedrey, *The World of John Cleaveland: Family and Community in Eighteenth-Century New England* (New York: W. W. Norton, 1979), pp. 17–57, 104–19. Epstein (see above, pp. 45–65) also discusses women's participation in the Second Great Awakening as do Nancy F. Cott in *The Bonds of Womanhood: "Woman's Sphere" in New England* (New Haven: Yale University Press, 1977), pp. 126–59, and "Young Women in the Second Great Awakening in New England," *Feminist Studies* 3 (Fall 1975): 15–29; and Mary P. Ryan, *Cradle of the Middle Class: The Family in Oneida County, New York, 1790–1865* (New York: Cambridge University Press, 1981), pp. 60–104.

Esther Edwards also learned that God's will for women was fundamentally different from his plan for men. While Puritan ideology dictated that both men and women were to follow a secular calling, a woman's calling was determined by her spouse's position and vocation. Race and economic position limited the work possibilities of many men, but most of the men of Esther Burr's acquaintance had options; they might, for instance, become merchants, ministers, educators, or gentleman farmers. For eighteenth-century women, there was little illusion of choice; they could either marry or remain single. Men's and women's duties further differed because through their occupations, men served only God, while women served both God and men. Therefore, for men to question their vocations in life was to question God, but for women to question theirs was to question the authority of both God and men. This was a lesson Puritan daughters learned early. Perhaps no event of Esther's childhood taught her that lesson more poignantly than her mother's final resignation to God, which took place when Esther was ten. Because throughout most of her own adult life Esther would yearn for a similar resignation, it is important to look more closely at her mother's experience.

Despite the idyllic pictures of the Edwardses' family life drawn by Jonathan's biographers, during the 1730s and 1740s it appears that Sarah was under considerable stress. By 1742 she had given birth to seven children, who then ranged in age from eighteen months to thirteen years. The primary responsibility for their care, including their education, fell on her shoulders. According to Samuel Hopkins, Sarah "took almost the whole care of the temporal affairs of the family, without doors and within," while Jonathan, who "chose to have no care of any worldly business . . . commonly spent thirteen hours every day in his study . . . [and] gave himself wholly to the work of the ministry."[19] After the 1734–35 revivals, Jonathan was even less accessible, as the time he devoted to lectures, travels, and the Awakening's defense increased markedly. At the same time, Sarah's burdens grew heavier. In addition to her usual household labors—and the additional "deputy husband" chores that probably fell to her as a result of Jonathan's preoccupation with the revivals—

19. Hopkins, *Edwards,* pp. 46, 57, 113.

it was Sarah who fed, housed, and entertained the numerous cler-
gymen and other visitors who flocked to seek her husband's spiritual
guidance and council. [20] Additional pressure during these years came
from opponents of the Awakening, many of whom were relatives
and neighbors who couched their criticism in the form of verbal
attacks on her and her husband. Jonathan could do battle with his
enemies from his pulpit and with his pen, but he expected his wife
to remain silent. [21]

Indeed, among the primary goals of Sarah Edwards's daily life
was the silent and steady performance of her multiplying duties as
wife and mother, a goal she set for herself and one set for her by
her society. As a Puritan, she was making her appointed contri-
butions to the ordering of God's creation. As a member of eighteenth-century society, she was to shine by the efficiency and grace
with which she imbued the home. Rebellion and complaint were
equally antithetical to both cultural norms, even though these were
norms that Sarah (and other religious women) found difficult either
to live up to or to discard. Sarah appears frequently to have dealt
with the frustrations and exhaustions of her life by retreats into
melancholy and outright physical illness. Even these strategies
brought little relief, however, because both she and her husband
perceived her depression and illness as spiritual failings—attributed
to her being "low in grace"—a consequence of a stubborn reluctance
to submit her will completely to God's. [22]

Her reluctance disappeared in 1742, after an ecstatic religious
experience. The change began in the latter part of January, just after
her husband had criticized her for her lack of "prudence" in a recent
conversation with one of his relatives and staunchest opponents.
Sarah responded by bursting into tears and by turning to God for
relief and comfort. Distraught lest she had lost the "esteem and just
treatment of the people of [the] town . . . and more especially, the
esteem, and love and kind treatment of [her] husband," she gave
herself entirely to God. For the next seventeen days, she was in "a

20. Laurel Thatcher Ulrich discusses the "deputy husband" functions of Puritan
women at length in *Good Wives*, pp. 35–50.
21. For more on Jonathan Edwards's responses to his opponents during this
period, see Tracy, *Jonathan Edwards, Pastor*, pp. 123–94.
22. Dwight, *Edwards*, p. 171.

kind of heavenly elysium," reaching heights of spiritual ecstasy such as she had never before known. When she finally emerged from her transports in early February, she was at peace with herself, her husband, and her God. She could say with equanimity: "if I were cast off by my nearest and dearest friends, and if the feelings and conduct of my husband were to be changed from tenderness and affection, to extreme hatred and cruelty, and that every day, I could so rest in God, that it would not touch my heart, or diminish my happiness." Her spiritual conflicts resolved, she could "work for God in the daytime, and at night . . . lie down under his smiles."[23]

Jonathan could not have been more pleased with Sarah's transformation. In his account of her experience, he deleted any mention of her sex and of the particular conjugal nature of the tensions, but he made it clear that her former failings had been overcome. Her most fervent turning to God was "attended," he said, "not only with a great increase of religious affections, but with a wonderful alteration of outward behavior." She had become "as it were a new person." After her resignation, her melancholy and bodily disorders vanished, and she performed her "relative and social duties . . . . with a continual, uninterrupted cheerfulness . . . and . . . great alacrity, as part of the service of God."[24] She had learned to "prefer others" to herself, or as Hopkins would later put it, to account it "her greatest glory, and that wherein she could best serve God and her generation, in being a means of promoting Mr. Edwards's comfort and usefulness. . . ."[25]

Sarah Edwards's spiritual resolution of her difficulties could not have gone unnoticed by her daughter, though Esther may not have perceived its meaning at the time. Esther herself was converted in her teens, but only as an adult did she share enough of her mother's temporal experiences to long for the same kind of resignation and assurance of her own salvation.

In 1752, at the age of twenty, Esther married Aaron Burr, a minister whose evangelical cast of mind was much like her own.

23. Dwight, *Edwards,* pp. 172, 178, 183, 188.
24. Goen, *Great Awakening,* pp. 334, 340.
25. Hopkins, *Edwards,* p. 112; Goen, *Great Awakening,* p. 335.

Aaron was sixteen years older than she, already pastor of Newark's Presbyterian church and president of the newly formed College of New Jersey (later to be called Princeton). Her courtship and "way of marrying" were exceptional enough to invite comment from family and friends.[26] Apparently Aaron traveled to Massachusetts from New Jersey with the express purpose of asking Esther to be his wife, "tho' he had no acquaintance" with her and had last seen her when she was just fourteen.[27] Within five days he had accomplished his end. Two weeks later, Esther was on her way to Newark to be married. Her mother was the only family member present at the ceremony.

The suddenness of Esther's decision may have had something to do with the most recent crisis in the Edwards family. In 1750 Jonathan Edwards was ousted from his Northampton pastorate after years of open disagreement with the church over his demands that all new communicants profess conversion.[28] Although the family remained in the King Street parsonage for nearly two years, they suffered both financially and socially. Jonathan continued to fill the pulpit often during this period, but he no longer received a regular salary. Apparently in an attempt to maintain the family's previous standard of living, the Edwards women made lace and painted fan mounts for sale through the agency of Sarah Prince's family in Boston. In the midst of this crisis, it is hardly surprising that the three eldest daughters all married—Esther, shortly after the family moved to her father's new post in frontier Stockbridge.

Newark and Princeton

Whether or not the uncertainty of the last years in Northampton hastened Esther's decision to marry, the move from Massachusetts to New Jersey brought increased financial stability and renewed social prominence. Although, like Jonathan Edwards, Aaron Burr

26. For the family's reaction, see Lucy Edwards to Mary Dwight, August 20, 1754 (AND); below, p. 289.

27. Joseph Shippen, Jr., a student at the College of New Jersey, also described the courtship and marriage of Esther and Aaron Burr in a letter to his father from Newark dated July 1752 (Princeton).

28. See Tracy, *Jonathan Edwards, Pastor,* pp. 147–94.

might be dismissed from his pulpit at any time, as the son of a wealthy Connecticut landowner his situation was more secure than most. But New Jersey, like Massachusetts, was still embroiled in the religious controversies spawned by the Great Awakening. The College of New Jersey, committed both to classical education *and* to demonstrable piety among its ministerial candidates, was itself a by-product of a schism between Presbyterian "New Sides" and "Old Sides." In 1745 this conflict had been institutionalized with the formation of the evangelical Synod of New York, many of whose members had been ejected from the older, more conservative Philadelphia Synod.[29] As the College's president, Aaron Burr was fully supportive of its evangelical goals, but he was also keenly aware of the young institution's need for broad-based support. Thus he remained dedicated to reuniting his church's warring factions. He could easily have become a target of deep-seated hostilities; and, as Esther Burr knew only too well from her mother's experiences in Northampton, so too could she. She began her life in New Jersey cognizant of the need to be cautious about what she said and to whom.

The move to New Jersey also separated Esther from family and friends and marked her transition from daughter to wife. She described her relationship with Aaron in affectionate, sometimes even playful terms, openly acknowledging the importance of his presence and the strength of the bond between them. But with Aaron traveling regularly, preaching and raising funds for the College, Esther's Newark and Princeton years were often intensely lonely. Traveling back to Massachusetts was not impossible, but for a young woman who expected to be pregnant or nursing a child most of the time, the hazards of several days on boat and horseback ruled out all but the most essential trips. Establishing new friendships, on the other

29. For a discussion of the schism in Middle Colonies Presbyterianism, see Leonard J. Trinterud, *The Forming of an American Tradition: A Re-Examination of Colonial Presbyterianism* (Philadelphia: Westminster Press, 1949), esp. pp. 109–34. The establishment of the College of New Jersey during these disputes is treated in Thomas J. Wertenbaker, *Princeton, 1746–1896* (Princeton: Princeton University Press, 1946), pp. 6–20; Archibald Alexander, *Biographical Sketches of the Founder and Principal Alumni of the Log College* (Philadelphia, 1851), pp. 7–85; and John Maclean, *History of the College of New Jersey . . .* (Philadelphia: J. B. Lippincott, 1877), 1:23–69.

hand, took time. The wives of her husband's associates tended to be considerably older than she, and Esther often found their daughters caught up in becoming "ladies"—an aspiration Esther found demeaning as well as meaningless. She felt isolated and ached for the company of young women with spiritual and intellectual interests similar to her own. She was also plagued during these early years with feelings of inadequacy. Though she had aided her mother in managing a large, busy household, she still felt herself ill-prepared for the enormous responsibilities she had undertaken in the Newark parsonage, as well as for the additional duties of a college president's wife.

Esther had been in New Jersey a year and a half when Sarah Prince journeyed from Boston for an extended stay in the Newark parsonage. The two women had known each other since childhood, when the events of the Great Awakening had brought their families together (Sarah's father, Thomas Prince, minister of Boston's Old South Church, was an early supporter of Jonathan Edwards's evangelical successes in Northampton). Esther's move to New Jersey had made regular contact between the two friends more difficult than ever before, so their time together was especially precious. We can only imagine what they talked about during the visit, but it was probably at this time that they decided to maintain their intimacy by keeping journals for one another. At the time, Esther was pregnant with her first child, Sally. Esther's mother was present for the delivery, and Sarah may also have stayed almost to the time of Esther's confinement in the spring of 1754. No doubt Esther named Sally (short for Sarah) for the two most important women in her life.

Most of what we know about Esther Burr's life during the next few years comes directly from the journal entries, which she began making on October 1, 1754. At the time, she, Aaron, and five-month-old Sally were living on the corner of Broad and William streets in Newark. College students met regularly in their house and in the Presbyterian meetinghouse nearby. Although most of the students boarded with neighbors, some lived temporarily in the Burr household. Esther was also obliged to provide food and lodging for parents, ministers, and trustees who visited the College, and for traveling friends and relatives.

Esther was preoccupied during her Newark years with church dissension and with the Newark congregation's reluctance to release Aaron so that he could devote his energies to the College and move with it to its Princeton location. She was also deeply concerned about the Seven Years' War, then raging in northern New York and western Pennsylvania. She was especially fearful of Indian attacks near her parents' Stockbridge home and angry that, even after a number of British defeats, the colonies were extremely slow to mobilize their military forces. Believing that the victories of the French and their Indian allies were God's way of punishing a backsliding impious people, she grew even more convinced of God's wrath after an earthquake shook the east coast in November 1755. Her sense of personal danger was heightened that winter as she prepared for the birth of her second child. Given her not unreasonable fear that she might die in childbirth, planning for her lying-in also meant preparing for death.

On February 6, 1756, somewhat earlier than expected, Esther gave birth to Aaron Burr, Jr. The difficulties of this birth seem to have been more emotional than physical: her husband was in Philadelphia at the time, and she delivered the baby without her mother or any friends present. Within seven weeks, however, Esther was strong enough to write Sarah that she had had a "fine time" in labor.[30] Spring and summer of that year were taken up with the new baby, preparations for the move to Princeton, and concern over Sarah Prince's ambivalence about marrying. In late August, at her parents' urging, Esther made the long wilderness trek to Stockbridge, carrying her young son with her. Arriving just when the threat of Indian attacks seemed greatest, she lived in daily fear for her own and her family's safety. To make matters worse, Sarah Edwards went to Northampton to attend her daughter Mary's lying-in, leaving the house a dark and lifeless place, as Esther always felt it when her mother was away. Finally, giving in to her fears and her homesickness for her husband and Sally, she returned to Newark after only four weeks instead of the six weeks she had planned.

By December 1756 the Burr family had moved with the College to Princeton, which was even further removed than Newark from

30. Below, Letter No. 20, March 26, 1756.

family and friends. The transition to Princeton was made easier, however, by the presence of Annis Boudinot, an aspiring young poet who lived nearby. Now, with even fewer places for visitors to stay in the town, Esther was busy with constant entertaining. No sooner had the Burrs settled in than a revival, reminiscent of the revivals of her youth, broke out at the College. "Concern" and "distress" prevailed at Nassau Hall as God "got possession" of the students' hearts. Though burdened with extra work and worried as a number of irate parents withdrew their sons from the College, Esther excitedly awaited dinner, when she would hear news of that day's "pouring out of the spirit."[31] Both for her and for her husband, the outburst of religious feeling was proof of Princeton's success in educating genuinely pious young men.

Over the spring and summer of 1757, Esther's letters to Sarah became shorter and less frequent. They were filled with complaints of exhaustion. Her husband, too, was terribly overworked. By late August, although he was probably not aware of it, Aaron was seriously ill. On September 2 Esther's journal ends abruptly with Aaron's departure for Elizabethtown to preach a funeral sermon for New Jersey's Governor Belcher. He returned a few days later shaking with the chills and fever of malaria. Three weeks later he was dead.

Esther's letters home during the next several months tell of her mourning and the comfort she found in her faith. Two other friends, Martha Smith and Experience Brainerd, died that fall, increasing her sense of personal loss and her need for God's aid. By November, however, she had achieved a degree of resignation. In a letter to her father she recounted her attempts to accept her husband's death and her son's threatening illness. She described an explicit covenant with God that enabled her to resign both herself and her children to his care. Later, while talking of the "glorious state. . .[of her] dear departed Husband," she said her soul "was carried out in such longing desires" that she had to leave the room. This "foretaste of Heaven" remained for a long while, and she finally felt ready to be "called hence."[32] While Esther's religious transports were neither as sustained nor as powerful as her mother's earlier experiences, they

31. Below, Letter No. 2, February 19, February 22, and February 23, 1757.
32. Esther Burr to Jonathan Edwards, November 2, 1757 (AND); below, p. 295–97.

clearly provided similar solace and strength during this time of sorrow.

Another hopeful note was the news that her father had accepted the presidency of the College of New Jersey. At least she could expect that her family would be with her. In February 1758 Jonathan Edwards arrived to assume his new duties while Sarah Edwards remained in Stockbridge to prepare the rest of the family for the move. But the Edwardses were not meant to be reunited. During a smallpox epidemic that winter, physician William Shippen inoculated both Esther and her father against the disease. Jonathan Edwards died from the inoculation on March 22, 1758. Shortly thereafter Esther developed a fever, the cause of which is unknown. She died on April 7, at the age of twenty-six.

The family's tragedies were not yet over. Devastated by her losses, Sarah Edwards journeyed to Philadelphia in late summer of 1758 to bring Esther's two children back with her to Stockbridge. En route, she contracted dysentery. She died in Philadelphia in October of that year.

Twenty-year-old Timothy Edwards, who as a student at the College had spent much of his time in the Burr household, took charge of his young niece and nephew. So it was that Esther's young Sally and Aaron were raised in the Elizabethtown and Stockbridge homes of Timothy and Rhoda Ogden Edwards and received their education at the hand of a talented young tutor, Tapping Reeve. Sally Burr later married Reeve and lived in Litchfield, Connecticut, where her husband established the state's first law school. Aaron Burr, Jr., grew up to become the second vice-president of the United States under Thomas Jefferson. The rest of his fascinating story is so well known that it does not bear retelling here, except to say that in her final journal entry, Esther Burr described her son as a "little dirty Noisy Boy, . . . sly and mischevious . . . [and] resolute," who needed "a good Governor to bring him to terms."[33]

The Journal

Over the more than two hundred years since Esther Burr's death,

33. Below, Letter No. 4, September 2, 1757.

her journal has been carefully preserved by her descendants, but it has gone largely unnoticed by scholars and, until now, unpublished. Reasons for this neglect are not hard to determine, for the journal adds little to previous knowledge about the men in the Edwards and Burr families, the founding of Princeton, or the Seven Years' War—topics historians have usually deemed important. To be sure, these people and events are present in the journal, as they must be in the writings of a woman committed to her family and actively interested in the events of her time. But the journal's center is elsewhere. It is first of all a woman's document, and its substance is domestic detail and other female concerns which have only recently been recognized as historically significant. It is precisely because the journal focuses on Esther Burr's own life that it most deserves our attention.

When Esther Burr and Sarah Prince decided not simply to write letters but to keep journals for one another, they had specific goals in mind. Most important, they wanted to monitor one another's spiritual and emotional growth. With religion central to both women's lives, they hoped that by sharing their daily struggles in the search for salvation, they might learn from one another's failures and triumphs. Both of these women were latter-day Puritans, and like other Puritans, they believed they were "called" to salvation. Each saw her life in terms of her soul's journey to God—an undertaking that began with conversion and assurance of God's grace, but that required lifelong vigilance against backsliding. One could never be sure of continued worthiness, and thus one lived with spiritual uncertainty. Among other mechanisms, the private diary provided Puritans with a vehicle for intense, and constant, self-appraisal. Readers of Esther Burr's journal will note that it too has this function. The journal is a continual self-examination, itself a spiritual quest rather than simply a description of a quest.[34] In this process Sarah Prince is an actor, not a passive observer, and her

34. Mary Jane Moffatt and Charlotte Painter examine extensively the meanings of diaries in women's lives. They find that, like Esther's journal, most women's diaries are documents of "psychic survival" providing not only an antidote to loneliness but also opportunities for "self-exploration" and emotional growth. See Moffatt and Painter, eds., *Revelations: Diaries of Women* (New York: Random House, 1974), esp. pp. 3–12.

presence intensifies rather than vitiates the monitoring function of the document. For this reason, although addressed to and regularly read by a second party, the journal can be located in the tradition of introspective Puritan diaries.[35]

The Puritan pilgrimage can also be viewed as a search for one's identity and purpose in the world. In this sense, the pilgrimage is bound up with the notion of a secular calling, or public vocation. Both Burr and Prince accepted the Puritan idea that they were created to be "helpmeets" to men, but they believed that their proper vocation also required them to teach others by the example of their striving and by the model they might provide as "godly women."[36] Herein lay a second purpose in writing. In addition to strengthening their own search for piety, they hoped that their correspondence would one day be published so that other people could benefit from their spiritual struggles.

At the heart of the second purpose lay a trying issue. Both Esther and Sarah knew that most Puritan men were hostile to the idea of women writing. As their occasional disparagements of their own literary aspirations suggest, to an extent they internalized that view themselves. Rather than subject themselves to ridicule, they kept their method of correspondence a secret from everyone but their families and a few sympathetic friends. Esther Burr's journal does reveal her anger at male presumptions of superiority, but she usually expresses that anger indirectly, through satire. Rare are the instances in which she risks direct confrontation with women's detractors.

35. For more on the spiritual quest that characterized Puritan journals, see Daniel B. Shea, Jr., *Spiritual Autobiography in Early America* (Princeton: Princeton University Press, 1968), pp. vii–xii, 87–233; and Cecelia Tichi, "Spiritual Biography and the 'Lord's Remembrancers,'" in Sacvan Bercovitch, ed., *The American Puritan Imagination: Essays in Reevaluation* (London and New York: Cambridge University Press, 1974), pp. 56–73.

36. Puritan ministers in the seventeenth and eighteenth centuries used these terms to describe women's religious and secular roles. See, for example, Cotton Mather, *Ornaments for the Daughters of Zion* (Boston, 1692), pp. 3–4, 48–49. For more on women's roles as pious exemplars, see Laurel Thatcher Ulrich, "Vertuous Women Found: New England Ministerial Literature, 1668–1735," in Vaughan and Bremer, *Puritan New England*, pp. 215–31, and Lonna M. Malmsheimer, "Daughters of Zion: New England Roots of American Feminism," *New England Quarterly* 50 (September 1977): 484–504.

Esther's and Sarah's ambivalence about writing reflected growing cultural ambiguities about female authorship. As early as the 1690s, Cotton Mather had noted that females converted to Calvinism in greater numbers than males. He exhorted pious women to record their religious experiences so that their lives could serve as models of Christian behavior.[37] Thomas Foxcroft, Benjamin Colman, and other eighteenth-century ministers followed Mather's example.[38] The religious awakenings of the 1730s and 1740s provided an even stronger impetus for change as ministers' teachings strengthened the association of women with spiritual concerns and prompted written expressions of affective religious experience to influence potential converts. Women had long been described as more emotional than men, and Jonathan Edwards's claim that a true understanding of divine things was a sixth sense—a sense of heart combining reason and emotion for the apprehension of religious truths—allowed a connection to be made between women's greater piety and their emotional natures.[39] It is not surprising that Edwards chose Phebe Bartlet, Abigail Hutchinson, and his wife Sarah as his three exemplars of heartfelt religion, and undoubtedly his lead encouraged evangelical women in particular to keep written accounts of their souls' concerns.[40]

Still, recognizing that women's lives might provide appropriate religious examples and favoring female authorship are two different matters. New England ministers wished to retain final control over what women said by describing women's experiences themselves, whether in funeral sermons or other prescriptive literature. Even though women were their most devoted adherents, the lessons of Anne Hutchinson, Ann Hibbins, Mary Dyer, and Anne Bradstreet

37. Mather, *Ornaments,* pp. 48–49.

38. See, for example, Benjamin Colman, *Reliquiae Turellae, et Lachrymae Paternae* . . . (Boston, 1735), and Thomas Foxcroft, *A Sermon Preach'd . . . after the Funeral of Mrs. Elizabeth Foxcroft* (Boston, 1721).

39. See Smith, *Religious Affections,* pp. 96–118.

40. Edwards's descriptions of the conversion experiences of Phebe Bartlet and Abigail Hutchinson were first published in their entirety in 1737 as *A Faithful Narrative of the Surprizing Work of God* . . . and can be found in Goen, *Great Awakening,* pp. 191–205.

had not been lost on the clergy.[41] If allowed to speak for themselves, women might take their equality before God to imply equality on earth. Better to draw on pious women's lives, or as Jonathan Edwards did, to edit their writings carefully, than to risk the possibility that women's voices might be raised independently.

European religious women in the early eighteenth century, however, were beginning to publish letters, memoirs, poetry, and other writings themselves; by their example, they nourished literary ambitions in other women. Elizabeth Singer Rowe's published letters, for instance, addressed to a circle of imaginary and real friends,[42] were obvious models for the correspondence of Esther Burr and Sarah Prince. Rowe's claim that her female sensibilities opened her heart and spirit to religious experience was not significantly different from Cotton Mather's supposition that women's greater piety could be explained by their experience *as women*. What was new was the implication that some women should actively and publicly participate in instructing Christians on issues of religion and morality. Indeed, as Puritans committed to becoming exemplars of piety, and as evangelicals encouraged to accept a definition of themselves as peculiarly attuned to religious affections, Esther Burr and Sarah Prince were quite ready to employ their pens in the service of God.

In the long run, the female pens that probably did most to prompt women to write were held not by real women but by the heroines of Samuel Richardson's epistolary novels. First published in the 1740s, Richardson's *Pamela* and *Clarissa* were avidly read by women in both Britain and America. As Ellen Moers explained in *Literary Women*, women "read the moral of *Pamela*" as not so much *Virtue Rewarded* (the novel's subtitle) as *"Writing Rewarded."* It was Pamela's

41. For more about these outspoken women, see David D. Hall, ed., *The Antinomian Controversy, 1636–1638: A Documentary History* (Middletown, Conn.: Wesleyan University Press, 1968); Selma R. Williams, *Divine Rebel: The Life of Anne Marbury Hutchinson* (New York: Holt, Rinehart and Winston, 1981); Kai T. Erikson, *Wayward Puritans: A Study in the Sociology of Deviance* (New York: John Wiley and Sons, 1966), pp. 71–136; Elizabeth Wade White, *Anne Bradstreet, "The Tenth Muse"* (New York: Oxford University Press, 1971); Lyle Koehler, *A Search for Power*, pp. 216–63; and Karlsen's forthcoming *The Devil in the Shape of a Woman*.

42. Elizabeth Singer Rowe, *Friendship in Death; in Twenty Letters from the Dead to the Living. To Which are Added, Letters Moral and Entertaining, in Prose and Verse . . .* (London: T. Worrall, 1733).

"positive self-assertion through letter writing," Moers pointed out, rather than her "merely negative defense of her virtue," that ulti- mately brought her wealth and happiness.[43] Esther Burr and Sarah Prince shared Richardson's concern for the plight of women in an increasingly secularized and market-oriented society. Anxious to reaffirm religious values in their own social worlds, Burr and Prince could easily accept Richardson's premise that pious women, armed with their letter-writing talents, had the power to influence their own destinies.[44]

The impact of these several developments was just beginning to be felt in America at the time Esther Burr and Sarah Prince wrote. Although it was not until the nineteenth century that men's op- position to female authorship was overcome sufficiently for women in any significant numbers to write deliberately for what Burr called "the Public," Burr's journal is an excellent example of women's literary efforts as they appeared in the mid-eighteenth century. Es- sentially a private document, the journal is written with only the faint possibility of a wider audience; in creating their unique com- bination of journal, letter, and spiritual meditation, she and Sarah Prince stayed within the boundaries of acceptable literary behavior for religious women. But in doing so they also participated in the emergence of private documents as a female literary genre.[45] In this sense, their writings belong to a tradition of American women writers from Anne Bradstreet to Harriet Beecher Stowe.

When Esther Burr sat down to write in her journal, the purpose uppermost in her mind was not the impact of her words on future readers. She wrote, on the simplest level, to articulate her sense of her own life and to communicate these thoughts and feelings to her friend. Out of her many concerns three themes emerge as paramount: religion, work, and sisterhood. Because for Esther Burr religion

43. See Ellen Moers, *Literary Women* (Garden City, N.Y.: Doubleday, 1976), pp. 114–16.
44. For an analysis of the implications for women of Richardson's work, see Ian Watt, *The Rise of the Novel: Studies in Defoe, Richardson, and Fielding* (Berkeley and Los Angeles: University of California Press, 1957), pp. 135–238.
45. For other examples of women writing in this genre, see Rowe, *Friendship in Death,* and the writings of Anne Finch, Mary Wortley Montagu, and Charlotte Smith in Katharine M. Rogers, ed., *Before Their Time: Six Women Writers of the Eighteenth Century* (New York: Frederick Ungar, 1979).

infused and was the context for every other aspect of experience, these themes appear in her journal in an inextricable connectedness.

"My time is not my own but God's"

On a Saturday morning in October 1754, Esther wrote to Sarah, "I write just when I can get time. My dear you must needs think I cant get much, for I hav my Sally to tend, and domesteck affairs to see to, and company to wait of besides my sewing, [so] that I am realy hurried."[46] In this manner, near the beginning of her journal, Esther divided her work into the three categories of household labor, social duties, and child-rearing. In the same sentence she introduced one of the main tensions of her Newark and Princeton years. Her daily work left little time for herself—most particularly, for her spiritual concerns and for her friendship with Sarah. She felt that her time was not her own to command, and she described herself as overburdened with work and repeatedly frustrated in her attempts, as she put it, to find "one vacant moment for my Life."[47]

The conflict between what Burr called her *life* and the ceaseless demands of domestic life is a familiar one in women's letters, diaries, and autobiographies, especially in the writings of married women.[48] Yet, like other women, Burr experienced this conflict in terms specific to her times. Both the content of what was considered work and the cultural meanings imposed on it were then undergoing changes. In order to understand Esther Burr's ongoing conflict, it is important to examine both the nature of her daily work and the significance she attached to it.

Although the general categories of household labor expected from a wife did not vary strikingly across class lines in the mid-eighteenth

46. Below, Letter No. 9, October 5, 1754.
47. Below, Letter No. 23, June 15, 1756. The theme of work as it appears in the journal, as well as the themes of religion and sisterhood, are discussed in greater detail in Laurie Crumpacker, "Esther Burr's Journal, 1754–1757: A Study of Evangelical Sisterhood," Ph.D. diss., Boston University, 1978.
48. See Moffatt and Painter, *Revelations,* pp. 3–12, for a discussion of the ways that conflicting demands often dominate the diaries of married women.

century,[49] a husband's class background and occupation dictated (both directly by the plenitude of his contribution and indirectly through the family's location) the way in which a woman would go about her work and the share of her day given to each category. By following her mother's example and marrying a clergyman, Esther Burr could expect to spend her days differently from her sister Sarah, who was married to a Stockbridge farmer, or her sister Mary, who married a Northampton merchant. She could also be assured that the conditions of her household work would be different from those of the women she occasionally hired to wet-nurse her children or help with her sewing. Though many of the tasks of maintaining a household and raising children were undoubtedly similar for all these women, Esther Burr's daily activities were largely determined by her position as Aaron Burr's wife.

By mid-century, women like Esther Burr were beginning to purchase some products that their grandmothers had either bartered for or produced themselves. Burr's rural and less prosperous urban contemporaries still provided a major portion of their families' needs by what they grew, processed, and manufactured in and about the household. As the colonies moved from a domestic toward a market economy, however, time-consuming production increasingly took place in commercial enterprises in other homes, small manufactories, and shops or, among more prosperous families, was relegated to servants or slaves. Moreover, expanded trade increased the availability of both domestic and foreign goods. While manufacturing did not replace home production on a large scale until the nineteenth century—and distribution networks remained primitive up to the eve of the Civil War—the impact of economic changes on the patterns of women's work was discernible among a number of women of Esther Burr's generation.

Esther Burr's household work marks her both as an essentially urban woman and as a transitional figure in an expanding economy.

49. This is to say, most wives were expected to cook, manage the larder and contribute to its supply, provide labor toward the clothing of the family, oversee internal distribution of food and clothing, clean and wash, contribute to the general equipping of the physical dwelling, supervise infants and older females in the household, provide nursing care, and assume whatever aspects of their husbands' responsibilities might be necessary.

Unlike many country women, she did not grow flax; neither did she process flax or wool, or weave cloth. She did spin some of her own thread or yarn, but not alone and not on a regular basis (as did many poorer women in need of trading credit). Instead she participated in "spinning frolics," where neighboring women gathered to spin for themselves and for one another. Her yarn and thread were probably woven into cloth by a nearby weaver.[50] Wearing apparel such as cloaks, hats, and boots she either bought on her "business" trips to New York or had Sarah purchase for her in Boston, as she did furniture and other domestic equipment. What distinguished Burr in this regard was less that she did not produce these items herself (many women obtained major clothing items from outside the household, and most wooden furnishings and household utensils were—and always had been in the colonies—manufactured by men) than that she apparently obtained them through cash purchase. Her daily schedule, however, still included such demanding labor as tailoring, plain sewing, mending and altering old clothes, quilting, "pin[ing] up" beds, reworking chair bottoms, ironing, whitewashing, and turning the house "up-side-down" for cleaning.[51] In addition, she provided large dinners and did most of her own baking.

While many rural women still maintained family gardens and orchards, tended domestic animals, and processed their own butter, cheese, cider, and other foods, Esther—like most town and city women—"rode out" for many of these provisions or bought them from local peddlers.[52] Thus she substituted the work of bargaining and establishing good supply sources for the labor of primary production. Esther had help with domestic duties, and thus, like other women throughout history, had considerable management respon-

50. It is not clear from Esther's journal whether she did any spinning outside of the shared work context of spinning frolics. Current research suggests that even among less prosperous families, married colonial women were less actively involved in clothing production than scholars have previously assumed. On this point, see Laurel Thatcher Ulrich, " 'A Friendly Neighbor': Social Dimensions of Daily Work in Northern Colonial New England," *Feminist Studies* 6 (Summer 1980): 393–95. For speculation on the conditions that might have made some groups of women more likely to engage in this labor than others, see Norton, *Liberty's Daughters,* pp. 15–20, and Ulrich, *Good Wives,* pp. 29–30, 45–46.

51. Below, Letter No. 17, September 6 and September 8, 1755.

52. Below, Letter No. 9, October 7, 1754.

sibility. This help accounted for Esther's occasional freedom to retire "whiles dinner was geting."[53] She was sometimes aided by her sisters, Lucy and Susanna, and by young Sukey Shippen—all of whom were "put out" to Esther for short periods to learn housewifery. Had the Burr household survived intact, Esther would one day have taught Sally these same skills—and in turn benefited from a daughter's help. Such sources of aid might have been available in households of almost any economic group, depending on their particular circumstances.

Esther was also sometimes able to hire neighboring females to assist her with washing, ironing, and other extensive tasks and may have commanded the services of both male and female slaves. While the hiring of temporary labor was common in the colonial period in all but the poorest households, especially in the absence of older daughters, slave ownership distinguished the Burr family (and their relatives and friends) from most of their contemporaries. Unfortunately, in part because of her own racism, it is hard to know from Esther's writing either how many of the people she mentioned were slaves or the extent to which they performed traditional female labor. Harry is the only person Esther talked about who was clearly a household slave (although Caesar, whom Aaron Burr purchased in 1756, could have worked for Aaron at the College or for the family), but there is little indication of his daily work except that he answered the door. We suspect, however, that some of the most arduous and time-consuming labor usually done by the women in less prosperous families—carting wood, tending fires, serving and cleaning up after meals—as well as some of the cleaning, whitewashing, gardening, and cooking, was done by either the male slave(s) or by Sukey, a young woman who appears to have been, at least for a time, a servant or slave in the Burr household. If so, their assistance would have lightened Esther's household labor considerably, just as the growing number of slaves and servants in the late eighteenth and early nineteenth centuries lightened the daily work loads of other well-off men and women.

Esther's household work blended imperceptibly with her social duties; at the same time, her social duties were sometimes indis-

53. Below, Letter No. 13, April 14, 1755.

tinguishable from her recreational activities. Spinning frolics in the Burr's house, for instance, were both work sessions and parties, requiring considerable preparation, including a day or two of cleaning and baking beforehand. These gatherings also met some of Esther's "deputy husband" obligations to entertain parishioners and the wives and daughters of trustees and ministers. As the word frolic suggests, like barn- and house-raisings, these occasions were also meant to combine work with pleasure, providing occasions for women to share news, discuss faraway friends, exchange advice on domestic matters, and form new friendships. Similarly, on trips to New York, Esther combined business transactions with social calls to her husband's colleagues and their wives. Visits to the sick, bereaved, and widowed in the community were sometimes little more than onerous duties, but often Esther acknowledged that she received as much support and comfort as she gave.

However enjoyable some of the visiting and entertaining was for Esther, it was nonetheless a task, required of her as the wife of a minister and college president. It was as much a demand on her time as her household work. "Indeed," she confided to Sarah after a particularly exhausting afternoon out on business, "vissiting is the heardest work that I do."[54] If the conversation had been intellectually or spiritually rewarding, or if her time had been employed for some benevolent purpose, she seldom complained; but too often her social obligations seemed to be trifling and meaningless encounters which interfered with more serious endeavors. Frequently one group of guests barely left before others arrived. At these times Esther felt helpless to control the pace of her existence; images of hurrying, flying, time lost, and time wasted dominate these pages of her journal. Her use of quantitative terms to describe company at these times—"An Army to Breakfast," "A drove of Women strangers to Tea," "Sundry Minnisters to dine"—reveals how overburdened she felt with her seemingly endless social responsibilities.[55]

Child care was also demanding work, especially when there were no other women in the house. Like most of her contemporaries, Esther could expect to have a large number of children, possibly

54. Below, Letter No. 18, October 2, 1755.
55. Below, Letter No. 3, May 16, May 18, and May 19, 1757.

ten or eleven at two-year intervals. Aaron was born when Sally was nearly two, and after weaning Aaron at thirteen months, Esther explained in a springtime letter to Sarah that she expected a third pregnancy would prevent a trip to Boston that very summer. With her husband frequently away and busy with his own work when home, Esther took on most of the responsibility for child care, much as her mother had done. And once Aaron was born, Esther began to realize how burdensome children could be. Late one night with her son at her breast, she wrote plaintively to Sarah of her plight. "When I had but one Child my hands were tied, but now I am tied hand and foot. (How I shall get along when I have got ½ dzn. or 10 Children I cant devise.)"[56] Although her children lessened her feelings of loneliness and although she clearly delighted in their playfulness and in their accomplishments, the task of caring for them added to her sense of never-ending obligations.

Besides their physical care, Esther was also responsible for her children's governance, the eighteenth-century term for moral training. Governance was a particularly time-consuming task for Esther during her children's early years because evangelical parents were expected to instill obedience at the beginning of a child's moral development.[57] Believing that willfulness in her children was a sign of their inheritance of original sin, and that failure to curb it might lead to their eternal damnation, Esther had to be ever watchful for stubbornness—for what Puritans called "natural pride." Even before Sally was ten months old, Esther said that the child had been "Whip'd once on *Old Adams* account."[58] Esther found stern chastisement difficult, however, perhaps because she was influenced by John Locke, Samuel Richardson, and others who challenged Puritan beliefs about children's innate depravity.[59] Her description of Sally

56. Below, Letter No. 21, April 13, 1756.

57. For an excellent discussion of differing interpretations of child governance in the colonial period, see Greven, *The Protestant Temperament*, pp. 87–124, 156–91, 269–91.

58. Below, Letter No. 11, February 28, 1755.

59. On changing child-rearing practices in the colonial period, see James Axtell, *The School upon a Hill: Education and Society in Colonial New England* (New Haven: Yale University Press, 1974), pp. 51–96; Daniel Blake Smith, *Inside the Great House: Planter Family Life in Eighteenth-Century Chesapeake Society* (Ithaca, N.Y.: Cornell University Press, 1980), pp. 25–125; and Greven (see above, note 57).

as a bird, who begins singing "as soon as she is awake," hardly fits with notions of children's natural sinfulness.[60] But although she was exposed to new ideas about children's innocence and the emerging romantic ideology that would dominate nineteenth-century thought and profoundly alter the experience of mothering,[61] Esther accepted religious teachings over other evidence and disciplined her children early and frequently. Obviously she shared with other evangelical parents the hope that, docile and obedient, her children could progress rapidly from innate sinfulness toward their potential as reborn Christians.[62]

When Puritan parents were reasonably certain of the hopeful state of their children's souls they might proceed to their second duty—educating them for a proper calling. Women managed this education, both for their own children and other young people who lived with them, for the first six to eight years, either at home or in dame schools. Later, boys were usually turned over to men for schooling or apprenticeship, while girls continued to learn religion and housewifery from older females. Esther Burr expected that her daughter Sally would attend school for a while, but that she would apprentice with Sarah Prince and other women in the same way that Esther's younger sisters and twelve-year-old Sukey Shippen apprenticed with her. The putting-out system not only allowed for the training of daughters by women other than their own mothers, but, in colonial households with few females, it provided for much-needed domestic help.

Esther Burr had difficulty finding young women to train, and she complained frequently about the lack of domestic assistance. Her own explanation of her problem was that the young women around her were "all Ladies," who found it "beneath them to go out,"[63] suggesting not only the decline of the putting-out system in the mid-eighteenth century, but also the ways in which this demise was

60. Below, Letter No. 9, October 10, 1754.
61. For more information on changing concepts of motherhood in the late eighteenth century, see Ruth H. Bloch, "American Feminine Ideals in Transition: The Rise of the Moral Mother, 1785–1815," *Feminist Studies* 4 (June 1978): 101–26.
62. Greven, *The Protestant Temperament,* pp. 32–99.
63. Below, Letter No. 21, April 13, 1756.

related to the growth of bourgeois values at the time. Encouraged by the polite literature of the day and by the declining status of housework in the face of growing market-consciousness,[64] daughters of the socially prominent aspired to more genteel pursuits. Both the emergence of female academies in the second half of the eighteenth century and the relegation of domestic service solely to women of other classes and races were the ultimate results.

For Esther Burr, who still believed in the Puritan ethic of hard work, these many changes had a distinct and at times troubling impact. The increased social duties expected of a woman in her position were added to her more traditional household labor—and at times there may have been less help with that labor. More disconcerting, all of her daily work—her visiting, entertaining, feeding and housing of student boarders and visitors, teaching young females housewifery, and caring for her own children, as well as the acquiring, producing, processing, and distributing functions that comprised the rest of her household tasks—was denied social recognition *as work*. With a developing bourgeois culture increasingly defining that work *as leisure*, Esther's sense of her own social value was tenuous. At times she simply gave in to the feeling that what she did was something other than work ("I am as tired *as if* I had been heard at work all day"), but more frequently she looked to her Puritan heritage for confirmation of reality.[65]

The desire for validation took Esther (and Sarah) to chapter 31 of Proverbs, the biblical passage Calvinist ministers favored in their discussions of women's calling.[66] Esther's attention to this scripture indicates that she saw her own working life as similar to the biblical model; indeed she strove to emulate the industry and devotion to family and neighbors advised by Lemuel's mother. The passage reinforced her Puritan belief that every chore, every duty, even her

64. For fuller development of these ideas, see Jeanne Boydston's forthcoming dissertation, tentatively entitled "Home and Work: The Industrialization of Housework in the United States" (Yale University). Boydston's extensive revision of conventional views of women's work in the eighteenth and nineteenth centuries has kept us from several critical errors in our analysis of Burr's experience. For many helpful discussions with her on this subject, we are especially appreciative.

65. Below, Letter No. 18, October 2, 1755, emphasis added.

66. Below, Letter No. 10, December 1 and December 12, 1754.

aches, pains, and exhaustion had social significance. Esther also believed, as the chapter itself suggests, that women's domestic labor had spiritual significance, that her reward was neither her husband's approval nor her society's recognition, but a humble and graceful soul, worthy of heavenly reception.

Esther's efforts to find personal meaning in a devalued labor system are not to be confused with the nineteenth-century cult of domesticity. Later generations of women might see their household work as a sacred duty, a way to earn God's grace directly.[67] In contrast, Esther saw her labor as properly humbling to sinners, a kind of mortification of the flesh, turning her mind away from earthly concerns toward dependence on God's grace.

There was yet another difficulty. However much she might experience her domestic work as a religious and secular calling, she found it hard to accept both how onerous some of her responsibilities were and how little time this work left for either her spiritual and intellectual concerns or her friendship with Sarah. The conflict was particularly wrenching because her religious world view denied the very possibility of dissatisfaction. She believed that God required her not only to carry out her domestic duties, but to carry them out joyfully, as an expression of her complete acceptance of his will. She worried aloud to Sarah that she did not sufficiently appreciate her fortunate position and that God would punish her for it. Any discontent with her daily work or what she called her "lot in life" appeared grievously sinful to her, a sign that she was undeserving of God's grace.[68] Her complaints, therefore, were also a sign of spiritual weakness. Public dissatisfaction was unthinkable; only in her letters to Sarah were such complaints permissible—but even then, they had important psychological consequences.

Whenever she allowed herself to express discontent in the journal (which she did often) her subsequent behavior followed a discernible pattern. She first expressed remorse at her ingratitude and wondered that God did not punish her more severely. She then endeavored to submit herself to God's will and to accept, as she said, that "my

67. On the emergence of the ideology of domesticity in the late eighteenth and early nineteenth centuries, see Cott, *The Bonds of Womanhood*, pp. 63–100, and Epstein, *The Politics of Domesticity*, pp. 67–87.

68. Below, Letter No. 11, February 21, 1755.

time is not my own but Gods."[69] At times resignation came fairly easily, but more often than not the struggle to submit was intense— and anger-producing. With no acceptable outlet for expression she turned her anger inward and became depressed. Her bouts of melancholy might be accompanied by physical illnesses: headaches, pains in her eyes and breasts, and other bodily disorders. At these times she would usually take to her bed for a while. Later, when she returned to her duties, she was sometimes still unwilling to submit; at other times she seemed at least mildly comforted that God had not forsaken her completely. Most often, however, she felt resigned to her circumstances and claimed that her suffering had brought her a measure of peace. But her serenity was seldom long-lasting. Word that a visit from Sarah had been postponed again or hours of preparation for a meeting of ministers in her home were enough to start all over again the cycle of discontent, depression, and attempts at resignation.

We have already suggested that Esther Burr's mother, Sarah Edwards, suffered from conflicts similar to her daughter's. But Sarah Edwards seemed to have resolved them through her highly emotional mystical experience, what Jonathan Edwards called her "resignation of all to God." Her melancholy and bodily disorders disappeared completely, according to her husband, after her "transporting views and rapturous affections." From then on, he said, she performed her "moral social duties . . . in a spirit of humility and meekness" and learned how to "prefer others to self . . . as part of the service of God."[70] While her husband was still alive, Esther Burr never learned to prefer others to self without resentment. Her journal ends without the assurance of salvation for which she longed.

Pious Sisters of the Heart

In one of her early letters, Esther confided to Sarah Prince, "I have not one Sister I can write so freely to as to you the Sister of my heart."[71] Throughout the rest of her journal she spoke often of

69. Below, Letter No. 3, April 10, 1757.
70. Jonathan Edwards, quoted in Goen, *Great Awakening,* pp. 333, 335, 340.
71. Below, Letter No. 9, October 11, 1754.

the special nature of their relationship, as she did about her other friendships with women. She referred to a group of women in Boston as "the Sisterhood,"[72] indicating here, as elsewhere, that she felt a special connection to women who shared similar experiences both as women and as evangelical Christians.[73] She devoted a great deal of thought and space in her journal to establishing a definition of friendship against which she measured her relations with these women. She and a number of other religious females were beginning to express to one another their feelings about their shared oppression. Their comments seldom took the form of general statements about women's common condition; rather, they described particular circumstances, and even then, their remarks were haltingly made, sometimes denied as quickly as they were said. But in their attempts to make sense of their own experiences, these women increasingly looked to one another for support and guidance. In doing so, they became conscious of themselves as sisters and of their strength as women—necessary preconditions for the overt activities of their female descendants of the nineteenth century.

As several historians have suggested, the history of self-conscious bonds among women belongs primarily to the late eighteenth century and to the nineteenth century.[74] But for some women, these bonds had their roots in the changing conditions of the early eighteenth century and in the religious revivals of the 1730s and 1740s. As noted above, Esther Burr was one of the women most quickly affected by the economic, social, and cultural changes of the period and was deeply involved in the religious ferment of the years following the revivals. It is hardly surprising, therefore, that one of the earliest-known expressions of sisterhood in America appears in

72. References to "the Sisterhood" abound throughout the journal. See below, for example, Letter No. 23, June 17, 1756.

73. This special connectedness to other evangelical women did not, however, extend to evangelical women of other races and classes.

74. In this introduction we have not presented a lengthy discussion of the basis of sisterhood in shared female rituals because Carroll Smith-Rosenberg has already discussed these themes in her path-breaking essay, "The Female World of Love and Ritual: Relations between Women in Nineteenth-Century America," *Signs* 1 (Autumn 1975): 1–29. Nancy Cott also discusses these themes as they pertain to New England women's lives in the late eighteenth and early nineteenth centuries in *The Bonds of Womanhood*, pp. 160–96. For studies of female bonding in the

her journal.[75] Because of the particular circumstances of her life, she is an important figure in the history of women's emerging consciousness of their common identity.

It was out of shared conditions of daily life that Esther Burr and a number of other women began to look to one another for support and for answers to their dilemmas.[76] Together they evaluated what religious and secular writers said about marriage and women's responsibilities. Together they searched for ways to justify their interests beyond their domestic work, and together they encouraged one another's attempts to describe and to attach significance to their experiences. As latter-day Puritans they chose the language most available to them—the language of evangelical religion.

This language provided these women with a way to redefine friendship to fit their relationships with other like-minded females. As Esther Burr described it, friendship combined the same rational and emotional elements as Jonathan Edwards's definition of love and other "religious affections." Friendship was a divinely inspired manifestation of Christian love, nearly as "refreshing to the soul" as is communion with God, she told Sarah; and as such, it was "becoming [to] the rational soul."[77] It was, she insisted, hardly the highly intellectual relation many men of the day assumed it to be. Esther vehemently objected to the assertions of one of the tutors of the College that women did not know *"what Friendship was,"* that *"they*

nineteenth and early twentieth centuries, see Claudia Bushman, ed., *Mormon Sisters: Women in Early Utah* (Cambridge, Mass.: Emmeline Press, 1976); Susan Porter Benson, "The Clerking Sisterhood: Rationalization and the Work Culture of Saleswomen, " *Radical America* 12 (March–April 1978): 41–55; Blanche Weisen Cook, "Female Support Networks and Political Activism: Lillian Wald, Crystal Eastman, Emma Goldman," in Cott and Pleck, *A Heritage of Her Own,* pp. 412–44; Thomas Dublin, *Women at Work: The Transformation of Work and Community in Lowell, Massachusetts, 1826–1860* (New York: Columbia University Press, 1979), pp. 58–107; and Estelle Freedman, "Separatism as Strategy: Female Institution Building and American Feminism, 1870–1930," *Feminist Studies* 5 (Fall 1979): 512–29.

75. By way of contrast, note the absence of themes of sisterhood in the journals discussed by Laurel Thatcher Ulrich in *Good Wives* or in the writings of seventeenth-century poet Anne Bradstreet, in Jeannine Hensley, ed., *The Works of Anne Bradstreet* (Cambridge: Harvard University Press, 1967).

76. See especially Smith-Rosenberg, "The Female World of Love and Ritual."

77. Below, Letter No. 20, January 23, 1756.

were hardly capable of anything so cool and rational as friendship."[78] For her, genuine friendships could not exist without their emotional component.

Admiration for another woman's piety was often the initial step in forming female friendships. The poet Annis Boudinot, Esther's Princeton friend, indicated the importance of religion in establishing sisterly connections when she wrote Esther, "When first I knew thy Heavenly Mind / I felt the sacred Flame / [of] Friendship rising in my Brest."[79] With such lofty expectations women needed considerable time for friendships to develop. Three years after she moved to Newark, Esther was still longing for such friends as Sarah had in Boston: *"friends,"* she said, "that one might unbosom their whole soul too. You are sensible my friend," she added emphatically, "that it is quite otherwise with *Me.* There is *not one person that will talk freely to me on relegion in this Town."*[80]

Sisterly relations also served to reinforce piety in women. Evangelical women offered one another instruction in religious matters, monitored one another's spiritual development, and looked to one another for advice and encouragement in the exercises of daily religion. Together they searched for the spiritual significance of everyday events, and this kind of spiritual support was an essential part of the sisterhood espoused by Esther and Sarah. It was also the mainstay of the prayer and literary groups to which many religious women belonged. Although initially formed for other purposes, by the 1770s these groups had extended sisterhood into the public sphere with relief efforts for the poor and support for the cause of American independence.[81] They were the forerunners of the nineteenth-century female reform associations, antislavery societies, and, ultimately, women's rights organizations.

While sisterhood in the eighteenth century was firmly rooted in the evangelism of the Great Awakening, the uniqueness and power of sisterly ties originated in shared female experience. Certainly this

78. Below, Letter No. 3, April 12, 1757.
79. Below, Letter No. 3, April 11, 1757.
80. Below, Letter No. 13, April 20, 1755.
81. See Laurie Crumpacker, "Sarah Prince Gill," in Lina Mainiero, ed., *American Women Writers* (New York: Frederick Ungar, 1980), 2:127–28; and Norton, *Liberty's Daughters,* pp. 155–94.

experience was varied, even for such a homogeneous group as the latter-day Puritans under discussion. But two aspects of evangelical women's lives were widely shared because of their sex. First, their primary work was the maintenance of daily life. They took charge of pregnancies and childbirths; they nurtured, socialized, and educated young children; they saw to it that their families were fed and clothed and their households clean; they nursed the sick and dying and laid out the dead. Second, and not unconnected with the first, they shared a strong, ascribed social identification because of their sex. Assumptions made about their so-called "natural" limitations not only severely restricted their choices of work, but also limited their access to education and other sources of social power. It was out of these two interrelated parts of their experience—their mutual ways of life and their mutual oppression—that these women developed enduring relations with one another.[82]

Esther Burr and Sarah Prince, like most females of their time, grew up surrounded by other women. They understood that men controlled their society, that in all areas of public and private life men's opinions and activities were deemed more important than theirs. No matter how close their relationships to individual men, women were expected to defer to them. Esther Burr sometimes resented assumptions of male superiority, but to express her anger would only have alienated her from her God and from the men closest to her. Only the separate world of her friendships with other women remained untouched by this pervasive sexual inequality. Sisterhood provided her with her sole opportunity for intellectual exchange, confidences, and support among equals.

A 1755 journal entry, in which Esther envisioned the scene of her husband's visit to Boston, illustrates male domination of even the domestic world—and thus, for women, the necessity and desirability of separate interactions:

I imagine now this Eve Mr Burr is at your house. *Father* is there and some others. You all set in the Middleroom, *Father* has the *talk,* and Mr Burr has the *Laugh,* Mr Prince gets room to stick in a word once in a while. The rest of you set and see, and hear, and make observations

82. See Smith-Rosenberg, "The Female World of Love and Ritual."

to yourselves . . . and when you get up stairs you tell what you think, and wish I was there two.[83]

Gatherings of women for religious, political, or literary discussion were clearly essential to their self-esteem. Out of these associations came the support necessary for them to take a public stance on the cultural devaluation of women. When a newspaper satire appeared stating that women's brains are controlled by whim and folly, Esther's friend Annis Boudinot noted in her journal that a group of women asked her to answer the verse as their deputy, "which was done," she said, "in [their] company and sent for the next week's paper."[84] Several years later, Boudinot published another, more militant, poem on the deliberate exclusion of women from assemblages intended for intellectual and business purposes.[85]

Her friendship with Annis may have fortified Esther for what she described to Sarah as her "smart Combat with Mr Ewing about our sex." John Ewing, a College of New Jersey tutor, had disparaged women's intellectual capabilities and had condescendingly remarked that women should limit their conversation to *"things that they understood."* Suspecting that Ewing meant that women should talk only about "fashions and dress," Esther could not restrain herself. "My Tongue, you know, hangs pretty loose," she told Sarah proudly:

Thoughts Crouded in—so I sputtered away for dear life. You may Guss what a large field this speach opened for me—I retorted several severe things upon him before he had time to speak again . . . . We carried on the dispute for an hour [and] I talked him quite silent.[86]

It appears, however, that such public outbursts were rare. Rather than expose herself to ridicule and male criticism, Esther usually shared her feelings only with female friends. Even here, most of her comments were cloaked in irony.

While sisterhood provided support for women's opposition to a devalued separate sphere, it also enabled them to redefine their roles

83. Below, Letter No. 9, October 13, 1754.
84. Annis Boudinot Stockton, "Colonial and Revolutionary Poems," n.d., n.p. (Princeton).
85. Ibid.
86. Below, Letter No. 3, April 12, 1757.

within that sphere in terms less trivial than men like Ewing would allow. It was clear to Esther and Sarah, for example, that a woman's marriage was a crucial event of her secular life—and a principal determinant of the quality of her adult experience. The two friends devoted a great deal of intellectual energy to evaluating what was written about courtship and marriage, drawing from the prescriptive literature what they approved and rejecting what they did not. Esther and Sarah's 1755 correspondence about Richardson's *Pamela* illustrates this dynamic process. Sarah had read the book first and told Esther that "it did not equel [*Clarissa*]"; Esther borrowed the book to "have a judgment of [her] own." Esther rejected Pamela's marriage to Mr. B and criticized the author for supposing that women were so lacking in moral discrimination that they willingly married their former tormentors. "He has degraded our sex most horridly," she said. Still the book contained "some excelent observations on the duties of the Married state," so Esther did not "repent [her] pains."[87] In this interchange and in a number of other discussions, the two women tried to articulate codes of behavior that would reconcile their sense of religious imperatives with the secular changes taking place around them.

In the journal, Esther and Sarah were able to reveal their ambivalence about marriage more openly than they ever could with men. Sarah was still single during the period of their correspondence,[88] and in defense of the single state, she did not hesitate to mount an attack on marriage and "poor fettered folks." Esther found Sarah's attack unacceptable because, she told her, "the new tryals that this new state must be incumbered with . . . [are] perhaps not so great as what they were exerscised with Whiles single."[89] In addition, Esther knew that Sarah was considering marriage. In her courtships Sarah sometimes dissembled and played the coy maiden—a behavioral lapse that Esther roundly criticized. She insisted on more forthright and honest behavior on the part of her friend, telling Sarah, "my dear no man likes a woman the better for being shy when she

---

87. Below, Letter No. 11, March 10, March 12, and March 20, 1755.
88. Sarah married at the age of thirty-one, a year after Esther's death.
89. Below, Letter No. 16, August 23, 1755; Letter No. 4, June 21, 1757.

means the very thing she pretends to be shy off."[90] At the same
time that she advised honesty with men, Esther herself sometimes
dissimulated. She particularly dreaded revealing the limits of spirit
or stamina which might be interpreted as failings. Men were to see
her as strong and uncomplaining. At one point, after days of waiting
on ministers and a retreat into illness, she told Sarah that she got
up when Aaron came home because "I hate he should come and find
me on the bed sick."[91] Only in her letters to Sarah did she express
both sides of her ambivalence about men and marriage.

Sisterhood also sustained women within their domestic roles. The
restriction of women to domestic work fostered an isolation that
was intensified by the migration of so many families into new communities. Correspondences, like the long visits that characterized
female friendships during this period, helped women to endure the
loneliness of their situations. With her husband frequently absent,
Esther Burr relied on her journal as a means of coping with her
conflicts and sharing her problems. Sarah's letters, in turn, were a
powerful antidote to Esther's isolation and depression. In 1755 Esther told Sarah that she "could not help *weeping* for joy" after receiving a long-anticipated letter from her. "I broke it open," she
exclaimed, "with [as] much egerness as ever a fond lover imbraced
the dearest joy and dlight of his soul."[92] Here, as elsewhere in the
journal, she indicated the intensity and intimacy eighteenth-century
women offered one another in the name of sisterhood.

The themes of work and sisterhood in Esther Burr's journal—
and the very existence of the document itself—cannot be fully ap-
preciated without understanding the profoundly religious orienta-
tion of the journal's author. Esther's evangelical world view not only
encouraged, justified, and shaped the content of her writing, but
it also fostered responses to her social environment that were si-
multaneously constructive and constraining. To her religious self-
definition is ascribable much of Esther's resistance to her culture's

90. Below, Letter No. 21, April 16, 1756.
91. Below, Letter No. 18, October 16, 1755.
92. Below, Letter No. 11, March 7, 1755.

devaluation of both women and their work, and much of her sense of identification with other like-minded women. At the same time, that self-definition both impeded direct confrontation with social restrictions on women and generated deep psychological conflicts.

Her roles as a woman prescribed by religious leaders, Esther was raised from early childhood to embrace a specifically female piety—to present a model of virtuous womanhood for other females to emulate. Discouraged from writing for "the public," she was nonetheless encouraged in the written expression of her spiritual quest. As she searched, in her letters to Sarah Prince, for the spiritual significance of her daily experience, her evangelical world view gave direction and meaning to that experience. Moreover, by drawing on the language of "religious affections," she was able to claim, with Sarah, a special, female understanding of human relationships, and to articulate a separate female identity based on self-esteem rather than inferiority.

Raised in a latter-day Puritan household to see her daily labor as a religious vocation of some importance, she was able to maintain that view much of the time, in the face of changes in the social and cultural context of that labor. As eighteenth-century women were increasingly encouraged by a secular literature to aspire to a bourgeois value system, Esther, supported by her faith, was able to resist some of the denigration of women and their work that the new system entailed.

Still, the older Puritan model of womanhood could not always help her deal with feelings that some of her daily work was trivial or with resentment that her work made it impossible for her to spend time in ways more spiritually, emotionally, and intellectually satisfying. Indeed, that model denied the very existence of dissatisfaction in a virtuous woman. It was only at the risk of spiritual assurance that Esther could acknowledge her deep ambivalence. Thus, most of the time Esther tried to push her discontent away, attempting to replace it with a "resignation of all to God." Throughout the journal, however, the psychological conflicts remained. Cycles of discontent, depression, resignation, and reassurance are the dominant rhythms as she writes about her work. Ironically, part of the reason Esther failed to break the cycle was that the Puritan emphasis on women's work as a religious vocation had, in fact, lost its validity in the more secular, market-oriented world of the 1750s.

It is important for readers of the journal to remember this multiple impact of religion on Esther Burr—that it was at once a cause of her oppression, an obstacle to overcoming it, and a source of strength under it. It is important to bear in mind as well that while this journal is a highly personal document through which one woman attempted to resolve the major tensions of her life, it also speaks to us of many other women's experiences, in Esther's time and in our own.

PART II

The Journal

{October 1, 1754}
Teusday Newark Oct 1. 1754

To my ever kind Friend

I shall begin with telling you that on Monday morn erly Mr Burr left me, and all the rest of the company with him. It is very hard to let Mr Burr go but O! if he should never return again! But this thought I must put out of my mind, or I must be obliged to lay down my pen.[2]

This Morn the Woman that helpt me Commencement time left me (who is a very valuable person and a person of [r]eading, and very good company, as well as good sense and piety and has some very just thoughts about friendship). She is a Elizabeth Town woman, [so] that I am now alone except my Brother.[3] I feel somthing gloomy but endeavour not to give way to it. For my amusement since Mr Burr left me I have been reading Dr Watts's Miscellaneous thoughts, which I never read before. I think them like the rest of that valluable gentlemans works. There is somthing in the good Docts writings differant from every bodys elce, more ingaging—but I need not tell you how good his works are.[4]

1. There were eight earlier Newark letters from Esther Burr to Sarah Prince, but these have not survived.

2. Aaron Burr was on his way to Boston, probably on one of his many trips to raise money for the College.

3. Sixteen-year-old Timothy Edwards, the eldest of Esther's three younger brothers, was at this time a student at the College and living in the Burr household. Esther referred to Timothy many times in the journal, usually simply as "my brother," but at least once as "Brother Sammy." Readers should note, however, that Esther sometimes called Samuel Foxcroft "Brother Sammy" (see note 1, Letter No. 10, below) and that it is not always clear which of the two she was discussing. McLachlan, pp. 182–85.

4. Isaac Watts was a popular English religious writer, best known for his hymns and children's verses. He was also a preacher, and Esther was probably reading his *Sermons on Various Subjects, Divine and Moral,* published 1721–23. *DNB,* 20:978–81.

I expect company every minit.

(I have forgot what page I left off with so I begin again. Plese send me word.)

Eve.

All solitary! Our house seems so still. I am alone, almost affraid to step about [*the*] house for fear of [mak]ing a disturbance. I hop I shant feel so lonely all the time Mr Burr is gon.

{*October 2, 1754*}
Wednsday Eve

I suppose you want to know how Mr and Mrs Cumming had like to have been affronted.[5] In as few words as possible I will tell you. You must know in the first place they did not lodge here because we were full, nor did they dine here Commencement day, which they did not take hard, for we never invite any but the Trustees. But the day after Commencement I expected they would, as well as a numbre of others, but throu Mr Burrs forgetfullness they were not invited. In the Morning Mr Whitefield preached[6] (I could not go out myself.) Mr Burr saw Mr Cumming and determined as soon as Meeting was out he would speak to 'em, but when it was out sombody spoke to Mr Burr about business and put it quite out of his mind. I knew then they would be offended—Next Morn by 7 they rode by our house going home without so much as calling— but the wind was so high that Mrs Cumming dare not go . . . and

5. Mr. and Mrs. Cumming, whom Esther and Sarah facetiously referred to as Mr. and Mrs. Fickle, were Alexander Cumming, originally from Freehold, New Jersey, and Eunice Polk Cumming, from Mecklenburg County, North Carolina. Alexander, who had recently resigned his position as associate pastor of New York's First Presbyterian Church (see note 30, Letter No. 9, below), had at one time been one of Sarah's suitors. Some of Esther's ambiguous remarks about the Cumming couple stemmed from Eunice's apparent jealousy of her husband's former relationship with Sarah. After Eunice objected to Alexander's escorting Sarah from Newark to Boston in the spring of 1754, Sarah had a disastrous journey. The strain between the Burrs and the Cummings is obvious in the early sections of the journal, but it eased over time; when Esther realized in 1758 that she was dying she asked Alexander to preach her funeral sermon. Sibley 12:120–25.

6. George Whitefield, the English evangelical preacher who has been credited with initiating the first Great Awakening in 1739, made numerous journeys to the colonies between 1738 and 1760. *DAB* 20:124–29.

with a deal of trouble we got em here to dinner. Mr Burr says, "Mrs
Cumming, be honest now and tell me if you was not affronted that
you was not invited here yesterday?" She replied, she thought [*it*]
a little strange. So Mr Burr and she talked it over and then she
seemd as she used to, but when she first came in I could plainly see
an alteration, a shyness. Some of our company was gon and they
lodged here. Mr Fickle said not one word about you pro nor Con—
About 8 in the Evening Mrs Fickle says, "Mrs Burr I have a great
deal to say to [*you*] but I am affraid I shall not have time."[7] I told
her we would walk up stairs if she pleasd so we went up. Mrs Fickle
says, "Is not Miss Prince offended at me?" I said not that I knew
of. (I take it that you are not in the least offended but rather grieved.)
Then she asked me if you had not wrote me an account of your
journey and Voyage. I told her I had sent desiring it, but you said
it was such a meloncolly story you would not send it, it would
grieve me. Then she undertook to relate facts, the story of laying
at Stonington, and your illness before that, then about Mrs Pem-
berto[n's] Girl, then who you should go to Boston with, then Mr
Pembertons fray after you got to Boston, and heaps of things.[8] I
did not lay 'em up, nor regard 'em, for I know you better than Mrs
Cumming does, and I know you will not act without reason. You
must think I had a very diffecult part to act for Mrs Cumming told
it as a profound secret. She said she had not told any body. And
now I will recollect what I said to Mrs Cumming in reply. After
she had done I said *if these things were true* (I chose to speak in this
manner that she might see that I surspected the truth of what she
had said, but she took know notice of it). I must say I never saw

7. See note 5, Letter No. 9, above.
8. The Pembertons were Catharine Stillwell and Ebenezer Pemberton of Boston, and Mrs. Pemberton's "Girl" was Catharine's servant or slave, not her daughter.
A Baptist and the daughter of Richard Stillwell, a wealthy New York merchant
and a founder of New York's First Baptist Church, Catharine had married Ebenezer
in 1752, when he was still pastor of New York's First Presbyterian Church. Ebenezer
had resigned his New York position late in 1753 (see note 30, Letter No. 9, below)
and, by the time of the "fray" Esther mentions, had probably been installed in his
new position as pastor of Boston's New Brick Church. Apparently when Sarah
returned to Boston that spring she was accompanied by Catharine Pemberton, who
had remained in New York over the winter to settle her husband's affairs. Sibley
6:535–46.

any thing in Miss Princes conduct or behaviour, any thing like what she had mentioned, and doubtless you had reasons for it. I told her I hoped she would not take a prejudice against you without reason, or words to that effect, and that you wrote very handsomly of 'em, and spoke of your regard to 'em very frequently. I told her I did not doubt but you had a sincere regard for 'em, and a desire of their happyness, and many kind things I said about you which I suppose you dont want to hear. Mrs Cumming said she did love you, she could not help it, you wrote charmingly the last time you wrote to her, and she intended to answer it. I said I was glad she did, and hoped she would continue to write. I turnd of [*off*] the subject as soon as I could handsomly, for you must needs think it was very disagreable to me. I took great care not to say anything that should look as if I joyned with her. She saw plainly I did not like it or she would not have been so willing to drop the discourse. If I said any thing that you had rather had been let alone pray let me know in your next. I did all for the best, and that with an heart full of affection and tenderness. It raised up all the tender passions in me. As soon as Mrs Cumming began to talk, I wished she would holde her tongue a dozen times, for I dont love to have a person that I love talked against, and there behaviour criticised upon. I believe Mrs nor Mr Cumming will never say anything to me on that head again. I hope they wont.

{*October 3, 1754*}
Thursday Eve

What I have wrote hetherto must be burnt.[9] I had not my thoughts about me or I should have wrote the story on a pice of paper by it self. It will do the publick no harm if tis all burnt, as what I now write is not paged in order but that I will leve to you. This day had company and a relation of Mr Burrs from Newengland. One thing more that Mrs Cumming said and then I will have done with that story, and that is this. She was very much affronted at first,

9. In addition to their letter-journals, Esther and Sarah sent secret letters to one another, which they called their "privacies." These letters were always sent with trusted friends and were burned as soon as they were read. Evidently Esther was suggesting that Sarah treat the Wednesday evening entry as she would one of the private letters.

but since she came home and has thought it all over she is no ways offended. And for my part I believe she is sorry she ever was. I think tis much best it should be forgot as much as possible by us both, and if it *could be, buried in oblivion.* Tis late so a good Night to you, and My Dear Mr Burr.

{October 4, 1754}
Fryday

Page 37 you ask me if I am not tired of these *dry* journals. I assure you I was never so *charmed* with Letters in my Life as since you have wrote in this method, so dont call 'em *dry* again. If you do I shall be affronted (for it will be saying that I have a taste only for dry matter, and you know I dont love to have my judgment slighted no better than other people do) for it is exactly the thing I have always wanted of my absent friends.

Your 9 observations of chusing a friend, I think very judicious, but the 7 I am pecularly pleased with as it is a thought, an observation new to me viz "That a time of prosperity will discover some persons real temper better than adversity." I esteem it a pecular blessing of heaven on me as well as on you that you are not so subject to melloncholly as you used to be, and if I have been any ways an instrument of bringing about this happy alteration, I desire to be thankfull I had the blessed oppertunity. Your welfare in the least shape rejoices my heart.

The question you ask page 44. with a desire I would answer it is, whether after supposed friends have betrayed ther trust they are to be trusted again without proppor humiliation for past offences (or words to the same sence.) I answer by no means—I think It would *not* only not be our duty, but our *sin.*

I must forgive you because you ask it, for I cant deny any thing you ask. But why did you My Dear burn those papers—If I thought you would shew any of my Letters I should not write with half the freedom that I do. But you have eased me quite.

I think Mr Dwight deserves to be licked.[10] Pray cant you send me that little Book you are writing? I want to see it very much.

10. Either merchant Timothy Dwight of Northampton, who had married Esther's younger sister Mary in 1750, or Colonel Joseph Dwight, who, along with his wife Abigail Williams Sergeant Dwight, was involved in the early 1750s in a protracted dispute with Esther's father over control of the Stockbridge Indian mission. Dexter 1:757–58; Sibley 7:56–66.

Page 53 you knock all my hopes of your coming here this winter in head, but I desire to be resighned to the will of God. He knows what is best. Perhaps tis best I should be alone. I have nither óf my Sisters come down, [so] that I expect to have no young woman in the house with me this Winter. The supplement I received.

{*October 5, 1754*}
Saturday Morn.

I write just when I can get time. My dear you must needs think I cant get much, for I hav my Sally to tend, and domesteck affairs to see to, and company to wait of besides my sewing, [so] that I am realy hurried.

Afternoon.

I dont much wonder that such a thought did come into your mind (as you mention page. 60.) as whether some folks would not try to break the friendship between us. It was what I expected, so *fore warned, fore armed.* But I should chide you for your second thought, that Possibly they might obtain their end. If *Soloman* had not said, *Tale-bearers seperate verry Friends.* All they have said has had no more influence on me, than a *Fether* would have to drive back the *Nor-west wind* if It were sent against it. If it had, to be sure I would tell you.

The observations you quote I think extreamly just. Dont regard fashion my dear but quote everything you think would profet me, for you know I hant much time for reading now I have a young Child. Page. 61. that of telling secrets. . . . Not long since Mrs Smith and I were talking of this *same thing,* and determined that whatsoever had been spoken in *Confidence* whiles there was supposed to be a friendship aught to be kept secret.[11] Altho the friend-ship was at an end, yet the obligation was as strong as ever, and Mrs Smith thinks stron[ger]. This is sertain, it is but adding *sin* to *sin.* I call it *sin,* for I look on the ties of Friendship as *sacred* and I am

11. Martha Dickinson Smith of Newark Mountains (later Orange, New Jersey) was one of Esther's close friends. Martha's father, Jonathan Dickinson, had preceded Aaron Burr as president of the College. Her husband, Caleb Smith, was minister of the Newark Mountains Church and one of the College's trustees. Esther referred to Martha and Caleb frequently in the journal, sometimes as Mr. and Mrs. Smith of the Mountains. Dexter 1:747–48.

of your mind, that it aught to be [a] matter of Solemn Prayer to God (where there is a friendship contracted) that it may be preserved. And it is what I have frequently done and shall continue to do.

{October 6, 1754}
Sabbath-day.

In the Morning I went to Meeting, heard Mr Joans Preach from 1. Corinthians. 12 Chap. 3 vers these words, "And that no Man can say that Jesus is the Lord, but by the holy Ghost."[12] A good profetable discourse tho not the best. I believe Mr. Joans to be a [. . .] good man. . . . Afternoon stayed at home with Sally. O I am ashamed, and that justly, that I spend my Sabbaths no better! I wonder God does not deprive me of these blessed oppertunitys! I am sure I deserve it!

Eve. If you knew my dear friend how gloomy our house was you would pety me. Mr Burr has been gon one long week and if every week seems as long as this, it will be *an Age* before Mr Burr comes home. I am so concernd about his helth (as he was poorly when he left) that at times I cant rest—I wish I could leve him in the hands of a kind and gracious God who has preserved him, and me, so many journeys. But I forget myself—you will pardon me my *dear*. "Out of the aboundance of the heart the mouth speaks."

{October 7, 1754}
Monday Eve.

This day I rode out to see some sick people, and to do cuntry business, such as speak for Winter Tirneps, Apples, and syder, and butter. This Eve not very well, somthing of a pain in my Brest— My Brother desires his regards to you, and bids me tell you he has by no means forgot you, and if ever he comes nere where you be he shall not do as Mr *Dwight* did. If his regards to you have not been mentioned in my Letters to you heretofore tis my fault, for he has often spoke to me about it. I feel so poorly I must lay down my pen.

12. Possibly Timothy Johnes, son of Samuel and Esther Stephens Johnes, who was a minister in Morristown and a College trustee. His wife was Kezia Oldfield Ludlow from Jamaica, Long Island. Dexter 1:577–79.

{October 8, 1754}
Teusday Eve.

I have no time to write this day. All the time I could get, I spent in writing my Privacies.

{October 9, 1754}
Wednsday Eve.

My time for writing is after I have got Sally a sleep. This day I rode out to see some sick people and Mrs Serjent amongst the rest tho' I hope she is not daingerous.[13] This afternoon Mrs Belcher and Mrs Woodruff came to drink Tea with me.[14] I have been very poorly all day with a pain in my brest and am now so ill I can but just set up. It is very late—a good Nights rest to you my dear friend. . . . I wonder if you have no Mr Burr in Boston by this time. I hope you have. I am glad you have his company since I hant.

{October 10, 1754}
Thursday

I am almost out of conceit of all the world—I wonder if it is in such a tumult at Boston as here. Everybody seem hurried. But I will not bring the hurrys of the world into my Letters to you nither. For they are all the diversion I have now, and most of my company. I have never felt so well since Mr Burr left me as when I am talking to you. But this *pen thinks it* has talked enough I beleive by the actions of it, so I will lay it aside and get another. . . . In the Morn Sally awakes me with her prattle. Like *other Birds* as soon as she is awake to singing. . . . The first thing after her Eyes are open is to look for me and as soon as she sees me a very pleasant smile, her

13. Abigail Dickinson Sergeant, originally of Elizabethtown, lived in Newark with her husband, Jonathan Sergeant, who was the College's treasurer from 1750 until 1777. Martha Dickinson Smith (see note 11, Letter No. 9, above) was her sister. McLachlan, pp. 407–11.

14. Mary Louisa Teal Belcher of Elizabethtown was married to New Jersey's governor, Jonathan Belcher. She was a Quaker when she married the elderly governor in 1748, and apparently she possessed a considerable fortune prior to her marriage. Her husband was a great friend to the College, granting its first permanent charter in 1748 and serving as a lay trustee until his death in 1757. Elizabeth Ogden Woodruff, also from Elizabethtown, was the wife of Samuel Woodruff, the mayor of his community, a wealthy merchant, and a College trustee. Sibley 4:434–49; McLachlan, pp. 88–90.

Eyes sparkling like *diamonds*. She is very good company when I have no other.

Mr Smith when he was here t'other day asked me what Miss that was at your house.[15] I told him Miss Jenny. He commended her much and said she was exceding prety. Every body takes notice of her, but *Doct Fickle*. . . . My thoughts this day have run much on the instability of Mankind. Dear Miss Prince we dont know *to day*, but we shall be left *tomorrow* to contradict all we have said or done in our whole lives. . . . You must know I have been hearing about some fickle folks who are just like a *wetherCock*, "turnd about by every blast."

{*October 11, 1754*}
Fryday

It is a great comfort to me when my friends are absent from me that I have 'em some where in the World, and you my dear for *one*, not of the least, for I esteem you one of the best, and in some respects nerer than any Sister I have. I have not one Sister I can write so freely to as to you the Sister of my heart. There is a friend nerer than a Brother, *sertainly*. . . . That old proverb is not a true one, out of sight out of mind.

{*October 12, 1754*}
Saturday.

I have been this afternoon to see Mrs Sergeant who is realy very sick, but she thinks her self much worse than she is. She is extreamly discouraged and sees nothing but *death* before her. She says Gods face is hid from her, and she fears she never beheld *him* a right, tho' this no one has reason to doubt. O my dear what a mercy tis to have the Light of Gods Countinance on a sick Bed! If I loose Mrs Sergeant I loose the best friend that Mr Burr or I have in this Town. I desire I may be fitted for Gods holy will and pleasure concerning her. . . . She is a hearty friend to you two, which makes her the more valluable to me. . . . It realy seems as if the time was come when friendship is going quite out of the World by one means or other, those that are formed for it taken away by death or threatned.

15. Caleb Smith. See note 11, Letter No. 9, above.

We, viz you and I, never shall forget the friends we have lost by death. I mean our *Sisters.*[16]

{October 13, 1754}
Sabbath

Had no Minister in the forenoon, stayed at home with Sally. Mr Brainerd who was to preach here this day has sent me word that he is very sick and cant come.[17] In the afternoon I went to the Mountains to hear Mr Smith. He preached better than ever I heard him before [*so*] that I was not sorry I took the pains.

Eve. O my dear it seems as if Mr Burr had been gon a little *Age!* and it is yet *but one Fortnight!* I dont know what I shall do with my self the rest of the time, I am out of patience already. I imagine now this Eve Mr Burr is at your house. *Father* is there and some others. You all set in the Middleroom, *Father* has the *talk,* and Mr Burr has the *Laugh,* Mr Prince gets room to stick in a word once in a while.[18] The rest of you set and see, and hear, and make observations to yourselves, Miss Janny amongst the rest, and when you get up stairs you tell what you think, and wish I was there

16. Esther's sister Jerusha Edwards had died at the age of seventeen in 1748. Sarah had lost all of her sisters—her infant sister Grace Prince in 1743, her twenty-year-old sister Deborah Prince in 1744, and her twenty-six-year-old sister Mercy Prince in 1752. *Edwards Genealogy,* p. 15; *NEHGR* 5:375–84.

17. John Brainerd, son of Hezekiah and Dorothy Hobart Brainerd of Haddam, Connecticut, was at this time missionary to a group of Delaware Indians in a settlement near Trenton. His brother, David Brainerd, who had died in 1747, had formerly held this position. In June 1755 John took over most of Aaron Burr's responsibilities as minister of Newark's Presbyterian church, but after a year on probation there, he decided to return to his Indian congregation, which was then resettled in New Brunswick. His wife, Experience Lyon Brainerd, became one of Esther's close friends during the Brainerds' year in Newark. Experience was the daughter of Experience and William Lyon of New Haven. She died just one week before Aaron Burr, in September 1757. Dexter 2:76–79.

18. Sarah's father, Thomas Prince, was minister of Boston's Old South Church, author of numerous books and articles on New England's early history, and one of the Great Awakening's most prominent supporters. His wife, Deborah Denny Prince, had grown up in England. She met Thomas when he was serving as minister to her congregation in Coombs in Suffolk (1711–17), and accompanied him to the colonies. The couple married in 1719. In 1754 Sarah was their only surviving child. Sibley 5:340–68; *NEHGR* 5:375–84.

two. Now is not this right, say? But I must *adone* or I shall think I am there of a truth.

{*October 14, 1754*}
Monday

A.M. Much hurried preparing for Company. This is our *grand* Training day, all the Militia in the County are coming into Town. . . . P.M. whiles I set waiting for the Governor to call me, and then I am to go up common to see 'em Train.[19] My head is so confused with the noise of Drums, Guns and Trumpets, I cant write so I'll stay till the Town is a little stiller. All the Rabble rout in Town goes by here [*so*] that I am almost crazy.

{*October 15, 1754*}
Teusday A.M.

The Town is prety still by this time. I went up on the common according to appointment tho' the Govournor did not come himself, the weather being not very good, and he not very well, but Madm came. It was a sight for me; for I never saw so many people togather before. There was eighteen Captain's Companys, and in all that were on the Common above two Thousand people. There never was such a Training in this Town before.

Eve. This P.M. I received a very affectionate Letter from Mr Burr, which did me more good than ever a Cordial did when I was faint. I was before extreamly low-spirited, but at once I felt as lively as ever I did in my life. What power these people have over us that have our hearts. They can do anything with us, at least with me— this P.M. Mrs Smith of the Mountains came to see me.

{*October 17, 1754*}
Thursday. Octr 17

I did not write yesterday because I felt so dull that I knew that what I should write would not be worth reading. . . . Dont you want to know how I spend my time now Mr Burr is gon? I [*suppose*] you do in reason. In the forenoon my Brother reads loud to me. In the P.M. we commonly Ride out frequently on business if I have not company. Eve My Brother reads again. We generaly set and

19. New Jersey's governor, Jonathan Belcher. See note 14, Letter No. 9, above.

chat alittle after dinner about Mr Burr and you and the rest of Boston good friends, Northhampton and Stockbridge which has no small share in our conversation as well as thoughts. Poor people! I fear they suffer a great deal! I wish they were some where elce out of dainger! You cant conceive the distress I have been in on their account[20]. . . . It is late so a good Nights rest to you My dear.

{October 20, 1754}
Sabbath Eve Octr 20.

You will excuse my not writing Fryday and Saturday. All the time I could get on fryday was taken up in writing to Mr Burr. Saturday I was busy about famaly affairs.

This day I was at Meeting all day. Heard Old Mr Pierson preach from 3 chap. Colossians 4 verse, "When Christ who is our Life shall appear" etc. . . . He preached with a good deal of life and spirit. I liked him well, but I know by the countinances of peopel in general that they did not like him. Tis truth that this people are very whmsical about preachers.[21]

20. Esther's concern for her family and friends in western Massachusetts stemmed from the danger of Indian attacks. The Seven Years' War (French and Indian War) was already underway, and although most of the Indians remaining in the area ultimately sided with the British against the French, not all of them did. In Stockbridge, where Esther's father was missionary to resettled groups of Mahicans, Mohawks, Oneidas, and Schaghticokes as well as minister to the small white population, the danger was particularly great. Long-term Indian resentment of white settlers had been heightened in the early 1750s by appropriations of Indian lands and by mismanagement of Indian school funds. After the killing of a Schaghticoke man by two white men and the refusal of the Massachusetts court to take the murder seriously, several Schaghticokes retaliated by killing four whites. Esther had probably just received news about these latter deaths, as well as word that a fort was being built around the Edwards house to shelter those white people who had not fled.

21. John Pierson, son of the Reverend Abraham and Abigail Clark Pierson, was minister of the Mendham, New Jersey, Presbyterian church and one of the College's first trustees. His wife was Judith Smith Pierson, probably from Jamaica, Long Island. In 1752, after thirty-five years as pastor of the Woodbridge church, John had resigned his position, having lost the support of his congregation in the aftermath of the Great Awakening. Esther's sympathy for him, and her musings about people's inconstancy, may have been evoked by the memory of her father's own experience in Northampton. Dexter 1:103–05.

{October 21, 1754}
Monday.

This afternoon I rode out to do some business, and to see the Widow, the fatherless and the sick. There is somthi[ng to] be learnd go where one will if we have but an heart [to] reflect and improve. I cant but be amazed that *ever* I was disposed to repine at the dispensations of Providence for when the dispensation has been most grievous how much more Mercyfull has God been to me than others that are far better than I. Sometimes I am affraid I am to have my portion in this life, and what a miserable portion will that be. O my dear let me begg my bread rather than a fullness on these terms!

{October 22, 1754}
Teusday Eve.

For a fortnight past I have enjoyed as good a state of helth as I did anytime last Winter. O that I might be excited to be devoted more entirely to that God that is so kind to me in so many respects! In the Morn I rise erly. My first business is to dress *Sally,* for I dont love to see Children naked till Noon. Then with a very good stomach to my breakfast (as I have to dinner and supper) then with a good heart to business which I go about with as much life and courge as ever I did in my Life. . . . Those people that are never sick dont know how great a mercy helth is. I am sure I should not, but you my dear as well [*as*] my self know enough of sickness to prize *helth* above *wealth.*

{October 26, 1754}
Saturday. Octbr 26.

These several days I could not get one minutes [rest] to say one word to you, for I had a quilt on the fra[me] and my Ironing to do, and could get no help. I expected I should have been quite sick before now but I holde we[ll] as yet. . . . This day Mr Badger comes to Town and brings me the joyfull News that Mr Burr will be at home on Wednsday Next week, and that he is much better than when he went from home.[22]

22. Jonathan Badger (1729–57) was a tutor at the College and possibly a candidate for the ministry. He was the son of Captain Daniel and Patience Durkee Badger of Union, Connecticut. McLachlan, p. 35.

{October 27, 1754}
Sabbath Eve.

Not very well, somthing of a Headach. Went to meeting, heard one Mr Whittaker, a young Preacher.[23] He was brought up at this College. He did better than I expected. I must lay down my pen for I am very vapory, and confused you can see.

{October 28, 1754}
Monday Eve.

O my dear Miss Prince, this afternoon to my unspeakable surprize my best self came home, all unexpected as much as the Man from the Moon. I could hardly believe my Eyes. He is very well and found us all so. The pacquet from you I have just looked into, and that is all.

{October 29, 1754}
Teusday Eve.

This afternoon I had a room full of company, amongst the rest Mr and Mrs Brwn [*Brown*]. She desires her very kind [r]egards to you, she has a very great respect for you.[24] I have stole a little time to read your dear Letter . . . by the way I had a Letter from Sister Dwight and another from sister *Nabby,* who informs me that Sister Dwight is nere her time of Laying.[25] I feel distresst for her. . . .

23. Nathaniel Whitaker, who graduated from the College in 1752, was the son of Elizabeth Jarvis and Jonathan Whitaker of Elizabethtown. In later years he played a crucial role in securing the funds that made the establishment of Dartmouth College possible. McLachlan, pp. 60–63.

24. We have not been successful in identifying Mrs. Browne, but her husband was Isaac Browne, who was both a physician and the Anglican rector of Trinity Church in Newark. Dexter 1:380–82.

25. Sister Dwight was twenty-year-old Mary Edwards Dwight. She is the most well known of the Edwards daughters, largely because her first son, Timothy Dwight, prominent author and minister as well as a president of Yale College, credited his success to her intellectual and religious training. Mary's husband was the Northampton merchant Timothy Dwight, son of Colonel Timothy and Experience King Dwight. Sister Nabby was eighteen-year-old Lucy Edwards. She later married Princeton graduate Jahleel Woodbridge, a young man whom she had grown up with in Stockbridge. *DAB* 5:573–77; Dexter 1:757–58; McLachlan, pp. 365–66.

{October 30, 1754}
Wednsday.

Now Mr Burr is come home *All the World and his Wife comes here* but the worst of it is they hinder me from better company, I mean company at Boston, and that vexes me to death.

{October 31, 1754}
Thursday Eve.

This afternoon went to make a *set* vissit. The Topick of conversation was the mischeif done at Stockbridge (and war in general.) I have avoided writing anything about My dear friends there because I should be two gloomy if I once begin. But O my dear friend tis impossible to conceive the anguish of my Mind on hearing the News first for it was told in the worst light it could be. Sombody comes, I am called.

{November 1, 1754}
Fryday. Novbr 1.

You say I have excepted the office of *Monitor* but on no other conditions than that you be one to me. *Mind that.*

I think it one of the great essentials of friendship [that] the parties tell one another their faults, and when they will [say] it and take it kindly it is one of the best evidences of true friendship, [I] think. Pray what are your thoughts. [*Note in margin unreadable.*]

{November 2, 1754}
Saturday P.M.

There is so much goodness, kindness, openness with every other good quallity, savoured with piety in your Letters that when I am read I am always charmed. Now dont say this is a complyment. I shall dislike it if you do, for I abhor em among friends and such a friendship as ours. I have such a *Duke of a pen* that I must be obliged to leve off. Pray be so good as to send me some, for them you was so kind as to leve me when you went home, suted me the best that any ever did. . . . I am of your mind, it is very needfull, this private way of corresponding, (I mean our billets to be burnt.) We can no other way be let into one anothers cercumstances, which would give us both much distress, but tis very hard to commit any thing of so dear a friends to the flames. It grieves me so I can hardly bare it. I have promisd and will not break my word, nor give you uneasyness.

{*November 3, 1754*}
Sabbath

A.M. Before meeting a Funeral attended. O that the Living would take warning! Mr Burr had a written sermon which he had thoughts of Preaching, but at the funeral his thoughts run on Hebrews XI. 13, "These all died in faith not having recived the promises etc.", the whole verse. He laid by his writen sermon and preached extemporary all day, shewing the necessity of faith to die by as well as to live by, and also how we aught to live as pilgrims and strangers. I think it was very suitable as well as very affecting.

{*November 6, 1754*}
Wednsday P.M.

Two days past I have been imployed in writing Letters to Stockbridge and Northampton, and am now down sick with an extream bad cold, and cant write any mor but that Mr Burr is gon to a Presbitry. He keeps the stroke going, as soon as come home gon again. Eve. I saw in the News just now that Miss Canning is come to Boston. I have a deal of curiosity about her. Pray my dear write me what you think of her.[26] I dont undertake to answer your last, because I expect every day to hear of an opportunity to send this, and shant have time to answer it so fully as I would chuse.

{*November 8, 1754*}
Fryday

Am a little better. A gentleman from Albany has been here to day and brings the sertain news that all the Indians in Stockbridge have left the place except two or three famalys. He say they are much disgusted, and say the white people are jelous of em and they will not live among em any longar. He said farther that they had a mind to send for a neighbouring Tribe to assist em to kill all the people in Stockbridge. O my dear what a dismal aspect things have! I am almost out of my witts! What will become of my Dear father

26. Elizabeth Canning was a young Englishwoman who was tried and convicted of perjury in 1754 and transported to the colonies for seven years. The case was the subject of a heated pamphlet war in England, including author Henry Fielding's "A Clear State of the Case of Elizabeth Canning . . ." (1753) and Canning's own "A Letter from an Unhappy Young Lady . . ." (1754). It also received wide publicity in the colonies. *DNB* 3:870–72.

and his afflicted family! O help me to commit em to God who orders all things in mercy, and dont willingly afflict nor grieve any of his Children! I am ready to say some times, why is it? Why does God suffer his own most dear children to be hunted about in this manner! But this is a very wrong temper of mind. I hope I may be enabled to crush it by divine assistance. This day was our prepareation day for a recseption of the holy ordinance of the Lords Supper

{November 9, 1754}
Saturday P.M.

The Governor and Lady just went from here. They drank Tea with me. He is as well as usial [*usual*]. I find in my distress about my friends, and great confusion in the house (this confusion was occasioned by a croud of people here all day, such a day as I have hardly seen since I have been here) I have wrote a most dolefull heap of scrawls as almost all my writing is. But if you cant read it or any other of my letters pray be so good as to put em into the fire. It is no wonder for all the time I do get to write I steal. As for coppiing, I never do. I am glad I can get time to scratch once, for my writing, and in such haste two, is but scratching. (I dont so much as look over what I send to you. You have my thoughts just as they then happen to be.)

{November 10, 1754}
Sabbath

A.M. Went to meeting. Heard a discourse from those words of Christs concerning John "What went ye out for to a Reed shaken of the wind?" which put us all upon enquiring what end we had in view when we came to the House of God and his ordinances etc. . . . I thought I felt some longings to meet Christ at his Table. I hope I felt a little more alive than I do commonly, but O my deadness! P.M. Stayed at home with Sally and Sue who is very poorly and has been so some time.[27] There is duty at home as well as at the house of God.

27. Sue, also called Sukey in the journal, was a young servant or slave in the Burr household. Readers should be aware that Esther also used the nicknames Sue and Sukey for her sister Susanna (see note 3, Letter No. 10, below) and Sukey for Susannah Shippen (see note 6, Letter No. 14, below). It is not always clear which of the three young women she was referring to.

{*November 11, 1754*}
Monday

In the morn Mr Burr sat out for Princeton. The same story—
P.M. A Room full of company, not the most agreable. I dont see
as I am like to have an opportunity of sending this so will answer
your last as I go along. Page 67 you speak of a desire of my pertaking
with you when you meet with any thing that is pleasing to you,
whether reading, or eating, or drinking, a desire of amost *nere
participation* as you call it, and desire me to give it a better word
which I am unable to do. I am of the mind my dear it is better
conceived of than expressed. I know what you mean. I have felt so
a Thousand times with respect to you and other of my dear friends,
and it did me good to meet with that passage in your letter, because
it was exactly what I had felt and thought.

I cant but love Mrs Mathews for her good advice to you. Pray
take it into serious consideration. Mr Burr has got a new thing of
one Miss Joans's puting out. The title is *Miscellanies in Prose and
Verse.* She has a turn for poetry, is quite lively in some places, but
in others flat which I wonder at. She has some fine strokes on
friendship which shews a turn for it, but no turn for relegion. I
believe her to be a Deist in principle. What a pity![28]

(You will excuse my writing on such poor paper. I had no better
nor could get any but now shall be able to send better for time to
come.)

{*November 12, 1754*}
Teusday Eve.

I am much pleased with the passage you quote out of Sir Charles
Grandson [*Grandison*] that says the Character of a friend, the greatest
that can be given, or to that purpose.[29] I have met with somthing
in Miss Joans to the same efect, which I shall give you.

She says in a poem to the memory of Miss Clayton.

28. Mary Jones was an English poet. Her *Miscellanies in Prose and Verse* was
published in 1752. S. Austin Allibone, *A Critical Dictionary of English Literature*
. . . (Philadelphia: Childs and Peterson, 1859), 1:989.
29. *The History of Sir Charles Grandison,* published in 1753, was novelist Samuel
Richardson's response to Henry Fielding's *Tom Jones. DNB* 16:1129–33.

And if some friend, when I'm no more, should strive
To future times my memory to extend,
Let this inscription on my tomb survive,
Here rests the ashes of a faithful friend.

I cant but hope my dear that the World is agoing to have better notions about friendship than they used to—it seems to me we did not use to meet with so many just thoughts on it as we do in late authors, or is it because friendship is going out of the World, and the judicious part of it see it, and are awake about it. If this is the case I wish they might awake others by what is printed.

Page 71 you say and seem quite peremtory too, that I must tell you all and every thing that is amiss in your private papers, and you seem to conclude before hand that if I dont find fault, it will be because I make *unreasonable allowances* for you. But if you do think so, I cant make em where there is none. For to tell all my heart, I could not complain of one sentence nor one word, nor think how you could have conducted more prudently, and shall indevour to take pattern. . . . I feel very dull, Mr Burr gon you know and am very tired so good Night to you.

{November 13, 1754}
Wednsday A.M.

You ask me page 72 whether you are right to send Letters three times to ⟨ . . . ⟩ and ⟨ . . . ⟩ without their sending to you once. I say I should not have been so good, but perhaps tis most prudent, but I think I would not send again least they think *you cant live without their smiles*. . . . They know you love em as you do your own soul. . . . My Brother has been at Newyork lately. Mr Fickle and Wife are gon to Freehold, so did not see em. *Brother Janey* is going after Mr *Bellamy*. Mr *Professor* sends him and says if the Presbitry would concur they should sertainly get him, for one of Mr *Bellamys* Deacons says he is convinced tis his duty to go to Newyork.

Mrs Professor said to my Brother, that she thought [*it*] very strang that I should go to advise Mr Bellamy not to settle in Newyork. She did not think I would have done such a thing. Now you know Mr Bellamy told her.[30]

30. Joseph Bellamy, son of Matthew and Sarah Wood Bellamy, had been pastor

{*November 14, 1754*}
Thursday A.M.

Just now I meet with a paragraph in Miss Joans that has disgusted me extreamly, and beclouded all her witt and good sense. I have a good mind I'll read no farther but thro aside the book, but this you will say is prejudice. In one of her letters she undertakes to prove that there are such beings as *Demons,* and that men are often under the influence of em. One instance she mentions as [undeniable?] proof is Mr Whitefield and all the Methodists. She dont speak his Name but she says, "Some have left their ca[l]ling and all visible means of subsisstance, for the Kingdom of heavens sake, are now seting out for the Wilderness in order to be fed by the Ravens" and a quotation to the margin, "*Georgia*" and a great deal more that would be tedious to transcribe. She sets all zeal in relegion in the most *abominable ridiculous* light.[31] I am very poor[ly], hardly able to set up.

of the Bethlehem, Connecticut, Congregational church since 1738. He was a close friend and disciple of Esther's father, and a major New Light figure. His wife was Frances Sherman Bellamy, daughter of Rebecca Burwell and Nathaniel Sherman of New Haven. Dexter 1:523–29.

With this mention of Joseph Bellamy, Esther began a discussion (not always easy to follow) of the internal disputes of the First Presbyterian Church in New York. These disputes had their roots in early eighteenth-century tensions between New England Congregationalism and Scottish Presbyterianism, and they reached a climax in the early 1750s when Ebenezer Pemberton and other church officials had tried to introduce into the service Isaac Watts's version of the Psalms. In the wake of the ensuing controversy, both Pemberton and his associate minister, Alexander Cumming, had resigned. Shortly thereafter, a call had been sent out to Bellamy to become the church's pastor. In part because the call was opposed by several prominent men in the church, both the negotiations and the heated quarrels had dragged on for many months—even after Bellamy's "final" refusal in July 1754. At this time (November 1754) Bellamy's supporters within the church were trying to reopen negotiations once again. Esther clearly thought Bellamy should stay where he was, but Aaron Burr wanted him to accept the call, hoping that he would ultimately unite the warring factions.

Brother Janey was probably Captain James Jauncey, wealthy New York merchant and husband of Maria Smith Jauncey. Our guess is that Mr. and Mrs. "Professor" were merchant Nathaniel Hazzard and Elizabeth Drummey Hazzard. All three were members of the New York congregation and among Bellamy's strongest advocates. Webster, pp. 628–50; McLachlan, pp. 430–32, 458–60.

31. Mary Jones was undoubtedly alluding to John Wesley, founder of the Methodist Church in England, and to his brother Charles, as well as to George

Pray let me know who [*it is*] that is going to be married as soon as she will let you. You say tis a *friend*. I cant affect to dislike your writing so much to me, for I cant dissemble, and I should most abominably if I should pretend such a thing, but I can advise you not to write so much to other people.

{*November 21, 1754*}
Thursday Novbr. 21.

You may remember that this day week I told you I was very poorly, and so have been ever since, some of the time very bad. The Doct was affraid I was taken with the long fever, and is still affraid it may prove that or some other bad fever. I have not been able to walk alone for almost a week past, but today as our people were all at meeting (This day is our thanksgiving. I am very uneasy that you have not heard from me since by Mr Burr) I crawld as far as the case of drawers and got my paper and thought I would try to write a little but can no more.

This afternoon Mr Phillips, the Gentleman that preaches at the Castle, drank Tea with me and says he is going to Boston as fast as he can, so I conclude to send this by him. I hope the opportunity is safe.

I think I am in a mending way. I hope I shall get out soon. The Week after next a Presbitry are to set here, and tis expected they will dismiss Mr Burr from this Church and Congregation.

I am so very poorly and confused that I cant ad but Cordial Salutations to all friends in which Mr Burr joyns me. You my dear have and ever shall have my prayers and best wishes's from your very affectionate friend

Esther Burr

Mrs Serjant is still very low but I hope not daingerous. She is

---

Whitefield. All three had come to Georgia in the 1730s to establish missions and schools. The Wesleys soon abandoned their ministries there, discouraged by the hostile reception they had received, but Whitefield established an orphanage in Bethesda, Georgia, which he continued to promote until his death in 1770. *DNB* 20:1209–13, 1214–25; *DAB* 20:124–29.

[. . . .] Mrs Ogdens Daughters desire their kind regards to you. They often ask after you.[32]

(No. 10.)

{November 24, 1754}
Newark Novbr—24. 1754.

Dear friend

Yesterday just as I had sent away my No 9. Mr Foxcrafts son came in with your dear Letter.[1]

I am much refreshed with the good News you tell me about Boston. O that it may continue to go on and increase mightily till Boston become a Mountain of holyness and praise! I rejoice with you my dear that you have found the Lord to be with you of a truth, and that you have experienced so much of his loving kindness to your soul, and have had his enlivneing and quickning presence. I pray God it may continue throu' out your life.

I hope and pray that dear Miss Janny may not Miss this goulden season. You my dear friend have great reason to hope, and go on praying for her at such a time as this when the spirit of God seems to be striving among some. I am unable to write any longar.

(My Brother desires his regards may be made acceptable to you.)

{November 25, 1754}
Monday A.M.

This day is the time apointed for our Wood-Carting.[2] You have heard me say what a time of confusion tis. I am almost crazy, am not so well as yesterday, but I dont wonder at that. You say my

32. Mrs. Ogden was Hannah Sayer Ogden of Newark. Her husband, John Ogden, son of David and Abigail Hammond Ogden, was a prominent Newark lawyer and judge. Their daughters were Hannah Ogden, Abigail Ogden, and Jemima, possibly already married to Stephen Johnson. Wheeler, pp. 51–52, 65.

1. Samuel Foxcroft was the eighteen-year-old son of Thomas and Anna Coney Foxcroft of Boston. His father was the distinguished pastor of Boston's First Church. Samuel probably came to the College to teach in the Latin grammar school and to study theology. In 1765 he was ordained minister of the First Congregational Church, New Gloucester, Maine. Esther sometimes called him "Brother Sammy" (see note 3, Letter No. 9, above). Sibley 13:410–13.

2. Woodcarting was the custom of parishioners' providing the minister with a year's supply of firewood.

dear you believe you shant answer Mrs Cummings Letter untill you hear from me. My first thoughts are that tis best to write to her, but it may be I shall alter my Mind soon. You have given em *no occasion* as yet, and I should be sorry to have you give em the least grounds to blame you, or to say you have treated em *unhandsomly,* or with the least *neglect.* But these are my sick thoughts—If you do write I immagin it must be with some *craft.* You must be *friendly* but not *free.* You must be *good natured but very causious that you dont seem to Court em, for they will be very apt to suppose such a thing.* I count they stand *Tip-toe* to have you *kneel* and *cringe* for their favour.

{November 27, 1754}
Wednsday

Last Eve who should come in but my Sister Susannah to my great surprize as well as joy.[3]

My good Father is recovering very fast, and my Mother is much better than she has been.

I hear also that they are all well at Northampton. My Sister Dwight is not yet a bed but looks every day. . . . I could not write yesterday for want of a pen and now I have such a dolefull one I dont believe you can reed any of it.

{November 28, 1754}
Thursday

Nothing worth writing except that I a little more poorly than yesterday.

{November 29, 1754}
Fryday P.M.

You say page 74. that you are determined to prevent the publication of any of your Letters, but I imagine tis not soully in your power, which I desire to be thankfull for.

Mr Burr said the other day as he was reading Miss Joans's Letters, that *Miss Princes* were Ten times as well worth Printing as hers. So

3. Fourteen-year-old Susanna Edwards (also called Sue and Sukey, as discussed in note 27, Letter No. 9, above) had come to Newark to visit the Burrs but also to learn housewifery under Esther's direction and to help her sister with her many domestic obligations. She later married Eleazer Porter of Hadley, Massachusetts. *Edwards Genealogy,* p. 16.

tis not worth your while to vex your self for nothing, for I believe we shall have some of em in the Press *first* or *last*—O dear this *dreadfull Pen.* Ill try another—sometimes I write with a pen mended with the sizzers.

In the same page you say you fear I am uneasy about what you said upon *Obligation.* At first I felt a little hurt just when I read it, but I sat and considered a minut, and I knew you did not mean me, for you would not have wrote so if you had, and so got quite over it at once. I can assure you my dear If such a thing had stayed by me you would have heard of it, for I make conscience of telling in case I am in the least dissattisfied with a friend. Such things should not lay *grumbling* within, untill they are forced to *belch* out all at once like a *floud.* This I suppose to be the case with Mr *Fickle* and his Wife, and we see the Consequences. So dont be affraid, if I dislike anything you write you may be sertain of hearing of it, and I shall expect the same from you.

{November 30, 1754}
Saturday

Rode out and received no hurt but I hope some good. We are much in a clutters today cleaning the house fit for the Presbytery next Week.

I am so poorly I am much concerned how I shall be able to entertain em as they deserve, but I shall do the best I can, and wish all was better. And so they must except the *will* for the *deed,* and I know some of 'em will. Considering my bad Cough I have recoverd quite fast.

{December 1, 1754}
Sabbath

A very dark dull day, and I feel just as the wether is. O I long for a Sabbaths frame of Mind! But insted of that my thoughts wander to the ends of the Erth!

And in what ever duty I am engaged, I am as could and Dead as a stone! My heart I see is on the World and not on God! I fear I have got little or no good by this sickness! Whiles I was under the Rod It seemd as if God was nere, and I felt resignation, and a desire to be and do just what God pleased. But O God has left me!

Eve. Saturday in my haste I have made a most Egregious blunder which I never discovered till this minute, but you will pardon this and all others. But I am realy ashamed. (I dont wonder at your surprize but plese to turn it up and you will see *whats the matter.*) I would burn this, but I cant possibly write it over again for want of time.[4] As soon as I discoverd this bottom upwards work, it brought to mind Ro[. . .] Letter wrote the day after he was married. Pray dont you remember that Letter?

I am desireous of writing all I can this Eve whiles our people are at meeting (you must know they are all gon to hear the Scholars answer questions) for I dont expect to get time to write any more this 4 days, or not much.

Brother *Sammy* lives with *US* at present. I think he is a prety Clever Boy. He did not come so soon as Mr Burr expected so he had engaged another schoolmaster before he came, and I believe Brother *Sammy* must go out of the house for the schoolmaster had moved in before he came. So much for *Sammy.*[5]

Your *dream,* that you enjoyed your Brother in so many agreable characters, I think resembled your short lived friendship with Mr Fickle, for when you awoke *behold it was a dream*[6]—Ah! and if that had been all it would not have cost you so many heart-aching spels (I mean if it had been a dream.) How much more agreabl would the reflection be if all was realy a dream—But as we hope it has been sanctifyed for your spirittual good we aught not to regret it. . . . Page. 80. You desire Mr Burrs and my thoughts about what Solomans good Woman kept a candle a burning all Night for, and query whether she did not set up to read, or rather seem to take it for granted that she did.

I have asked Mr Burr for his thoughts, and he will not be serious about it but said in a jest that she kept a candle burning for the reason that Mr Pemberton did, but I intend to ask him again. . . . My thoughts are these—first her Candle goeth not out *by Night* (viz) *as soon as tis Night.* You know tis a common way of speaking, as for instance, such a person *did not get up by day.* We dont mean that he lay aBed *all day,* but he did not get up as soon as the day Broke—

4. Esther had written this page upside-down.

5. Samuel Foxcroft. See note 1, Letter No. 10, above.

6. Sarah's only brother, Thomas Prince, had died at the age of twenty-six in 1748. *NEHGR* 5:375–84.

our People are coming—you shall have more of this subject the first opportunity I can get to write.

{December 2, 1754}
Monday.

Extreamly hurried prepareing for the Presbytery.

{December 3, 1754}
Teusday.

Provided a dinner and nobody came till afternoon. That was enough to try a bodies patience was not it? But in the eve they come fast and thick.

{December 4, 1754}
Wednsday.

Dined eight Minnisters. In the forenoon a Sermon, in the afternoon the Presbytery sat upon our affairs, and adjourned till some time in Jannawary. Our people are in a great fude, some of em shew a very bad spirit.

{December 5, 1754}
Thursday

Dined 10 minnisters. In the forenoon was a sermon.

This day was spent in examening a young candidate for the Minnistry, one that is to go to one of the Dutch Islands in the West Indias that has applied for an English Minnister, and make very handsome offers to such an one. . . . Towards Night most of em went home.

{December 6, 1754}
Fryday

Company stays yet, the wether being very bad.

I am by this time almost wore out as I believe you think when you consider that last Saturday was the first of my going out. Indeed my dear I am quite sick. I wish you was here to pity me a little, but hold! What signifys wishing—I can write no more this day.

{December 9, 1754}
Monday

At last the house cleard of company. Yesterday Doct Smith tarryed

and preached all day. He is the Loyers Brother.[7] I am quite vext
that I cant get time to write more.

{December 10, 1754}
Teusday Eve

Know sooner is the house emptyd but filled again. Just now came
in Mr Tennent of Freehold, and his Wife, and two sons that he has
brought to put under Mr Burrs care.[8] I am of the mind that my
days are to be spent in a hurry of business, such sort of business as
this that I have mentioned.

{December 11, 1754}
Wednsday Eve.

Mr Tennent looks at me and says, "Poor creature, she is to have
no comfort in life I see! but always to be hurried to Death." But
Mr Tennent is misstaken for even in my being hurried I take pleasure, for it has always been recond by me amongst my greatest
pleasures to wait on my friends. Tis true sometimes I have those to
attend on that are not the most agreable, but how many I am rejoiced

7. John Smith, son of Thomas and Susannah Odell Smith, of Guilford, Con-
necticut, was a physician and a minister. He served as pastor to Presbyterian
congregations in both Rye and White Plains, New York. His wife, whom he
married in 1724 in Guilford, was Mehitabel Hooker Smith. His elder brother,
New York lawyer William Smith, is best known for defending Peter Zenger, the
New York publisher and printer who was tried in a celebrated libel case in 1735.
He was also one of the College's first trustees and a member of New York's First
Presbyterian Church. William's wife, Mary Het, daughter of French merchant
René Het and Blanche DuBois Het, had died earlier that year. Their son, William
Smith II, later wrote the recently reprinted *History of the Province of New York*, ed.
Michael Kammen (Cambridge: Harvard University Press, 1972), which was first
published in 1757. Dexter 1:207–11, 359–60.

8. William Tennent II, minister of the Freehold, New Jersey, Presbyterian
church and trustee of the College, was one of Aaron's closest friends and a much
sought-after preacher. He was the son of William Tennent, founder of the Log
College at Neshaminy, Pennsylvania, and Catharine Kennedy Tennent. His wife,
whom he had married in 1738 within a week of meeting her, was Catharine Van
Brugh Tennent. Most references in the journal to Mr. and Mrs. Tennent are to
this couple. Their two sons, John Van Brugh and William, were about to enter
the College's grammar school; they spent their first month in Newark in the Burr
household. Gilbert Tennent (see note 32, Letter No. 10, below), the most con-
troversial preacher in the family, was William II's brother. *DAB* 18:370–71;
McLachlan, pp. 247–51.

to see enter my doors—Went down to Elizabethtown with Mr and Mrs Tennent, dined at Mr Woodruffs, drank Tea at the Governors.[9] Found him and Madm very well.

{December 12, 1754}
Thursday

Made a visit at Parson Browns, the conversation as agreable as could be expected. They are well at Mr Browns.

Mr Burr is gon to preach at Newyork. One Mr Allin preaches here.[10]

Eve. I have received your agreable letter just now, and hear Mr Whitefield is this side Newhaven. I hope he will come to Newark once more. O that my heart might be prepared to receive good by him!

But to return to my good Woman which I had like to have forgot. By her Candles not going out by Night, or as soon as Night, May shew her industry, that her business did not cease as soon as night came. She was not in a hurry to lay all aside and go to bed as lazy people do. . . . It could not be that she sat up till two, or three, o' the Clock or great part of the Night as you seem to suppose, for tis said of her Vers 15, "She ariseth also while it is yet Night," etc. . . . Now I query whether tis possible for her to arise so erly (if she sat up so late as you suppose) and live under it, unless she was made of some other sort of *Matter* than we be, which is not very likely, for Soloman speaks of her as one of *US,* and that makes him *wonder so much, and admire her so greatly as to set her price far above Rubies.* I apeal to your own experience. You know you cant get up erly in the Morn if you set up very late, dont you, *say?* But if you have any objections to what I have said, pray let me know it in your next.

9. Mr. Woodruff was Samuel Woodruff. See note 14, Letter No. 9, above.

10. Probably Timothy Allen, son of Rachel Bushnell and Timothy Allen of Norwich, Connecticut, and husband of Mary Bishop Allen. At this time Timothy was pastor of the Presbyterian church in New Providence, New Jersey. During the Great Awakening he had been a leader of Separatist groups in Connecticut. He is most remembered today as the founder of the Shepherd's Tent, a short-lived seminary for training evangelical ministers. Dexter 1:551–55.

{December 16, 1754}
Monday Morn

Saturday Night about bed time I received a paquet from you I
suppose by the superscription but no Letter to my great disapoint-
ment. I cant but think there is one somewhere. I fear tis lost. . . .
In the bundle one lb of Cruels, and a pair of shoes for Sally, some
books, and two pair of Gloves seald up by themselves and directed
to Mr Burr and me.[11] The writing is not yours but I think tis Mrs
Funnils.[12] Who ever sent em we are greatly obliged to em. They
are charming Gloves—For those other things I return you hearty
thanks, and *think* my self laid under further obligations to you.
Altho' you will not let me say so, I may *think* if I mant speak.
Saturday Mr Burr sat out for Newyork but hearing Mr Whitefield
was there, returned—I fear he will not come here, he is in such a
hurry.

P.M. Mr Whitefield sends for Mr Burr to go to Elizabeth Town
for he is in such hast he cant come up here, which I am exceding
sorry for. I loted much on his company and conversation as well as
preaching, but submission becomes me.[13] I should have gon down
with Mr Burr but he was sent for to go directly, which he did in
about 10 minuts, and then I am prepareing to go to york on business.

{December 17, 1754}
Newyork Teusday Night

All at once about 10 in the Morn I concluded to come to york
it being a very fine day, for I was obliged to come soon on some
business that I chose to do my self. . . . About one oth Clock we
set sail and reached here about six in the Eve.[14] My Brother came

11. Crewels were bobbins of thin worsted yarn or thread used for embroidery
and tapestry. *OED*.

12. Mary Cutler Faneuil was the daughter of Timothy Cutler, Anglican pastor
of Boston's Trinity Church. She is remembered by her descendants as a well-educated
and literary woman who wrote poetry. Her husband was merchant Benjamin Faneuil, brother of the Peter Faneuil who gave Faneuil Hall to the town of Boston.
The couple's son Peter, whom Esther mentioned several times in the journal, was
a student at the College. McLachlan, pp. 185–86.

13. To lot on something meant to count on it. *OED*.

14. Travel from Newark to New York City was by boat across what are now
Newark and Upper Bays.

with me, for it will not do for Mr Burr and I both to be gon at once, *just Now*. Come to Doct Fickles, found Mrs Fickle Ill with the Head-ach, but seem to be very glad to see me, both of them.

{December 18, 1754}
Wednsday.

Rain all day. I sat in the house (and never so much as stept out) with Mrs Fickle and helpt her Make her Children some Hats. As for the Doct, he was in his study all day, could hardly allow him self time to eat. We talked about one thing and another, and amongst the things, and folkes, you my dear came on the Carpet, and engrossed no small part of the conversation I assure you—See an account of what Mrs Fickle said of and about you, in the private paquet to be burnt—As for the Doct, he said not one wor[d] about you good, nor bad.

Eve. Miss Nancy came to see me, and all the talk was *Bellamy, Bellamy,* and reflections on the Minnisters this way. She said that all they did in that affair was *lame.*[15] Twas evident they did not want Mr Bellamy to come amongst em.

{December 19, 1754}
Thursday

Out erly in the Morn on business, got Me a long Scarlet Cloth Cloke and some other things for famaly use. Mr and Mrs Bryant came to see me, and dined at the Doct. Mrs Bryant talked about you a great deal, and longs to see you. She says if you lived no farther off than Amboy she would go to see you directly. Capt Bryant says they have four *Popes* in Newyork, *women popes,* and who do you think they be? Mrs Mercy, and Mrs Hazzard—Mrs Breese and Miss Nancy Smith—Mrs Breese is *pope jone* he says—tis impossible to concive the Confusion that this place is in—What with

15. Miss Nancy was Ann Smith, a member of New York's First Presbyterian Church and a daughter of Captain William and Sarah Het Smith. Her father had recently died, and she lived in the household of Elizabeth Drummey and Nathaniel Hazzard. In 1756 she married minister Benjamin Hait, son of Elizabeth Jagger and Benjamin Hait, and moved to Reaville, New Jersey, where her spouse was pastor of the Amwell Presbyterian church. William Pelletreau, *Wills of the Smith Families of New York and Long Island, 1664–1794* (New York: Francis Harper, 1898), pp. 38–39; Webster, pp. 643–44; McLachlan, pp. 99–100.

Mr Bellamy, and what with the College, tis almost a Bethlehem! I tell em I would not live here a fortnight for any Money. . . . Eve. Supt at Mrs Mercy's. Mr Hazzard was there and Miss Nancy lives there. Came to the Doct and found Mrs Donaldson and Miss Kitty and Cousen Frank. All were very glad to see me.[16]

{December 22, 1754}
Sabbath Eve Decmbr 22.

Fryday Morn (Cousen Frank comes to bring compliments as usual) out on business. Dined at Capt Bryants with the Doct and Lady. After dinner returnd to the Docts, and in our return we were surprised with the Cry of Fire, and where should it be but at the City-hall (poor Mrs Cumming was almost affrighted to death) but in the space of 10 minutes was put out. . . . Sat drinking a Cup of Coffee and my Brother came in and said there was a Boat going to Staten Island in about a quarter of an hour, (it was now grown so extream coald that I dare not venture in our Newark Boats) so in the greatest hast got ready and went off with such a wind that carried us over the Bay in 40 minuts. It was so late when I landed that I concluded to lodge there that Night. It was well I did for I found my self sick with the coold when I sat down and considered of it. . . . Saturday about one oh Clock arrived safe at my dear home. Found my famaly all well, *Brother Sammy* gone to Mr Tennents to keep a school. . . . This day I found my self prety much fatigued, but went to Meeting in afternoon and eve.

16. Most if not all of the persons mentioned in this entry were members of New York's First Presbyterian Church. The Bryants were Captain William and Eleanor Bryant, later of Elizabethtown. Mrs. Mercy was Ann Bradford Mercier, daughter of printer William Bradford and wife of Captain William Mercier. Mrs. Hazzard was Elizabeth Drummey Hazzard (see note 30, Letter No. 9, above). Mrs. Breeze was Elizabeth Anderson Breeze, wife of Samuel Breeze, and daughter of James Anderson, the church's first minister, and Suitt Garland Anderson. Miss Kitty was Kitty Bradley. William Bryant's comment about the "women popes" was probably generated by the unusually active role these four women played in the controversy over the calling of a new minister (see note 30, Letter No. 9, above). Webster, pp. 332, 628–50; Dexter 2:107–08; McLachlan, pp. 395–97, 458–60.

Wednsday. 25. Christmas day.

Mr Burr went to Church very devoutly, and heard an old sermon preached three years ago. Mr Smith and Mr Allin a neighboring minnister, dined here. I have been so crouded with famaly affairs that I could not get time to write two days past—Sue is sick as is very common you know. I dont know but her illness will be a means of making me sick two, but that I must submit. I am realy very unwell. My Cough that I have spoke of above, has not left me but increases greatly. Last Night I did not know but I should have died with nothing but Coughing—I am so ill I must beg to be excused from writing any more this Night, so as a good Nights rest to you my *ever dear friend*.

Janary 1. about Noon

This day insted of being a play day is turnd into a fast which reaches as far as the bounds of our Presbytery. Was at meeting this A.M. Heard a sermon from Hosea 9th and 12 vers, "Though they bring up their Children etc." The discourse was very propor for the occasion. O my dear what reason have we to be humbled under the present thretnings of heaven which are very just and what troubles may we not expect at this day when iniquity abounds, and the *love of even Gods own Children waxes* cold. Indeed my dear friend we have reason to expect such times as this land never saw. Tis very probable *you* and *I* may live to see persecution, and may be called to give up every thing for the cause of God and a good Concience, even to *burn at the stake*—O Lord look in infinite mercy on us, and save this wicked land for the *Ten Righteous sake!*

It is extreem cold. My fingers are so numb that I cant write any more. . . . Eve. This P.M. an excelent discourse from the same Tex [*Text*]. I think there could not be any thing more propor for the occasion. In the first place was shewn somthing of the state of our Nation and the French Nation, and how probable it was that the French might overcome in their desighns as to this Country, then told us what might be the consequences in a very affecting manner.

I have not seen an assembly so affected this many years.[17] O that there might be some lasting affect on the hearts of the hearers! I have not wrote any thing this several days. I have been very busy about some other writing, as well as some famaly affairs which I find increas upon me.

{January 2, 1755}
Thursday

I am very glad to see people in any measure awake with a concern about the dainger of being swallowed up by our popish enimies. How much easyer this is, than to awaken sleepy souls (in the greatest dainger from their infinitly more tirrable foe the Devil) to the least concern about it. What blessed times would it be if all were as much ingaged in conversation about the grand concerns of their never dieing souls, as they are about their bodies and estates, when they immagine them in a little dainger of being injured.

Made a vissit at Colonel Ogdens[18] . . . had company to dine with me. Mr Sprout was amongst em. Perhaps you knew him in the New-light times.[19]

{January 3, 1755}
Fryday

I expected company but they did not come, the wether being bad—I sat down with a desighn to write, but my spirits are depresst with somthing I just now heard [*so*] that I cant write any more. When I hear more fully of the matter I will tell you. I suppose I shall to morrow.

17. This sermon, which was preached by Aaron Burr, was later published as *A Discourse Delivered at New-Ark, in New-Jersey, January 1, 1755. Being a Day Set Apart for Solemn Fasting and Prayer, on Account of the Late Encroachments of the French, and Their Designs against the British Colonies in America* . . . (Philadelphia and New York, 1755).

18. Seventy-five-year-old Colonel Josiah Ogden was the son of David and Elizabeth Swaine Ward Ogden. His wife at that time was Mary Banks Ogden. Wheeler, p. 45.

19. James Sproat, minister of the Guilford, Connecticut, Congregational church, was the son of Ebenezer and Experience Sproat. His spouse, Sarah Smith Sproat, was a sister of the Reverend Caleb Smith (see note 11, Letter No. 9, above). Dexter 1:690–92.

{January 4, 1755}
Saturday

You know my dear that Peter Funil studies here. Well, he takes it into his head to talk about Suky, my Sister that is here. Thus far was hinted to me yesterday, no more. Today I have inquired in to what he has said, and am glad to find not so much in it as I feard, tho' tis true he has been foolish, yet has not said any thing very bad about her—I am very sorry for his dear Mamma sake that he is such *a trifling good-for-nothing Chap.* It looke very doubtfull to me whether he will be able to get safe through College.[20] Had company to dine here today.

{January 5, 1755}
Sabbath Eve

I was at meeting all day and evening but have reason to lament and mourn my unprofetableness under such excelent means, and such a variety. In the afternoon and Eve Mr Sprout preached to universal acceptance. O my dear I hoped to have meet My Lord and Savior at his Table. But to my grief find no great alteration tho I think I was brought to some sense of my own utter innability to do anything for myself and my whole dependence on God alone. I expect that nobody see, or hear, anything I write about my soul['s] concerns.

{January 6, 1755}
Monday Eve

I think we go along much as we used to last winter (I hope you have not forgot that *It did'nt use to be so.*) You know how that was— dont you remember we made a vissit at Mrs Ogdens last Winter about this time?[21] Well I have made another today, and Sally with me. Mr Burr gone to Elizabeth Town as he used to do all the cold days last Winter (for you must know the weather is very cold.) Mrs Ogden and her Daughters are very well. Miss Abigail is nere marrying, as is usual for all young people *but Miss Prince.*[22] I know I talk a little (and not a *very* little nither) confused and at random,

20. Peter Faneuil. See note 12, Letter No. 10, above.
21. Hannah Sayer Ogden. See note 32, Letter No. 9, above.
22. Abigail Ogden, daughter of Hannah Sayer and John Ogden, married David Crane of Newark the next day. Wheeler, p. 65.

but I feel so, and my pen is so two, for tis one of the worst I ever took in hand. Sometimes it won[t] make any mark, then the Ink comes *pop out.*

I feel two silly to write anymore, so I think I'll leve off—No I wont nither. Pray what do you think every body marrys in, or about Winter for? Tis quite merry, is'nt it? I realy belive tis for fear of laying cold, and for the want of a bedfellow. Well, my advice to such is the same with the Apostles, LET THEM MARRY—and you know the reason given by him, as well as I do—TIS BETTER TO MARRY THEN TO _____.

I always said I would never be marryed in the Fall nor Winter, and I did as I said, and am glad of it. (I have been reading over my scrawls—And I dont know *whats the Matter.* It did not use to be just so bad I think.)

{January 12, 1755}
Sabbath Eve Janu. 12.

At last I have got time to break silence to my great joy—for a whole week past I may say I have conversed with nobody but my other self, for Conversasion with any body elce I have about me, I dont call Conversasion. I dont know what to call it, but I believe *Chit-Chat* will do as well as any name, for indeed tis no easy matter to give a name to *Nothing.*

To give you some general acount what has past since my last date, which was a week ago, and make such an excuse for my silence as your candour and good nature will except as suffisent, I shall begin with Teusday last—To my surprize had an invitation to Mr Ogdens in the Eve to see Miss Abbey married, for when I was there but the day before I did not mistrust she was to be yoked in two or three weeks—but they are to be pardoned. I suppose they did not know how to wait any longer. Wednsday, invited to dine with Mrs Bride, who is now Mrs Crane. Had a very good dinner, Turkey, and Plumb pudding etc. . . . I never saw Mr Burr in such a Weddingish humour since he was Married himself.

My thoughts run faster than my pen [*so*] that I leve out half.

Thursday, Fryday and Saturday, nothing remarkable but the weather very cold and I extreamly hurryed. My Wench is not so good as she used to be, which makes me an unknown deal of diffeculty. But I wont trouble you with my troubles (when you are at such a distance—But if you were here you should know all)— but just enough for an excuse for my silence, which was a vast mortifycation to me, and no disadvantage to you, but rather an advantage. For your precious time, that is every hour and minute of it devoted to some valuable purpose (except when to the reading of my Letters) is not so much of it wasted—*but stop pen* or you will get a reproof, when you dont desigh[n] it, nor mean any such thing as a complyment, but only just the natural breathings of thy soul— Not well this day and stayed at home all day. Adieu for this Night.

{January 13, 1755}
Monday.

I wonder what sort of Ideas you have of Mrs *Rowe,* I believe the same that I have. I have been reading some of her Real Letters. They are very fine. I wish I could see and convers with her. She was, to my notion hardly a mortal altho she did die. She seemed to live among the ded, and Angels and departed spirits. I wish she and Doct Watts had got togather and had one Child [*so*] that [we] might see what they could do.[23]

{January 14, 1755}
Teusday

To morrow the Presbytyry are to meet here, so you may think I am prety busy in the Citchin, making Mince-pyes and Cocoa-nut Tarts etc.

{January 15, 1755}
Wednsday Eve.

The Reverend Presbytry are now and have been ever since dinner setting. What they have done or will do I know not, they keep all to themselves. I feel very easy about the matter whether we stay or go. I suppose you have still a profound regard for our famaly, and would be glad to hear of the welfare of anyone of em.[24]

23. Elizabeth Singer Rowe (1674–1737) was an English religious poet and essayist. Esther may have been reading her *Letters, Moral and Entertaining, in Prose and Verse,* published 1729–33. *DNB* 17:338–39.

24. The Presbytery was meeting to decide whether Aaron Burr should be released from his position as minister of the Newark church. His congregation was reluctant to allow him to devote his time fully to the College presidency.

Brother Tomy is come [*to*] Town, dined here this day. I think he looks prety much as he used to but only about Ten Years older. I guss he begins to pine *about, and for the want of a Wife.*

{*January 16, 1755*}
Thursday Eve.

I am realy my dear, *very* uneasy, and *much* concernd that I hear *nothing* from you for so long a time—Are you alive? You are *sick,* and have kept your Chamber this *six weeks,* and perhaps will *die* before I can hear one word from you—But *stop*—I should not anticipate such tirrable evils—No, my *dear* lives and is happy, and injoys a good state of helth. She has sent me a long Letter two, but only it is unhappily lodged on sombodys *Mantletree-shelf.* I *will* hope the best.

This morn Mr Burr was sent to Newyork by the Presbytyry, to look into their affairs, and see if somthing could not be done for their reunion and happy settlement once more. . . . Four of the Minnisters stayd and dined with me. After dinner they all went a way, and I went out to make a visit at Colonel Jonsons. She was a *Newengland* woman, a *Oliver* woman. You know she *must* be of consequence.

{*January 17, 1755*}
Fry-day

I dont know but I write the same thing *over and over again,* and again, for as soon as I have laid down my pen, I have perfectly forgot what I have been writing about and I dare not read it over, for it appears so *silly* that I cant bare to send it out of my hands, and I hate to have such a mean opinion of my self—I believe if I should read [*it*] all over, I should not find but about one fourth part fit to send to you. . . . Our house is very gloomy, as tis *always* when Mr Burr is gone. I am ready to immagine the *sun* does not give so much light as it did when my best self was at home, and *I* am in the glooms two, half *ded,* my *Head* gone. Behead a person and they will soon *die.* . . . Strang tis no Vessels come, nor go, to Boston. I am realy impatient. You want to hear from me two.

{*January 18, 1755*}
Satur-day

Barrenness posseses me *wholy,* I have *nothing* to say any more than a *Dumb* Man, or an *Irrational Beast.* In short, my few, weak faculties that I once had in possession, are *gone,* for ever *gone* so far as I know! If Mr Burr should come home before I have been *dead* so long as to stink in the nostrils of all that are about me, *tis barely possible* I may (after my head is fixed in its propor place) recover to life, and the faculties of reason once more. Adieu.

{January 19, 1755}
Sabbath A.M.

Heard Mr Smith from 1 Peter IV Chap 8 vers, "and above all-things have fervent Charity among your selves: for Charity shall cover the multitude of sins." The drift of the discourse you know must be Charity, or Christian Love. So far as he has gone tis well done, but I shall by the leve of providence hear farther in the afternoon.

P.M. The subject finished, and very well done. I wish what I have heard this day may abide by me. Sure I am nobody needs such a lesson so much as I do. O how do I fall, *greatly* fall short of the Rules, the golden rules, that Christ and his Apostles gave us, not only in words and letter, but in deed and Practise! Mr Prince, Mr Smith and Mr Burr, are the most (I was going to say the only) suitable persons in our world to preach on this most excelent and divine subject. They do realy *abound* in Charrity. No dainger that the World will cry out Physicians, heal your selves, as they might If *I* were to preach on the subject.

{January 20, 1755}
Monday A.M.

Feel dull, heavy and stupid, can nither speak nor write, but I hope to find myself in the afternoon, a little more like a reasonable creature.

P.M. Miss Polly Banks I expect in to see me every minute, so cant add but only I have heard from Mr Burr [*that*] he is to be at home this day, good gentleman.[25] I wish he was here now. . . . Eve. Something happend to make us extreamly merry this eve. You

25. Twenty-year-old Mary (Polly) Banks was the daughter of Mary Ogden and James Banks of Newark. She was the granddaughter of Colonel Josiah Ogden and his first wife, Catharine Hardenbroeck Ogden (see note 18, Letter No. 10, above). In 1758 she married Princeton graduate Jesse Root, son of Sarah Strong and Ebenezer Root. Wheeler, p. 70; McLachlan, pp. 163–66.

will wonder what it should be, so to put you out of pain I'll tell you—I had orders from *Cousen Billy Vance* to dress *Brother Sammy* (this is my Brother you know) in womens Cloths, in order to act part of a play, which was done quite privately, and with no other desighn than to Lern the young sparks a good dilivery.

{January 21, 1755}
Teusday Eve.

Last Eve prety late Mr Burr came home almost sick, as he always is after a Newyork jant [*jaunt*], but he has *settled* the *Nation* for em, has got em all to a *man* to unite in sending for Mr McGegore [*MacGregore*] to come and settle among em, not as a probationer.[26] But I need not tell you. Mr Burr says he has sent to your good Papa about it. Mr Burr says that *Mrs Robie* is greatly altered for the wors by Marrying. He says, *that Life* and *Pleasantry* that she used to carry in her countinance is almost all gone. I thought so when I saw her but would not tell you till Mr Burr had seen her.

{January 22, 1755}
Wednsday

Mr Burr says Mrs Cumming is greatly affraid of the French and trys to get Mr Cumming to be willing to move to Boston, but he will not hear nor think any thing about the French, and dont care *two pence* for all the french. They are as safe at York as anywhere, there is no dainger, etc. Mrs Brese asks if the witnesses are yet slain. If they are not I suppose she thinks she shall *go to it.* Mr Burr told her that Mr Edwards thought that they were slain, and that seemd to make her feel prety secure. I have such a dreadfull pen, I am out of all patience!

{January 23, 1755}
Thursday A.M.

I had intirely forgot to tell you the result of our last Presbytry. They have concluded on the impertunity of the People, to continue

26. David MacGregore, son of Marion Cargil and James MacGregore, was born in Londonderry, Ireland. He moved with his parents to Londonderry, New Hampshire, where he became the town's West Parish minister in the 1730s. He ultimately declined the New York church's offer. Webster, p. 650; Frederick Weis, *The Colonial Clergy and the Colonial Churches of New England* (Lancaster, Mass.: Society of the Descendants of the Colonial Clergy, 1936), p. 132.

Mr Burr as their pastor for the present, at least till next Presbytry, but at the same time have recommended it to the people to be looking out for a Minnister, on a dependence that Mr Burr will sertainly leve em as soon as the College is fit for the reception of the scholars.

P.M. Made a vissit at Mrs Burnets.[27] The weather very fine, the roads begin to settle as if Winter had done its *due*. Things begin to sprout in the gardens—and upon the whole life looks a little more inviting than it did a month ago. Now if you was but here!

{January 24, 1755}
Fryday

You my dear cant immagine how much pleased of late Mr Burr is with his little Daughter. He begins to think she is good to kiss, and thinks he sees a great many beauties in her, that he used to be perfectly blind to. He complains she is another temptation to him, to spend two much time with her—he does love to play with her dearly. . . . O my dear how apt be we to set our hearts on the injoyments of time and sense.

{January 25, 1755}
Saturday P.M.

Tis an Age since I have heard whether you are an inhabitant of this little Earth, or whether you are safely arrived to the Regions above to Mantions of glory, as I am ready to immagine some times. O the happy day when we shall meet never to part! No such thing as distance of place or length of time to intercept our joys.

{January 26, 1755}
Sabbath A.M.

Was at meeting. Text Hosea XIV. 1 2 3 4 verses, "O Isreal return unto the Lord thy God: for thou hast fallen by thine iniquity" etc.

The subject was very applicable to the present day as you will see the words of the Text are if you turn to 'em.

P.M. The same subject with an exortation to our young people

27. Either Mary Camp Burnet, who married young Newark physician William Burnet in 1754, or Mary's mother-in-law, Hannah Burnet, whose husband Ichabod was also a doctor in nearby Lyon's Farms. McLachlan, p. 17–18.

who in a very *emphatical* maner may be called *Proud backsliders.* Indeed our youth make them selves vile and are not restraind, as was very justly observed from the Pulpit this day. They do indeed add iniquity to iniquity, and openly boast themselves and *glory* in their shame, and one of 'em was heard to say of a very good Man in the Town that observed some of their vile practises, that he wished him *in Hell* making room for *him.* O my dear friend what can such a people expect but the *vengence of Heaven* in a very remarkable and distinguishing maner!

{January 27, 1755}
Monday P.M.

We have just been talking about a journey in the spring some where. Mr Burr says I must go either to Boston or Philedelphia. I say if I dont go to Boston next spring I shall never go, but I can go any time to Philedelphia when we are once got so nere as Princeton. Now what do you think is best? (I wish you here to advise.) I should be not at a loss if it suted Mr Burr equelly, but he is obliged to go to Philedelphia in the spring, and cant possibly go to Boston, and poor *I* must go pokeing alone, which I dont half like—We have hung it up to consider on for the present—But this depend on without *ifs* or *ands* that if I do go I'll not return without you with me—I am resolved on't.

Eve 9 oth Clock. Mrs Brown, Colonel Ogdens Wife, Justis Ogdens Wife, and the Widow Ogden, all came and spent the afternoon here.[28] A very pleasant time we had of it. I do assure you, all I wanted was to have had your good company amongst the rest. Just about sun set Mr Tennent came in very unexpectedly. As it happned Mr Burr has appointed a meeting for the scholars to answer questions. As soon as he came in Mr Burr told him he must preach. He

28. Colonel Ogden's wife was Mary Banks Ogden (see note 18, Letter No. 10, above). Justice Ogden's wife was either Hannah Sayer Ogden (see note 32, Letter No. 9, above) or Elizabeth Charlotte Thébaut Ogden, who was married to Uzal Ogden; the husbands of both of these women were judges and both men were referred to repeatedly in public records as Justice Ogden. Widow Ogden we assume to have been Catharine Ogden Ogden, daughter of Catharine Hardenbroeck and Colonel Josiah Ogden; her spouse, who had died in 1750, had been her cousin David, son of Abigail Hammond and David Ogden. All were Newark people. Wheeler, pp. 51–64.

made a most *tirable* out cry about it, but nothing would do, so it must be, and after the Bell began to ring Mr Tennent had a Text to find. We went to meeting and he dilivered a charming discourse from Acts, those words, "The Will of the Lord be done."

{January 29, 1755}
Wednsday A.M.

We hear a deal about the two Governments in Newengland going on an Expedition some where, but that is kept a secret, which is politick. Be it where it will, my desire and fervent prayer is the Lord go with them and prosper them.[29] It does me good to hear any are engaged for their Country and the Relegion we profess. But alas! Here is our dainger, tis only profession—hold—I am two uncharritable, but you will forgive me. I beleive I feel a little as *David* did when he said all Men were liars. As for US here we act as if their was never such a thing to be as *War*. Newyork have but two guns that can be fired. They have been so neglected that they are rusty and got quite out of order, and more than that they have carried all their gun-powder to the French, and have not enough in the City to fire them [. . .] guns above twice. Did you ever hear the like![30]

Yesterday I went a vissiting.

{January 30, 1755}
Thursday

Mr Burr is writing a copy for the press of part of the sermon I mentioned preached on a fast-day.[31] He withstood a vast deal of impertunity before he consented but at last, as the unjust judge,

29. The "secret" here was that Massachusetts Governor William Shirley would be leading an overland expedition during the coming summer to capture Fort Niagara and that Robert Monckton would be leading a naval force to capture Fort Beauséjour and expel the Acadians from Nova Scotia. These two campaigns, planned late in 1754, were part of the first British effort of this war to drive the French out of North America.

30. Esther's cynicism was based on the reluctance of local assemblies to provide either funds or men for the colonies' defense. With the French and their Indian allies hundreds of miles away, and with widespread suspicion of the motives of both the British and other colonists, efforts to get the assemblies to support the war had gone largely unheeded.

31. See note 17, Letter No. 10, above.

was forced to yeald because of their impertunity. You my dear shall have one of em as soon as ever they come out.

{January 31, 1755}
Fryday.

Our Chairs lay a sleep and have done no work since you was their School-Mistress. I was looking of em to day, and concluded that they would sleep till Sally was big enough to set em a working agin.

{February 1, 1755}
Saturday. Feb the 1.

I feel very gloomy today, the weather is dark and black. I am so connected with it that it never changes but I change two. I think to send this Letter Next week to York. There is some prospect of a conveyance soon. I know you want to hear from me, *and how much,* I judge by myself. As *Face* answers to *Face* so does the *heart* of a *friend* to a *friend.*

{February 2, 1755}
Sabbath Eve

Two excelent sermons My dear I must say from Deuteronomy the 21 chap, 218. 19. 20. 21. verses. Pray my dear be so good as to turn to the passag. Tis so remarkable a paragraph that I think no one can read it and not feel mooved. Tis true, lamantably true that we have many of these Rebellious stubborn Sons, and Daughters two, amongst us. Never did our young people get to such a higth of wickedness as now. They are come to that, to go to pulling down buildings in the day time, and then so dareing as to say in excuse for them selves, "O we were drunk"—Drunkness and uncleanness prevail aboundantly. O my dear I am sick of this World!

{February 3, 1755}
Monday

I have an opportunity to write to Stockbridge so have time to say only this, that I am a widdow again. Mr Burr sat out this Morn erly for Princton.

{*February 4, 1755*}

Teusday A.M.

Messrs Tennent and Davies are returnd home safe. They have collected three Thousand Pounds Sterling.[32]

Now Mr Burr is freed from the obligation I spake of, of going to Philadelphia in the spring—but I dare not hope that we shall go to Boston.

P.M. *No* my dear we sha'nt go to Boston in the spring dont *hope* for it. I am sorry I have said any thing about it, for to give *hope,* and then to disappoint is a most *vexsatious* thing. Conclude we shall not come, and then all the better if we do, then there is no disappointment if we do not.

Pray my dear send my stays as soon as possible, for I am not fit to go out of my doors with these old jumps. If you dont think best to get em at Boston, pray send me word as soon as you can. I feel very poorly today being much disturbed last Night by Sally. My hand shakes so I can hardly hold my pen, but sick or well, I am your *most sincere friend.*

{*February 5, 1755*}

Wednsday Eve.

To my unspeakable surprize Mr Burr came home about Noon. I did not expect him in the least till tomorrow, to be sure. I shall Chalk it up. Tis very strang I can tell you for him to come home before the time set or I should not dwell on't so much.

{*February 6, 1755*}

Thursday Eve.

What a mess of stuf 'tis I send you. I am realy ashamed, and have almost come to a conclusion never to write any more. Indeed my dear I am quite sick of my self, and all I do, but especualy what

---

32. Gilbert Tennent, brother of William (see note 8, Letter No. 10, above) and one of the most powerful of the Great Awakening's evangelical preachers, was at this time minister of the Second Presbyterian Church in Philadelphia. His second wife, Cornelia DePeyster Tennent, had died in 1753. Samuel Davies was minister to a Hanover County, Virginia, congregation. His wife was Jane Holt Davies, from Williamsburg. The two men had just returned from Great Britain, where they had been seeking funds for the College. In 1759 Samuel Davies became the College's fourth president. *DAB* 5:102–03; 18:366–69; McLachlan, pp. 490–92.

I send you—To tell the truth I love my self two well to be indifferent whether I write or no, but in *down right compassion* to you 'tis that I have taken into consideration whether I shall write *yea,* or *nay.* Be not you tired of reading one page after another? *Say,* now be honest.

{February 7, 1755}
Fryday. P.M.

I'll begin to wind up for fear the Letter will be called for on a sudden and I have time to say only that I am your _____ etc. As to my going to Boston in the spring, to be serious, tis not possible as I can see. Many things are in the way which I could mention if it would not be two tedious. That I do long to see Boston once more is all I can say.

My dear, I depend on your coming here *before* or *by* next fall. Tis more than possible you may see Mr Burr at your House in that time tho' I am not quite sure, but he gives me a great charge to tell you that he depends on your coming whether he or I go or not. We are affraid you dont think of it in ernest.

{February 8, 1755}
Saturday

This Letter or what ever tis most proppor to call it is to set out on its journey on Monday next. I wish it a good journey and a spedy one. I almost begrudge its happyness of seeing the Face of my dear Miss Prince when I am deprived.

What! These scrawls injoy the privilege of being handled in the most free and intimate manner and I deprived! *In short I have a good mind to seal up my self in the Letter and try if I cant Rival it. . . .* I was at Mr Smiths today, they are well.

{February 9, 1755}
Sabbath Eve. February 9.

At meeting all day. Mr Burr preached in the forenoon, and Mr Knox in the afternoon, a very ingenious good young Man.[33] Mrs

33. A graduate of the College in 1754, Hugh Knox had emigrated to the colonies from Ireland only a few years before. After receiving his degree, he continued to study with Aaron Burr. Later in 1755 he became a missionary in Saba, a Dutch Windward Island in the Caribbean under the jurisdiction of the New York Presbytery. Many years later he married a Miss Simmons, the fourteen-year-old daughter of the island's governor. McLachlan, pp. 101–05.

Sergeant came out to meeting to day. This is the first time. Poor woman has under gone no tongue can tell how much.

Now my dear I must bid you farewell. I can only say the Lord be with you, and bless you, and make you a great, a Rich, a long and lasting blessing to me, to all your friends, and your self. . . . Mr Burr joyns with me in a vast deal of kindness and friendship more than I can express. And also our duty to your ever honored parents, and love to Dear Miss Jany, who I love sincerely. My kind regards to Constantia, Mrs and Miss Hunt, Mrs Royal that good woman.[34] My Complyments where you think proppor. . . . Adieu my dear and be happy. You may be sure you have an intrest in the daily prayers (I cant forget to pray for you unless I do for my self) of your unfeighned and very Affectionate Friend—

Esther Burr.

(No. 11.)

{February 12, 1755}
Wednsday Newark February 12.

To my very dear Miss Prince.

I have not been able to write since I sent away No 10. by reason of illness in my famaly. Old Mingo has been very ill with a sort of Plurasy but is recovering very fast.[1]

34. Constantia was a Latin pen name of one of Esther's and Sarah's Boston friends. In their correspondence eighteenth-century women sometimes used pen names that suggested their own names or some desirable quality. Hence Esther was Burrissa and Sarah, Fidelia. Although none of the women subsequently mentioned by pen name in the journal can be identified, some of them were no doubt members of the Old South Church women's prayer group to which Sarah belonged.

Mrs. Hunt may have been Sarah Wendell Hunt, a member of the Old South Church; she was the daughter of Jacob Wendell and the wife of John Hunt. We think Mrs. Royall was Elizabeth McIntosh Royall of Medford, who is well known among colonial scholars because the portraits of her and her family, painted by Robert Feke and John Singleton Copley, are among the earliest American paintings. Elizabeth was the daughter of Elizabeth and Lachlan McIntosh and the wife of merchant Isaac Royall, Jr. Sibley 9:412–13; Gladys Hoover, *The Elegant Royalls of Colonial New England* (New York: Vantage Press, 1974), pp. 24–28.

1. "Old Mingo" was probably a servant or slave in the Burr household. Mingo may have been a nickname for the Burrs' slave Harry (see note 11, Letter No. 11, below).

This morn Mr Burr went down to Elizabeth Town to a meeting of the Trustees. . . . Doct *Fickle* is going for Europe in about six weeks.[2] Mrs *Fickle* is either coming here to live or at Elizabeth Town till he returns. Pray dont you *congratulate* me on this *joyfull ocasion?*

{February 14, 1755}
Fryday Eve.

Yesterday was a day of as much confusion as I have known this great while. After-noon before we went to Bed there was Thirty, or Thirty one people came here, and most of 'em vissitors, and I hardly able to keep off the Bed. Amongst em those that you know was Loyer Ogden and Lady, Colonel Ogdens Lady, and widow Ogden who cant be content with having had one Husband, but must try again, and a young one two, about twelve years younger than her self—this is just what you have preached so often.[3] Towards night Mr Burr came home and Mr Spencer with him.[4] The Trustees have *settled the Nation.* At last something is concluded. Mr Smith of Philadelphia they have agreed with for the Whole (that is the College) for 4960£ . . . —the Trustees find stone, and Timber, and Mr Smith all other materials, and finishes the Library and 28 Rooms, and ingages to do that by August next a year.[5] . . . *Then to Princeton.*

2. Alexander Cumming was planning a trip to Great Britain to raise money for the College. He never made the journey.

3. Lawyer Ogden was David Ogden of Newark, son of Colonel Josiah and Catharine Hardenbroeck Ogden and husband of Gertrude Gouverneur Ogden. The couple had two sons at the College and one in the grammar school. This branch of the Ogden family was Anglican and had been since 1735 when Josiah Ogden, censured by the Presbyterian congregation for clearing a hay field on a rainy Sunday, left the church to establish Newark's Trinity Episcopal Church. In 1757, when a religious revival broke out among the students, David Ogden called his sons home abruptly and encouraged other opponents of evangelical fervor to do so as well. David's sister, widow Catharine Ogden (see note 28, Letter No. 10, above) did remarry but not until 1761, when she wed widower Isaac Longworth of Newark. McLachlan, pp. 161, 238–40; Wheeler, pp. 52–54, 65–70.

4. Elihu Spencer, son of Isaac and Mary Selden Spencer of East Haddam, Connecticut, was pastor of the Presbyterian church in Elizabethtown. His wife was Joanna Eaton Spencer, daughter of Joanna and John Eaton of Eatontown, New Jersey. Dexter 2:89–92.

5. Architect and master builder Robert Smith had been hired to construct the College's buildings at its new Princeton location, including both the main building, Nassau Hall, and the president's house, which Esther and Aaron occupied in 1756.

But I am realy tired of the World, and indeed such a day (as yesterday) is enough to tire a person that loves it the most.

How happy is the holy Hermits lot!
The World forgetting, by the world forgot.

P.M. Made a vissit at Mr Browns. Mr Burr went with me. She is very well. I believe you wish I would leve off, so good Night.

{February 15, 1755}
Saturday.

How *vain and empty* is the World and all its injoyments. Tis enough to make one weary of life and all its charms, but just now it han't many charms to me, altho' few have so many of its comforts and conveniences allotted to 'em as I have, nay I believe nobody. I am sure I would not change my circumstances for any one living. Do you think I would change my *good Mr Burr* for any person, or thing, or all things on the Erth? *No sure!* Not for a Million such Worlds as this that had *no Mr Burr in it.* But I must ask your pardon. You will think I am not so very indifferent to everything in the world nither, but to tell the truth when I speak of the *world,* and the things that are in the *World,* I dont mean *friends,* for *friendship* does not belong to the *world. True friendship* is first inkindled by a spark from *Heaven,* and *heaven* will never suffer it to go out, but it will *burn* to all *Eternity.* I am apt to think that the *indifferance* I feel, is not from a weanedness from sensual injoyments, no I am not in so good a frame, but arises from bodily disorder, and a degree of low spiritedness, tho' I am better than I was yesterday.

{February 16, 1755}
Sabbath Eve.

At meeting all day. Mr Burr is still insisting on a reformation in famalies, and tells the people they must expect that this will be the burthen of his sermons until he sees reformation beginning. He has been remarkably stired up to be fervent in his preaching of late. O that the Lord would bless his labours! You my dear will joyn heartily in this petetion.

The Princeton designs were two of Smith's earliest; he was later recognized as one of the colonial period's finest architects. His wife's name was either Esther or Hester. Both husband and wife appear to have been Quakers. *DAB* 17:335–36.

{February 17, 1755}
Monday with a dreadfull pen.

P.M. I am realy sorry for poor Mrs Cumming. When I put the tryal *home* it touches me in a tender spot for the poor woman. . . . I guss she had *almost* as leve you should have had the *Revd Doct—* as that he should die at sea.

{February 18, 1755}
Teusday Eve.

This affternoon sat out to take a ride with my Brother, but meet a woman coming to make me a vissit and so turnd back. That was mortifying, was not it? Tis late, and I have nothing to say for I am one half ded and half a sleep as you see by my blunders. I'ene to bed. I wish you a very goodnight.

{February 19, 1755}
Wednsday.

P.M. Rode out to make a vissit, but was sent for home because a woman was come to see me that head not been at the house for a year, and after I had been at home a little while a company of little *Flurting* Misses came in. In short I was a good deal vexed about it, to be sent for home from a vissit that I had been contriving to make a long time to wait on a parsel of triflers.

{February 20, 1755}
Thursday Eve.

Snow all day. It seems as if winter was just seting in now. . . . Last Eve some travilers came here to lodge, this Morn went away. P.M. Mr Smith came here. It seems as if nothing went forward but coming, and going. I wish now I could take wing and fly to Boston into your Chamber, and set and chat about two days without any interruption. No body should know where I was gone, nor any body in Boston know that I was there. I am tyred of this Tedious round. I thought to have wrote a little more but I have got to the bottom of page and tis most convenient to leve off, for you must know it must cost me the trouble of geting some more paper out of the chamber and that is a pety, ant it. You shall never have reason to complain, as you have done, of Newark Blank paper.

{February 21, 1755}
Fryday.

A degree of melancholy has seezed me a few days past. I can give no reason why, nothing in petecular troubles me. I hope nothing, nor fear much, from the world. I am perfectly satisfyed with my lot in life, and can say as Miss Joans in one of her poems to a Lady. "The summit reached of Erthly joys."

I want nothing that the world can give, but feel perfectly contented. I believe this gloom arises from bodily disorder; I am not so hearty of late as I have been most of the winter. Tis common for me to begin to fail in February.

{February 22, 1755}
Satturday A.M.

This morn erly Mr Princes Letter came to Mr Burr with a few lines from my dear *Fidelia*. O how refreshing tis to finde you on this Erth yet! Indeed I cant be willing to wish you so happy as to be amongst the stars. I am govournd by a spirit of self-love two much to consent to have you shining in the heavens yet. I will not call it self-love wholy nither, for in pety to a poor degenerate age I would pray that your valluable life may be lengthened to a *good old Age*. Mr Prince says you are all in usual helth. This is beyond all my hopes. I expected at least to hear you was confined to your Chamber, and Miss Jany is with you two, dear little creature. In short all is as I would have it, if I must be deprived of your company. Those lines you speak of in Mr Princes Letter, that you recommend to my serious thoughts, I shall consider in a short Letter by the Post for the sake of a spedy conveyance.

I am just ready to set out and go to Boston for that Letter. I hope it will not be long before it comes.

{February 23, 1755}
Sabbath Eve.

At meeting all day. A.M. A very awakening sermon to young people. P.M. A discourse to rouse old peopel to do thier duty to their Children and servants, in counciling, instructing, and restraining 'em—I cant but hope some good will be spedily done in this place. Mr Burr is in a very uncommon digree stired up to sound the alarm of the Gospel.

{February 24, 1755}
Monday Eve.

A very stormy day, snow and Rain, N.W. wind blows very hard. It seems more like winter than any day this year.

Mr. Burr is exceding Ill with a bad cold, and Teeth-ach, head-ach and a fever. This P.M. have put a blister-plaster on his neck. Added to *all,* one of the scholars have a *bad* report raised about em and I fear not without some grounds. This sinks Mr. Burr into the Earth, [*so*] that he cant sleep—so on the whole you may conclude we are not very bright to day.

{*February 28, 1755*}
Fryday P.M. February the last Day.
Mr Burrs illness and my own has prevented my writing any thing since monday except the Billet in Mr. Burrs Letter to your good Papa. I am still very poorly with a bad Head-ach. We have a vast deal of company of late, much more than when you was here. I am almost wore out and tired of *staying* here, for living I cant call it. Tis all tumult and confusion, going and coming, tis this, that, and every body. O for some calm retreat, far from the busy World!

I had almost forgot to tell you that I have begun to govourn Sally. She has been Whip'd once on *Old Adams* account, and she knows the differance betwen a smile and a frown as well as I do. When she has done any thing that she surspects is wrong, will look with concern to see what Mama says, and if I only knit my brow she will cry till I smile, and altho' she is not quite Ten months old, yet when she knows so much, I think tis time she should be taught. But none but a parent can concieve how hard it is to chastise your *own most tender self.* I confess I never had a right idea of the mothers heart at such a time before. I did it my self two, and it did her a vast deal of good. If you was here I would tell you the effect it had on her.

{*March 1, 1755*}
Saturday March 1. day
A woman here Ironing for me, and I am very busy mending stockings and one thing and another, so would beg your pardon for this day.

{*March 2, 1755*}
Sabbath Eve.
A.M. A discourse exhorting Christians to the great duty of ad-monishing one another in a kind friendly manner.

P.M. A sermon from those words, "Husbands love your Wifes; and let the Wife see that she reverence her husband."

You can guss what sort of a sermon we had. It was realy to the purpose.

{March 3, 1755}
Monday. A.M.

I am of Solomans mind that there is no New thing under the sun. I am sure I have nothing new to tell you unless it is strange that we have company always, and at all seasons. This Morn a gentleman of the Court was here before we had done breakfast—O I have somthing new to tell you that was quite out of my mind! It is a brand New thing, such an one as never done under the sun before. Our assembly have voted *500. pounds in full,* to help carry on the war. Did you ever hear of such *generous* people before, *say*? I dont believe that Boston can for their lives produce such a number of *generous-sould Patriots.* Our assembly have been in Travil this several months, and we all in pain to have her delivered least she should die in the cause, and we have nothing brought fourth. But somthing is come at last—You my dear remember the Mountain that Traviled and brought fourth a Mouse.[6]

{March 4–5, 1755}
Teusday, Wednsday.

Nothing material except extreme cold. Vissited some of our good honest Christians. True it is that religion dwells among the poor— low and despised. I had some agreable conversasion with some of 'em. O how good is it!

{March 6, 1755}
Thursday Eve.

Mr Burr took it into his head to go down to Elizabeth Town in a *slay*—we went. I did not go to the Governors, but staied with good Mrs Woodruff whiles Mr Burr and Mr Sergeant went to wait of his Excelency, who is very hearty for him.[7] (Tis very strange that I should forget to tell you that this day Sally began to speak so as

6. The assembly also stipulated that the funds could only be used to provision British troops marching through New Jersey.

7. Jonathan Sergeant. See note 13, Letter No. 9, above.

to be understood—she trys to say Mamma and very pretely brings
out Mam—which is above half the word.)

{*March 7, 1755*}
Fryday P.M.

How over joyed I have just now been! I could not help *weeping*
for joy to hear once more from my *dear, very dear Fidelia*—and do
you yet live! Mr Burr was not within when the Letter came. The
cover was a little worn [*so*] that I could see just one or two words,
found it to be your dear hand. I broke it open with [as] much
egerness as ever a fond lover imbraced the dearest joy and dlight of
his soul . . . . And you are very well two. O how kind is God to
me! But in the midst of my joy I am half *mad* at you for paying
the Postage—pray did you think I could begrudge anything for
such a line—or did you suppose we had no money. If I had not I
have some credit. I could be trusted for a small sum.

{*March 8, 1755*}
Saturday P.M.

The sermon is come out of the press. I suppose it to be the only
one we shall ever get in the press. You my friend shall have one of
em as soon as an opportunity serves. Tis a little odd, there is no
text, and not much method compared to your New England sermons, and for that reason may be rejected by those nice people that
cant swallow anything but Text and Doctrine first, second propo-
sition, then inferences in just such an order. Mr Burr says you must
tell 'em that people this way are prerejudiced against the Scriptures,
and the discourse would not go down so well. If at the beginning
stood a text of Scripture, they would perhaps be so frightend with
that and the authors being a Presbyterian that they would not dare
to venture any farther.[8] . . . Rode out in the slay.

{*March 9, 1755*}
Sabbath Eve.

Our sacrament day. I dont remember I was ever so afflicted with
vain wandering thoughts at such a season in my life, but God be
praised, by the assistance of his holy spirit I got the mastery in

8. Aaron Burr's January 1, 1755 sermon. See note 17, Letter No. 10, above.

some measure in the P.M. . . . I thought to have wrote a little more but my intollerable pen obliges me to leve you for your nights rest.

{*March 10, 1755*}
Monday P.M.

Phoo, folks always coming. Eve. I have borrowed Pamelia and am reading it now. I fancy I sha'nt like it so well as I did Clarissa, but prejudice must have its weight. I remember you said that in your opinnion it did not equel her.[9] Your judgment my dear has a very great influence on mine. Nay I would venture to report that such a Book surpast such an one, if you said so, if I had never laid my Eyes on 'em—but forall I intend not to be so complaisant but I will have a judgment of my own. Tis quite late. May guardian angels protect my dear friend this night.

{*March 11, 1755*}
Teusday. P.M.

I say nothing to your repeated proposal yet, because we have a third time taken it into consideration.

Eve. Pray my dear how could Pamela forgive Mr. B. all his Devilish conduct so as to consent to marry him? Sertainly this does not well agree with so much virtue and piety. Nay I think it a very great defect in the performance, and then is'n't it seting up Riches and honnour as the great essentials of happyness in a married state? Perhaps I am two rash in my judgment for I have not read it half out tho' I have enough to see the Devil in the Man.

{*March 12, 1755*}
Wednsday P.M.

I thought to have gone out this P.M. but honest Mr Greene came to dine with us and spends the rest of the day here, so here am I.[10] . . . Your dear kind letter is so full of comfort concerning the troubles we lay justly exposed to from enimies within and without, that I am quite revived. We are at last listing Men here, but not

9. Samuel Richardson's two novels: *Pamela*, published in 1740, and *Clarissa*, published in 1747–48. *DNB* 16:1129–33.

10. Possibly William Green, husband of Lydia Armitage Green, who was a farmer and an elder of the Presbyterian church in Trenton. The Greens' son Enoch later became a student at the College. McLachlan, pp. 310–12.

to send abroad. No to be sure, they are only for our own defence. This is much better than nothing. Nay tis necessary we have sombody to appear in case the French undertake to drive the Country, tho' I think they say that if Newyork is invaded they are to be so neighbourly as to help 'em—hark—here comes sombody—Rap, rap—O! It is Mr Smith of the Mountains—I must run to the door, Harry is not within.[11]

Eve. I am quite angry with Mr Fielding.[12] He has degraded our sex most horridly, to go and represent such virtue as Pamela, falling in love with Mr. B in the midst of such foul and abominable actions. I could never pardon him if he had not made it up in Clarissia. I guss he found his mistake, so took care to mend the first opportunity.

{March 13, 1755}
Thursday A.M.

Mr. Brainerd comes to make us a vissit, and I hope will stay the Sabbath over, the weather being very bad. His little Daughter has met with a most sad mischance. About six weeks ago she fell into the fire and burnt her hands and face most tirrably, but is like to recover with the loss of one of her fingers.[13] O why was not this my tryal! But perhaps greater tryals await me—O to be fitted for Gods holy will and pleasure in every thing!

P.M. The rain stops nobody. Just now comes Mr Thane and Mr Sergeant.[14] I perceive more folks are expected here on some business—but here they come sure—Mr Woodruff, Mr Spencer wet as drownded Rats. I go to wait on em—Another gentleman from Elizabeth Town. I think peopel are beg——d to run about so in the rain. Tis a very stormy day as I have known this great while.

11. Harry was a slave owned by Aaron Burr. We have not been able to ascertain his full name or any other information about him.

12. Esther was confusing Henry Fielding with Samuel Richardson.

13. Sophia Brainerd was just nineteen months old. She only lived a month beyond her fifth birthday. David D. Field, *The Genealogy of the Brainerd Family* . . . (New York: John F. Trow, 1857), pp. 285–86.

14. Scotland-born Daniel Thane was one of the College's first graduates. He was minister of the Presbyterian church in Connecticut Farms, New Jersey, today part of Elizabeth. His wife, Mary Clowes Thane, was from Long Island. McLachlan, pp. 11–12.

{*March 14, 1755*}
Fryday A.M.

Jist now Mr Burr with Mr Brainerd sat out for York. Mr Burr will spend the Sabbath there. I hear Mrs Fickle has concluded to take lodgings in this place whiles the Doct is gone.

Eve.

Made a vissit at Colonel Ogdens, and Mrs Sergeants. She continues low, is discouraged. She now looks every hour for her time of Travil. . . . I may without a spirit of prophesy venture to say I shall never see Boston if I dont this spring or next fall, at least not for many years. Yet I cant see it duty to go this spring, altho' I have a very great desire to it. Mr Burr two is urgent that I should if that scheme fails that I sent by the post, and I fear it will. I am affraid you will never come here again if I dont go after you—I am so vapory I know hardly anything but that I am your tender-hearted friend—so good-Night—I hope to be better able to write about it tomorrow.

{*March 15, 1755*}

Satturday. So very busy that I cant get time to write.

{*March 16, 1755*}
Sabbath. Eve.

Last Eve, about 7 in the Eve Mr Brainerd came to spend the Sabbath with us. He found he could not get home to his Indians so Mr Burr prevaild on him to come and preach here. He left Mr Burr well. Mr Brainerd has given us two excelent sermons. He seemed much engaged as if he could pour out his whol soul if by any means he might do some little good. After meeting, Mr Badger and Knox came to see Mr Brainerd. The conversation turnd naturally on relegion—O my dear how Charming tis to set and hear such excelent persons convers on the experimentals of relegion! It seemd like old times, but this was two good to last long. Soon we had a room full of vissitants.

{*March 17, 1755*}
Monday. Eve.

Mr. Burr not come home—how impatient to see those we love and love us, tho' they have been gone but a very short time. I believe

I have looked out for Mr Burr since Noon an 100. times, and have avoided looking as much as possible two—every minute seems an hour—I wonder I am so foolish—but I cant help it, and I will look, and will hope, tis hope that keeps persons alive—pray what would life be without hope—hope is almost every thing—they that have most of it are the hapiest I believe—but hark—I think I hear a horse—I must go and look. . . . Well the dear gentleman is come sure enough—goodnight.

{March 18, 1755}
Teusday A.M.

I can only tell you my kind friend that Mr Burr brought your kind paquet which contained as follows—A billet in confidence, another called memorandem, Memoirs of the Illustrious most Noble William Flutterbox Esq and his companions. The Fable of the Rose Bush, which nither Mr Burr nor I have sense enough to understand so as to apply, so much desire further explaination—A Key, which I shall keep, as you kindly give leve, and that I may safely, for nobody can use it but me. . . . Miss Jannys Letter. Pleas to give my love to the dear Girl and tell her I shall answer it as soon as possible but she must not wait for that.

You can excuse me when I tell you I am making Cake for spinning-frollick to day, which is to be attended tomorrow and several days after as I suppose. (I forgot to tell you that Doct Fickle came here today and is going to Freehold to take leve of friends.)

{March 20, 1755}
Thursday. P.M.

Yesterday spinning, Mrs Brown was here amongst the rest— I hear there is a Vessal to sail soon for Boston so must begin to winde up.

There is a great many things that make it impossible for me to think of going to Boston this spring, as I told you before. It would be two tedious to give all the reasons in Black and White. I think I shall go next fall *if another Voyage does not prevent between this and then, which is very possible.* Dont let anybody see this. This aught to have been on a billet to be burnt but tis down.

I find I was not settled till I had a Child, and now I am effectually settled, a journey seems a Vast thing. I am to go to Princeton soon, which seems like Ansors voyage almost.

I think there is some excelent observations on the duties of the Married state in *Pamela*. I shant repent my pains I guss.

{*March 21, 1755*}
Friday. Eve.

This day a messenger came from Fairfield with the news that Mr Thaddeus Burr was at the point of death and desired to see his son who sat out immediately.[15]

O how unsertain is Life! We know not what a day may bring forth! I thought to have wrote a deal to day because I shall send this away to morrow, but a vast deal of company has prevented, *Uncle Tuttle*—pray dont you remember him?[16]—Mr Spencer and Wife,[17] people from Newengland—scholars in great plenty—spinning folks—Pedlars—The Oister man, and a Wash Woman—But why do I trifle thus—Plese to make my Duty acceptable to your honored Papa and Mamma.[18] My kind love to Miss *Julia* and *Constancia*. . . . My service to *Marinus* and *Marina,* also to Confidenta, Laura, Simpathia, Leomira and Mrs Hunt. . . . Mr Burr and my Brother joyn in tender affectionate regards to you my dear friend as

15. Thaddeus Burr was one of Aaron's cousins. He was a wealthy landowner in Aaron's native Fairfield, Connecticut. His wife, Abigail Sturges Burr, had died two years before. He died just a week after his son was called home. Young Thaddeus, who inherited a sizable portion of his father's estate, was then a student at the College. He had lived with Esther and Aaron for at least a brief period. He later returned to Fairfield, where he married Eunice Dennie, daughter of James and Eunice Sturges Dennie, and became active in Connecticut politics. McLachlan, pp. 135–37.

16. Uncle Tuttle was Esther's uncle Moses, son of John and Hannah Humiston Tuttle of New Haven. He had married Jonathan Edwards's youngest sister, Martha, and had been a minister in Granville, Massachusetts, until 1752 or 1753, when he was dismissed. Possibly he was without a regular church until 1756; at that time he was minister of a Presbyterian congregation in Kent County, Delaware. Dexter 2:66–69.

17. Mr. Spencer's wife was Joanna Eaton Spencer (see note 4, Letter No. 11, above).

18. Sarah's mother was Deborah Denny Prince. See note 18, Letter No. 9, above.

also to your good parents. Farewell my dear and be happy says your affectionate,

Burissa

(No. 12.)

{March 27, 1755}
Newark. March 27 day. 1755

To My dear Miss Prince

Tis *long,* very *long* since I have said one word to you, a whole Week, for which I should be utterly inexcuseabl were it not from necessity. I shall endeavour to be as petecular as I can think your kindness could desire. . . . The last I wrote I belive was Fryday last Week. Nothing remarkable of a Saturday except that P.M. Rode out with Mr Burr, which is a little uncommon of late. He has been much taken up otherwise.

Monday Eve Doct Fickle returnd from Freehold in order to take leve of his friends here, and to see the Lodgings we had taken for his Lady in his absence, which he is pleased to approve off. Teusday it Rain'd all day very hard [*so*] that the poor Doct could not stir one step—this was very mortifying indeed as he confessed—and to tell the truth I could not help being hurt for the honest Man. His time with his *Honey* was then but about Ten days—pray dont you think twas a tryal. . . . Wednsday the Rev'd Presbytry sat. They over persuaded the Doct to give 'em one more sermon before he left them, which he did by opening the Presbytry with an excelent discourse as they say. I could not be out my self—then he took leve of us, and seem'd affected. It really hurt me, and I said in my heart I never shall see him again.

Then we went to dinner and very good company of Ministers I had around my Table—I do love to entertain good Ministers, that [*is*] sertain—O—I forgot to tell you that in the Morn I received a Letter from Mrs *Fickle,* begging of me and Mr Burr to use all our influence with the Doct not to go, and proposed him for a Minister for Newark, but that wo'nt do I know—She wrote in such a distressed manner that I could not help being touched at the very heart, and when I put my self in her circumstances I could weep for her if it would do any good. . . . P.M. Presbytrey sat on our affairs, and on thoro' deliberation, after seeking to God for direction, and obtaining the consent of the people so far as to say if it must be done we think it would be best to have it done now, they proceeded to dessolve the Pastoral relation between Mr Burr and this People. . . . Thursday Presbytery sat erly in the Morn. Some of 'em went out of Town before dinner but not all. We had a prety good Tablefull. After they had dined they all went. . . . Eve. And here I be—writing to my *Fidelia*. I begin to feel as If I had recoverd my senses again. Indeed I have not felt right since I neglected writing to you—I will hope I shall never be prevented so long again.

{*March 28, 1755*}
Fryday

Your goodness will excuse me to day, I have several Letters to write home by my Brother.

{*March 29, 1755*}
Saturday.

We hear nothing of Capt Wimble yet, I am affraid he is cast away—The match you propose we had thought of before, and Mr Burr concluded to give him a hint the first oppertunity. I wish the good gentleman might succeed with all my heart. He deserves better fortune in the World that [*is*] sertain, than he has yet had.

{*March 30, 1755*}
Sabbath P.M.

I have been at Meeting all day. A.M. Mr Burr preached from Jeremiah—"They have forsaken me the fountain of living waters etc"—A good practical discourse. P.M. Mr Knox the young gentleman I have mentioned several times preach a good sermon from Romans III. chap. 28 vers. . . . After meeting he and My dear Mr Burr sat and talked on some very important points of our holy relegion—realy my dear I am under *many, many* advantages to know and do duty, and the servant that know his Lords will and did it [*not*] was beaten with many stripes—O how great will my condemnation be if I fail of the grace of God! O my dear pray for me!

{*March 31, 1755*}
Monday.

Excedingly busy, expect company, and our Negroes are gone to seek a Master. Realy my dear I shall be thankfull if I can get rid of 'em.

My heart was up at my mouth when I come to that Passage in your Memorandom, "If a French War dont come etc."—this you crost out but you was kind enough to leve it in such a manner that I could easily read it—but pray why need War hinder you? You can come by Land if not by water. (Mr Tennant came to see us.)

{April 1, 1755}
Teusday Eve.

A great deal of company this afternoon—I am almost tired to *death*. Vacancy began to day.[1] My Brother is gone home, the Scholars are all gone almost.

Tomorrow Mr *Burr* and *Brother Sammy* and *I* am invited to dine with the Govenor—O—I had like to have forgot it! Cousen Billy Vance is going to be Married—did you ever hear the like? Pray what can he do with a Wife?—he is more of a Woman than of a Man.

{April 2, 1755}
Wednsday A.M.

It rains very hard so we all stay at home and eat our own dinner— rain stops nobody from coming here altho' it does us from going abroad—Tomorrow if the weather is tollerable we shall procede to take this *wonderfull* dinner that we have attempted so frequently. If we are disappointed again I shall think a fatallity attends the poor *dinner* or rather poor *us*—I am highly pleased with some of *Pamelas* remarks on Married life, as well as her conduct in it—She was more than Woman—An *Angel imbodied*.

I sent for Doct Farrand. He seemd concernd for the Child, and ordered a portion Physick, which I gave about 1 o'Clock.[2] It does not yet opperate, but the Childs Fever has increased much this P.M.—God only knows what his will may be, but this is my comfort that she is in the hands of a mercyfull God, who has said, *Suffer little Children to come unto me and forbid 'em not*—I have *again,* and *again,* given her to God and I hope by *faith*—I think if I know my own heart, I can trust her in the hands of that God I have indeavoured

1. The College's recess.
2. This was Newark physician Daniel Farrand, who had graduated from Yale College in 1743. His wife was Margaret Farrand. Dexter 1:734.

to give her to, after death—But O my dear when this Letter comes to hand (altho' you ma'nt know what God has been pleased to do with the Child) pray for me ernestly that I may not be found wanting in my duty to this my dear Child whether in *Life,* or *death!* I wish I could say somthing a little more comfortable before I send this away, but I am affraid Mr Oliver will be gone.[3] I can only add that I have had the pleasure of hearing from Northampton, and that they are all well. Sister Dwight has another fine *Son,* which I suppose you have heard[4]—Brother Dwight says he heard from Stockbridge some time in Feburary, and my Mother had about that time had a very bad fall from a Horse, but was mending. This is all we have heard from there this five months.

Pleas to give Duty Love and service to all that you pleas, to your honored Parents, Miss Jany etc—Think my dear how gloomy I must feel, Mr Burr gone a long journey who I may say is all my comfort when at home, and when gone I seem to have none left. And I am affraid I provoke God the giver of all my many comforts by seting my heart two much on this dear gentleman, to take him from me— and—Alas what would all the world be to me if he were out of it!

But hold—I am two gloomy—you must not let any body see what I have wrote. Out of the aboundance of my heart my pen has spoken—Farewel my dear friend—says your ever affectionate

Esther Burr

{April 7, 1755}

Monday Morn. Sally is a Little better.

---

3. Our best guess is that Esther was referring here to Andrew Oliver of Boston, son of Elizabeth Belcher and Daniel Oliver, and nephew of New Jersey's Governor Jonathan Belcher. He was a member of both the Massachusetts Provincial Council and Boston's Old South Church. His wife was Mary Sanford Oliver, daughter of William Sanford. In 1771 Andrew became Lieutenant-Governor of Massachusetts, but he is best known as the stamp officer targeted by Boston mobs after passage of the Stamp Act in 1765. Sibley 7:383–413.

4. Mary Edwards Dwight had given birth to her second child, Sereno Edwards Dwight, on December 10, 1754. Benjamin W. Dwight, *The History of the Descendants of John Dwight of Dedham, Mass.* (New York: John F. Trow, 1874), 1:140.

(No. 13.)

{April 7,1755}

Newark. April 7th. 1755.

Dear (and ever shall be) Miss Prince.

This Morning (Monday Morn) I sent away No. 12. to go by Mr Oliver—I feel but very indifferently to day, what with [be]ing disturbed for several Nights past, and what with Drums, [G]uns, Trumpets, and [F]iddles, I have a very bad Head-ach—tis Training-day h[er]e. I wish I was out of the noise of it.

{April 8, 1755}

Teusday.

Sally recovers very [fa]st but is very cross. I am affraid this illness will cost [her] a whiping spel.

To day I have [been] reading an account of Mr *B.s* going after the *Coun*[*tess*] of ———. This appears very strange to me considering the [title] of the Book, which is, *Virtue rewarded*—I could but ju[st] stomach to allow it that title before, for he was a sad fello[w] to be sure, had one Child, *bastard,* and did his indevour to get many more as it seems by *Lady Davers,* and his own confession two—but I dont know—I have a poor judgme[n]t of my own. I wish you would be so good as to let me ha[ve] your thoughts on this affair, and I should be glad if it is not two much trouble on the whole History. I know you have made every usefull remark that could be made—there is sertainly many excellent observations and rules laid down [*so*] that I shall never regret my pains—you need not wonder if I write a little upon the scrawl for I have Sally in my Lap—In my humble opinion *Riches,* and *honour,* are set up two much—can Money reward virtue? And besides Mr *Bs* being a *libertine* he was a *dreadfull high-spirited Man, impatient of contradiction* as he says of himself—*Pamela* had a task of it, with all Mr *Bs* good qual[i]ties. She was as much affraid of him as of a Lyon—If the author had [le]ft it to me to have intitled the Books, I think I should hav[e] chose *Virtue tryed,* instead of *rewarded*—In that af[fai]r of the Contess he was vastly to blame, and would no dou[bt] have kept with her some part of his time at least, as his [wife?] if he had not been prevented just when he was.

{*April 10, 1755*}
Thursd[ay] Eve.

I have been to make a *set* v[isit] at the Loyers.[1] T'was as agreable
as could be expected. . . . I could get no time to write yesterday
nor can I to-day, altho' I am very loth to be deprived of this very
agreable imployment, and amusement, one day, and doubley so
when I cons[id]er it gives my dear friend pleasure at the same time
that I do m[y]self.

{*April 11, 1755*}
Fryday [A.]M.

Well—*Pamelas* virtue is *rewarded* at last, Mr *B.* is become a good
Man. I confess I had waited for this *reward* 'till I was quite discouraged, and after that *black* affair of the Countess I wholy dispared
of a *reward* in this World—but I want to find a little fault for-all—
Might not Mr *Fielding* as well have spared himself the pains of this
last tryal? Was not her virtue thoroughly tryed before? P.M. Have
been to see Mrs Sergeant—she is in a fine way to get up well. The
Child is very hear[ty].

{*April 12, 1755*}
Saturday. P.M.

The weather is [ve]ry fine. I am glad [of] it for Mr Burrs sake
and Mr Cummings, wh[o] I have heard to d[ay] is gone into Newengland with Mr B[ur]r. Cap' Wi[mb]le is arrived at last. I have
sent this day to see what he has brought from you. Indeed I cant
bear i[t t]o think that I cant have anything but a small Letter [now]
and then, I want a *Long Letter* as long as from here to Bost[o]n. . . .
Well I have finnished *Pamela.* Tis realy a ve[ry] good thing for all
my ill nature about it—I always [thin]k of Miss *Jenny,* when I read
of Miss *Sally Goodwin,* y[ou] remember her—but I guss Miss Jenny
has more soft[nes]s in her temper.

{*April 13, 1755*}
Sabbath Eve.

After a vast deal of p[ai]ns, Runing, writing, and Rideing, we
got two Minister[s] for the P.M. but none for the Morn so our good
Deacon [pr]ayd and Mr Foxcroft read.

1. Lawyer David Ogden. See note 3, Letter No. 11, above.

P.M. Two sermons. Mr Smith preached one, and a very good sermon it was—tho' I have great reason to lament I was not in a good frame to hear. I am so bad—that a little matter puts me out of a good frame, which makes me fear I never was truly in a go[o]d frame. Company comes in—Good Night [my] dear.

{April 14, 1755}
Monday A.M.

I have a short Letter from Miss Kit[ty] Bradly in answer to one I wrote on business and with it [a] sermon of Mr Princes on the death of Mrs Cary from [M]r Cary to Mr Burr.[2] Eve. I hear Mr Cu[mm]ing is not [go]ing to Europe for the present, but is [abo]ut to remove to [B]runswick with his famaly, and it l[ooks] very likely he w[ill] settle there, for Brunswick peopel ha[ve] had a great n[ee]d for him some time but he refused 'em. . . . T'other [nigh]t I had a most Charming dream—I thought one day just [be]fore dinner *your own dear self,* and *Miss Jenny* came, you said just to look on me, and to return after dinn[er]—I was over joyed at the sight, but said how could [you t]hink to go so soon—you said that you and Miss Jen[ny o]nely rode out for a day or two, and was to return, but th[e w]eather being very fine you concluded just to *step* to N[ew]ark and see *me* and my little *Sally,* and return with all [pos]sible speed, for nobody knew where you was, and there w[oul]d be a dreadfull uproar after you. So I could say noth[ing] then but be thankfull that I could have your company one [sin]gle hour. So we two retired whiles dinner was geting to unboosom our souls to one-another, and we had no soonner began to feel our happyness, and alas my Visionary Bliss was gone for I awoke!

{April 15, 1755}
Teusday Morn.

It was very late last Night when I wrote, or I should have troubled you with some of my reflections on that agreable *dream,* which then

2. The sermon Esther attributed to Thomas Prince was probably Thomas Prentice's *The Believer's Triumph over Death, and the Grave. A Sermon Occasion'd by the Decease of Mrs. Anna Cary, Late Consort of Mr. Richard Cary of Charlestown; and Preached There (the Sabbath after) March 2, 1755. And Now Published at His Desire. . . .* (Boston, 1755). Prentice was minister of the Charlestown, Massachusetts, Congregational church. Sibley 8:81–89.

were fresh in my mind, but I have now lost 'em—Tho' my dear I cant but think it was an emblem of a persons being called out of the World by death (perhaps you will think it more like being brought from death to life, as sleep resembles death) which often hapens at a time which perhaps those persons of all times of their lives would chuse to live, or perhaps at a time when the World is fullist of Charms—realy my dear their was somthing so Charming in you as I thought, that I was heardly perswaded that it was a dream, and to be sure should have been exceding glad if the airy Phantasy had been indulgd me till our sweet Conversation was ended. But if it had I should have had the mortifycation to have parted with you so soon. . . . I have been interrupted by company coming in five or six times so you will pardon my scattered broken thoughts.

Eve. The *Governor,* and *Lady,* and Mr *Oliver,* rode up this P.M. and drank Tea with me. Just now I received a Letter from Mrs Cumming—Adieu.

{April 16, 1755}
Wednsday P.M.

Mrs Banks has this day actually left her husband and gone out of Town. She was in to bid me farwel and said she was ruened soul and body, and cryed as if her heart would break, and I cry'd two. 'Twas very affecting indeed. O my dear what am I better than she that it was not my portion to be Bound to such a *Beast,* Nay *Devil* he is more like!

I am no better, yet how different are my circumstances from this poor Woman. I have all that is kind and Pleasant, whiles she, all that is unkind and disagreable—I have all my grasping Mind could wish, whiles she meets with nothing but disappointments in all her desires—O my dear pray for me that I may live answerable to the mercies I have and am daily receiving!

{April 18, 1755}
Fryday Eve.

Yesterday I spent in rideing about on business—Today the same—The married Woman careth for the things of the World etc. You my dear are not interrupted by such affairs as takes up most of my time.

At last the long looked-for and long-wished-for is come, your dear *social-thoughts,* and with it my stays, a bunch of pens, a pacquet directed to Mr Donaldson, a number of Pamphlets—(little Sallys sugar plumbs which she is very fond of—altho' she did not know what to do with [em?]). Every thing you send you contrive should be of use, so much as the paper you put about the pens is a prety thing. Words cant express my joy and gratitude, my joy that you are so comfortable and still allowed to me, my gratitude for kindnes's—It will take sometime to read the charming journal (which my impatience to read will hardly allow me time to return thanks for) so I fear I shant be able to say much for a day or two throu' the multiplicity of business I am ingaged in.

With your pacquet I received Letters from Stockbridge and Northampton informing that all are well.

{April 19, 1755}
Saturday P.M.

(Spent A.M. in vissiting some *sick,* and the poor *Prisoners* that you know are very near to me—poor Doct Burnet is very ill, not likely to live—tis thought he is poisond by his Wentch.)[3]

In what Language shall I address you? Or what [strain?] can equel that of my *Fidelias?* Sure you are more than your self or anybody else! I am *ashamed,* and *confounded* to think of useing my pen for you any more—Excuse me my dear, and be content to let me set at the feet of my dear friend and lern of her everything that is excellent.

O how do you surpass me in everything! I am left *far very far* behind in the Christian race to bemoan my own *deplorable* case, and can only look to the example of my beloved friend, and wish I was what she is! O Lord quicken me by thy unerring grace! And O let me never be content untill I arrive to that state of perfection that my dear Miss Prince is so much nearer than I am!

---

3. Either Dr. Ichabod Burnet or Dr. William Burnet. See note 27, Letter No. 10, above.

{April 20, 1755}
Sabbath.

I hope your *Charming* Letter has been in some measure Blessed to me—O my friend how much good you do wherever you turn your self, whether in Conversation or writing. At meeting all day. Heard Mr Clark on the glory of Christ and his being the Life of the Saints.[4] This is a charming theme—I thought it good to go to the house of God and meet his Saints, but *alas* for me, I cant attain to what my *dear Instructris* has, yet! God of his infinite mercy grant that I may be quickned by your surprizing example—I should highly value (as you my dear do) such *charming friends* as you have about you—*friends* that one might unbosom their whole soul too. You are sensible my friend that it is quite otherwise with *Me*. There is *not one person that will talk freely to me on relegion in this Town* —out of our own house—Not *even Mrs Sargeant*. She is very reserved on *these accounts*—but I feel thankfull that you are so *blessed*—Tis not fit that I should have everything agreable. I have already a *Thousand, Thousand,* more mercies than I make a good improvement of—I esteem *relegious Conversation* one of the best helps to keep up relegion in the soul, excepting *secret devotion,* I dont know but the very best—Then what a lamentable thing that tis so neglected by Gods own Children—Ah! Relegion thou gettest many a stab from thy *professed Friends!* Joab like!

(I understand your Rose-Bush fable now.)

{April 21, 1755}
Monday. just at eve.

About 8 O'Clock Mr Burr comes *pop* in greatly to my joy and surprize as you will guss, for he told me he should not be at home till the middle of the week. I am extreamly grieved about your and our disappointment—how was it? I feel as if I could not be passafied. My dear why could you not have sent us such word soon in the spring. If you had I should have been in Boston by the beginning of April that is sertain and Mr Burr would have come to us from Pelham to have waited of us here. I know I must submit—No I

4. We think this was John Clark, a Presbyterian minister who graduated from the College in 1759, when he was about forty-one years old. Little is known about his life prior to his graduation. McLachlan, pp. 266–68.

cant nither—You *must* come, and Mr Burr says *shall* if he sends on purpose. He is much distresst for you altho we dont *know,* yet we can *surspect*—Mr Burr has a scheam in his head that I hope will do, so I hope you will keep in readiness. We shall write by the post.

{April 22, 1755}
Teusday Morn, fine weather.

This Morn in the famaly we all joind to sing *for you* and *our selves* the Psalm you mention. Tis a charming psalm and very suitabl to our case as well as yours.

Yesterday I wrote, and sent your Packet to Newyork. I hope Mrs Donnaldson will not refuse my paying the Postage of your Letter, and to inforce it I told her that we had dealings togather. I should think it time to make up accounts with you if their was not a great prospect of your coming soon, and then we can make up much easyer than by writing—I am concernd because I know I am in your debt.

P.M. Mr Burr perswaded me to go to Elizabeth Town with him. We went to Mr Spencers but they were from home so I did not deliver your pamphlet. Saw Mrs Belcher [*and*] Mr Woodruff.

{April 23, 1755}
Wednsday P.M.

I am charm'd with your verses on my little Sally. I insist upon it that you send me more of it, let it be on what it will. You are used to the work or you would never be so expert without time or thought—Why if I was to study a Month (I might as well have said all my life) I should not be able to make such a vers. I have not a tallant that way no more than an *Ass* to play on instruments of musick. You'll excuse this cours comparison it just *popt* into my mind as I was writing—but for all that I love versifying in others. (I desighned by all means to have wrote to Miss Janny but tis impossible—I hope she will write by you to your humble servant.)

{April 27, 1755}
Sabbath Eve

Tis several days since I have said one word to you, but my heart has been at Boston with you very often.

My dear Little Sally has been very sick and as we feard near to death, (she was taken on Wednsday Eve, altho' she had been drooping before) but Gods goodness is continued and repeated in spareing her as yet, perhaps only to give us time to prepare us for the sore tryal we have apprehended so nigh.

She is still quite low and as I apprehend not out of dainger. The Doct think she has had somthing of a Pleursy, to be sure she has had a very violent feaver. She has been extreamly tendsome, would go to no stranger, so Sukey and I have been obliged to watch every Night ever since her sickness [so] that I am almost got to be as bad as the Child.

Two O.Clock in the Night as Sally is a sleep in the Cradle and I a rocking.

As I am alone I wanted amusement to keep me from sleeping, so I thought I would scratch a little to you whiles you are asleep. How extreamly the silence of the Night resembles the silence of the grave. Mr Hervy has most butifully painted in his Contemplations on the nig[ht]—and Doct. Young in his Night-thoughts which you are better acquainted with than I am.[5]

I have been reading till I am so blind that I cant see to write.

{April 30, 1755}
Wednsday Eve.

I am forced to neglect you soarly against my inclination.

I have the pleasure to tell you that my Sally recovers very fast, but is extreamly cross, crying all day *Mam-Mam* if I hant her in my Arms, [so] that she is more troublesom than when she was sicker altho' tis not so distressing.

I have been distrest to death since I wrote last—Mr Spencer comes up and says he cant go to Boston, his Wife is not willing (Mr Spencer is under peticoat govourment that is sertain—) altho' tis plain he has a great mind to go. *Nay,* Mr Burr thinks [he] could be perswaded for all but tis not best to urge the matter two much—Who knows but she may *think, and fear, as a sertain Lady has done before her*— Not that I have the least reason for this suspicion—but

5. Writers James Hervey and Edward Young were both Englishmen. Esther was referring here to Hervey's "Contemplations on the Night," in vol. 2 of his *Contemplations and Meditations,* published in 1747, and Young's *The Complaint: or Night Thoughts on Life, Death, and Immortality,* published 1742–45. DNB 9:733–35; 21:1283–88.

you and I have seen and heard such strange things that one may be almost allowed to surspect any thing—That same Lady mooves to Brunswick this Week.[6]

But I hope all is for the best yet. Mr Burr has concluded to send Mr Knox the gentleman I have had ocasion to name several times. He has no Wife to ask about the matter, which I suppose you won't be glad to hear of, but no dainger of talk, for he is soon to sail for the West-Indias to the Island of Saba and does not think of a Wife no more than he does of a Crown. He is quite a charming Man. I hope he will sute as well as Mr Spencer, and Mr Burr thinks much better—I was going to give him a character but you will see for yourself what a clever man he is better than I can tell you. I shant be able to say one tenth part of what I desighned for the gentleman goes to morrow as far as Newyork, and I am a little affraid wont go at last, for I perceive Newyork is to be consulted on the affair. But if he should happen to fail you can come with Mr Smith. Mr Burr will write a letter to him by Mr Knox to be dilivered in case he should fail, that is if Newyork dont chuse him to go but chuse rather to send two of their own members which is not likely in the least.

I leve your last Letter wholy unanswered for want of time and a dependence on an oppertunity to answer it Personaly (Since I think of it, it would be nonsense for me to write much if I had time— you would be so hurried abot coming away that you would not get time to read.)—Come you must if you are alive—sick or well you must come—I shant be able to support under the disappointment so I wont think it possible.

My Duty to your honored Papa and Mamma. Love to Miss Jenny and all the Sisterhood—I am so ill I can say no more but that I shall be much more ill if you dont come to see your Most affectionate friend

Esther Burr

I was up with Sally almost the whole Night last night so you wont wonder to see such scraches and scrawls from your—Burissa. April 30. 1755.

---

6. The "certain lady" was Eunice Polk Cumming. See note 5, Letter No. 9, above.

(No. 14.)

{May 9, 1755}
Newark. May the 9th. 1755.

To my ever dear, and much respected Miss Prince.

I had concluded not to write any more untill I saw you, but Alas for me I fear tis all over! You will not come I fear! Things have turnd out very strangely! Mr Spencer is an unaccountable Man! Mr Burr says it seems to him that he has contrived to disappoint in as many respects as he could possibly.

In the first place when Mr Burr mentioned his dependence on him to go to Boston, *forsuth* he would not hear a word of it. *"His Wife would not consent,"* he said—Well as soon as Mr Burr had contrived another method to get you here which would sertainly have done excedingly well Mr Spencer sends up [*that*] he would go by all means—Mr Burr was vexed to be Nosed about by him but said if he could but get you here in a way that would be agreable to you he did not much care. Now Mr Knox was gone to Newyork and carried our Letters so Mr Burr sets out erly the next Morn to tell Mr Spencer that he must not fail to call on Mr Knox for the Letters and to contrive the best and most comfortable way for your coming. Mr Burr could think of no way that would be convenient but the way you came before—but Mr Spencer could not go by Water. He said he should go all the way by land and, in short, Mr Burr said the ungreatfull creature did not care whether you came or not, nor whether he obliged or disobliged us.

Mr Burr came home very much displeased and said if he had thought Mr Spencer would not have been glad to [*have*] waited of you here he would have seen him to *Bantum* before he should have gone, for Newyork were not very willing he should go[1]—Then after all this, to compleat our uneasiness and distress, My Lord Spencer goes throu Newyork *Pilgarlick* and never calls for the Letters nor so much as inquires after Mr Knox[2]—We have been excedingly distressed to know what to do. Sometimes we thought to write by the

1. Bantam was an area in Java from which Europeans imported domestic fowl. *OED*.

2. According to the *OED*, pilgarlick derived from "peel-garlic" and was a slang term for a bald-headed fool.

next Post, but it could not get to you in season—I do feel angry at Mr Spencer. I cant help it—but tis all the ordering of a wise providence and becomes me to Eye the hand of God and not the hand of man—Perhaps I lotted two much on it—I thought so before but now I am convinced of [*it*]—But some hopes will remain yet for I have received your gound and scirt which looks like a foreRunner of somebody.

My head achs very bad so Adieu. Be you where you will, I will love you. (Your Application to Doct Wig[*glesworth?*]s sermon is much to the purpos and if Mr Burr had wrote one I beleve twod be much [such?] an one.)³ (Never fear—Mr nor Mrs Fickle have never seene one word you have wrote me, nor never shall with out your leve nor then nither if they dont think it worth asking for.)

{June 3, 1755}
June the 3 day—Teusday P.M.

Tis three long weeks since I have wrote one word to you, for between hope and fear I knew not what to do—when I thought of writing this would be upon my mind, why I shall see Miss Prince soon and then I can say much better what I think than I can write. (You desire me to send word by what vessels I send, but this I cant do for I dont know myself. I send my Letters to Mr Livingston and trust to his prudence.)⁴

When I thought it was possible that you might not come, I was so confounded that I had nothing to say, so I have lived along untill my return from Philadelphia which was yesterday—I shall give you

3. Esther was probably talking here about one of two sermons: *Some Distinguishing Characters of the Extraordinary and Ordinary Ministers of the Church of Christ* (1754) or *Some Evidences of the Divine Inspiration of the Scriptures of the Old Testament* (1755). Both were written by Edward Wigglesworth, professor of divinity at Harvard College and staunch critic of George Whitefield in particular and the Great Awakening in general. Wigglesworth was the son of the eminent Puritan divine Michael Wigglesworth and Sybil Sparhawk Wigglesworth. Sibley 5:546–55.

4. Peter Van Brugh Livingston, son of Philip and Catharine Van Brugh Livingston and husband of Mary Alexander Livingston, was a prosperous New York merchant, a member of New York's First Presbyterian Church, and an active participant in provincial politics. He was also one of the original trustees of the College, where two of his sons would receive their degrees. Dexter 1:430–31; McLachlan, pp. 232–35.

as petecular an account of my journey and what I saw, and heard, as I think will be agreable, as it is a part of the Country you have never seen.

This will take me time for I am much fatigued with the hurry of the journey, and heat of the Weather, and besides I have a great many Letters to Write to one and another—by the Way I have recieved No. 10. and 11., the last by Mr. Spencer. O my friend this Letter was not what I expected—no—I expected nothing less than your OWN DEAR SELF—but alas how disappointed! How vain all my hopes!

O help me to consider that God has done it and so I will hope tis for the best.

I am greatly grieved that you have meet with so much affliction and I am senscible some things come very nere which you dont and perhaps cant tell me off, for it you could you would I am sure—but again my dear you are greatly blessed with the divine presence which makes every affliction not only tollerable but comfortable, and we have reason at such seasons to say that it is good for us that we have been afflicted.

Your resignation to the divine will in everything is truly examplary, and I hope I shall indeavor to follow your blessed steps, who have so far out run me.

{June 4, 1755}
Wednsday A.M.

As you say, I believe tis true that I love you too much, that is I am too fond of you, but I cant esteem and vallue too greatly, that is sertain—Consider my friend how rare a thing tis to meet with such a friend as I have in *my Fidelia*—Who would not vallue and prize such a friend above gold, or honour, or any thing that the World can afford?

You must not talk about dieing soon—I cant bare it—I could not help weeping whiles I read pages 205–6–7–8–etc. I am trying to be weaned from you my dear, and all other dear friends, but for the present it seems vain—I seem more atached to 'em then ever—If God does not teach me the vanity of all things under the sun I shall never be taught—perhaps he designs to teach me by affliction and bereavement—O to be fitted for all his holy will!

{June 5, 1755}
Thursday.

Poor paper, but the best I can get.

You will kindly excuse me today because I am hurried with writing home by an unexpected oppertunity.

{June 6, 1755}
Fryday Eve. (A fast day on account of the drought.)

God has in a very remarkable maner shewed himself a God hearing prayer—We had hardly got home from Meeting in the P.M. but a fine showr came up and it looks likely to turn to a settld Rain—O how good is our God! He not only gives us temporal blessings freely, but *spiritual* and *heavenly* blessings!

{June 7, 1755}
Saturday

I see I was much out of the way in not continuing my journal, for now I have nothing to send to you, and if I had done as I aught I could have dispatched a paquit for you immediately as soon as I see you was not come, but I will send as soon as I have given you an account of my journey, which I cant do to day I am so busy— this going abroad makes a deal of work—and all for nothing I was going to say. (Received a Letter by the Post from my dear Fidelia informing of me that she cant come yet but hopes to see me before Winter.)

{June 9, 1755}
Monday

Last Eve I spent in writing to my two Sisters at Northampton.[5] And now I will give you some account of my journey—on Monday Morn very erly before we had eat Break-fast we sat out and got to Brunswick about eleven o'Clock. Went to Mr Cummings and dined. About one o'Clock we set forward, got to Princeton by Five at which time the Trustees were to meet—I went up to College but was two much tired to look much.

Teusday Morn erly we set forward, joind by Mr Tennent, and came safe to Philadelphia by Tea time in the afternoon—this was

5. Mary Edwards Dwight and eight-year-old Elizabeth (Betty) Edwards. Young Betty was then living with her older sister's family. *Edwards Genealogy*, p. 16.

quite smart Rideing to go with a Chair 90 Miles in two days, but I found myself much wearied when Night came—We were received with great kindness and respect by Doct' Shippen and his famaly where we lodged[6]—Wednsday Morn one Mr Smith (he was borne and brought up in Boston so I call him a Boston man) came to see us and invited us to dine with him but Mrs Shippen said that I must dine with her that day, and Thursday she and all of us would go togather. Wednsday P.M. Mr Smith brought his Lady to see me, and her two Daughters and Sons Wife came to see me, all of em very agreable Ladies much like Boston Ladies, free and easy in their behaviour and friendly—With these Ladies we spent the P.M. in a most Pleasant and agreable manner that ever I did amongst total strangers in my life. We seemd acquainted at once—to be sure I was pleased highly and I believe they were not displeasd by there looks and actions.[7]

{June 10, 1755}
Teusday Eve.

Today dined at Govourner Belchers. He and Madam are well.

But to procede with my journal—on Thursday A.M. we dressd and went to the Accademy to see the young gentlemen deliver of

6. William Shippen, son of Abigail Grosse and Joseph Shippen, was a prominent Philadelphia physician. He is also known for assisting Robert Smith (see note 5, Letter No. 11, above) with the plans for Nassau Hall. He married Susannah Harrison Shippen, daughter of Joseph and Catherine Harrison, in 1735. The couple had four surviving children, one of whom was Susannah (Sukey), who came to live with Esther and Aaron later in 1755 to be trained by Esther in housewifery and the essentials of evangelical religion. In 1767 she married Samuel Blair, a minister of Boston's Old South Church. Susannah's eldest brother, William, who would later distinguish himself as a pioneer professor of anatomy and midwifery at the College of Philadelphia (later the University of Pennsylvania), had just graduated from the College of New Jersey. Her brother John (Jackey) was a student in the College's grammar school and would enter the College itself in the fall. McLachlan, pp. 118–22, 243–44, 302–06.

7. These Philadelphia Smiths were probably merchant Samuel Smith, a founding trustee of Philadelphia's Second Presbyterian Church; his wife, Mary Harrison Smith, who may have been a sister of Susannah Harrison Shippen (see note 6, Letter No. 14, above); and their two daughters and their daughter-in-law, none of whom we can identify by name. Samuel and Mary also had two younger sons, Jonathan and William, both of whom later entered the College of New Jersey. MacLachlan, pp. 326–28, 593–94.

pieces, some out of plays, some out of Mr Hervys meditations, and one of Popes Pastrols.[8] Part of it was acted very Naturaly by three Lads of about 10. or 11. years of age. One Child of about 7 years of age dilivered somthing on the art of writing very pretyly indeed— last of all some young Men came on the stage, and they were so much a mind to act nature that it quite spoild it, tho' one of 'em did prety well. Yet there was two much jesture to appear natural. After this exercise we went to Mr Smiths and a splended entertainment was provided. We were a larg company of about 16. or 18.

After dinner we went to Mr Smiths Daughters that was Married and drank Tea—after Tea we went to one Mr Grants, a very Clever gentleman and has a very clever Wife two. She was one of Mr Whitefields Orphans.[9]

Fryday we went to young Mr Smiths to dine, a very fine entertainment again, and almost the same company that we had on Thursday—soon after dinner we were obliged to take leve and go to our lodgings to prepare for our journey, for Mr Burr was obliged to set forward that Eve. But we got time to make one visit more to one Mrs Stanleys, a very prety Lady.[10]

After Tea we set forward accompanied by Ten Gentlemen and Ladies about 6 Miles out of Town.

Saturday we got to Princeton by Noon.

{June 11, 1755}
Wednsday, erly in the morn.

Saturday P.M. we went up to College and took a very petecular view of it. It is a Monsterous House.[11] I wish I had a plan of it to send to you—the workmen gon on very fast, they had put in the

8. The Academy was the Philadelphia Academy, which was associated with the College of Philadelphia. *Pastorals,* written by Alexander Pope when he was still in his teens, was first published in 1709. *DNB* 16:109–27.

9. Apparently Mrs. Grant had been raised at George Whitefield's orphanage in Bethesda, Georgia.

10. This may have been Susannah Chevalier Standley, who lived two doors from the Shippens. Her husband, Valentine Standley, was a prosperous potter and brewer. At his death in 1781, he left his pottery business to Susannah, although it was carried on in her son's name. *Pennsylvania Magazine of History and Biography* 54 (1930): 108–12.

11. Nassau Hall. See note 5, Letter No. 11, above.

first Row of Windows and doors when I was there—Sabbath Mr Burr Preached in his New Barn. He had a pretty large Congregation, I think Two Thirds as many people as we have at our meeting here. In the Eve after sun set we thought it best to set forward and go a little ways to make the journey easier the next day, but we had a sad time of it. It was Cloudy, and soon grew very dark, and we were forcd to trust wholy to the Horses prudence and good conduct, for we found he knew more about it then we did. We did not go but seven miles, and I was as much wearied with it as I was with any days ride—Monday Morn we came to Mr Cummings just as their Brakefast was ready, eat and went forward to Amboy which was six miles out of our way, but business Obliged—came to Woodbridge and dined, to Elizabethtown, drank Tea and there received your paquet by Mr Spencer and had the mortifycation to hear that you was not come—about sunset we arrived safe home, and here I desire to stay for the present—Philadelphia is much larger than I thought it had been. The streets are wide, but not paved, which makes it very uncomfortable.

I [. . .] if you can read what I have wrote. My hand has got into the way of shaking very badly.

{*June 12, 1755*}
Thursday Eve.

Mr. Brainerd is come into Town with his famaly. I went to see 'em this P.M. They were all in confusion for they got here but a little before noon. He lives in the House that was Treat Cranes, the house that Mrs Cumming was to live in if she had come here.

Your notions about Love page 165 are extreamly just and so are all your thoughts.

As for getting your Letters out of Mr Cummings hand I dont know how I can contrive that matter but if anything can be done I will do it—I wish I had known of your desire before I was there for tis not likely that I shall see him a great while—but I question if he will give em up. He will say they are his but tis best triing.

{*June 13, 1755*}
Fryday.

I am in great hast to see your piece of poetry that you have begun—I have a thought in my head but I w'not tell you now—

dont forget to tel me in your next *what that other reason for your not coming is that relates to another person.*[12]

{June 14, 1755}
Saturday Morn.

Mr Burr is going to York to preach on the Sabbath and I have thoughts of sending this along—I know you want to hear from me—But I must tell you one or two more things first. You must write me word as soon as you can when you think you shall be here.

We have a very fine *Microscope,* and *Telescope.* Indeed we have Two microscopes—and we make great discoveries tho' not yet any new ones that I know of. The Microscope Magnifies a Lous[*louse*] to be 8 feet long upon the wall—The Telescope is very short not above 14 inches but we can see to read small print as small as in our common Bibles acros the streat, which is about 7 Rod, and we can see *Jupiters* Moons—I want you here prodigeously to see and wonder with us.

I said somthing (in my private papers) about promising myself comfort in the company and conversation of Mrs Brainerd. I think I may flatter myself for a friend in her because she is no new friend, but an old acquaintance of my Mothers, and she has a very great opinnion of her as a faithfull friend. Then I have had some acquaintance with her myself, and I find her in all respects to exceed my expectations.

God is very kind to me. When he denies me one friend he sends

12. This is the first of several cryptic references in the journal to men who courted Sarah Prince. Esther and Sarah alluded to these suitors variously as "Jesuit," "Cats-paw," and "Widower." They have succeeded in their secrecy here, as we have not been able to identify any of these men. It is clear, however, that Sarah was ambivalent about marrying, and it appears that she was the object of considerable gossip because she remained single for so long. She finally married Charlestown, Massachusetts, merchant Moses Gill in April 1759, when she was thirty-one and Moses twenty-six. They had no children, although at some point Moses adopted his brother's son, Moses. After 1767 the couple lived in Princeton, Massachusetts, on land Sarah apparently inherited from her father. Sarah died in 1771 at the age of forty-three. Moses died in 1800, after serving as lieutenant governor and then acting governor of Massachusetts. Thomas Bellows Wyman, *The Genealogies and Estates of Charlestown, Massachusetts, 1629–1818* (Boston: David Clapp and Son, 1879), pp. 408–11, and Francis E. Blake, *History of the Town of Princeton* . . . (Princeton, Mass., 1915), 1:109–21, 270–77; 2:113–15.

another, when it would be just in him to Cut me off from all friendship and society, for my abuse of friendships that I have heretofore injoied.

I wish I had time to fill up this sheet but I must conclude—Mrs Brown is in a very poor state of helth—Mrs Sergeant is as well as usual. She has a very prety Daughter.

(I am a blundering thing. I have wrote on this sheet rong but you can put it as it should be.)

Pleas to present my Duty to Mr and Mrs Prince, Love to Julia and all the Sisterhood.

From my dear friend your most affectionate Sister, and alway will be I trust yours—

Esther Burr

(No. 15.)

{June 14, 1755}
June 14th, Saturday

Dear Friend

Once more I am allowed to call you *friend,* which I hope I am thankfull for. Tis God that gives us friends, and *he* that preserves the friendship he has graciously begun.

You desire my thoughts on the different sorts of knowledge of God etc. My thoughts are very poor, not half so good as your own, so I'll not trouble you with many of 'em.

That knowledge of God that does not produce a love to him and a desire to be like him is not a true knowledge—That knowledge of any thing that produces *love* will also produce a desire to be like what we know and *Love*—That the fallen Angels know much of God is sertain, and that the more they know of him, the more they hate him is as sertain, and that because their hearts are filled with enmity to all good—Perhaps those perfections of God as Love and goodness etc are not discovered to 'em in any clear maner. But his justice, Power, strength, and Infinite hatetred to sin, etc.—they have a most dreadfull sense of.

{June 15, 1755}
Sabbath—at Meeting allday.

Mr Brainerd preached two very good sermons from those Words, "Lord is it I?" Shewed us the nesessity of applying the word preached and the Scriptures to our selves and say am *I* the person here discribed etc.

But O my barrenness, unfruitfulness, under all the precious privileges I have injoied my whol Life!

O how much shall I have to answer for! If I fail at last I shall be the servant that shall be Beaten with many stripes! Tis grown so very dark all at once that I cant see to write one letter more.

Eve. We have had a fine shower again. O that Men would prais the Lord for his goodness, and wonderfull works to the Children of men—We have had a very hard Thunder as I expected we should by its being so very dark.

There is somthing very solemn in the sound of Thunder—Elihus poetical discription of it 37 chapter of Job is extreamly Natureal, and striking. I dont think it is half so elegantly painted by any poet as that just mentioned, tho Mr Hervy has done it extreamly well— And if same may be said of all parts of Scripture they are in all respects the best writings, the most Butyfull.

{June 16, 1755}
Monday Eve.

Mr Burr is come home and brought back your Letter. He said there was no Vessel going so he did not leve it—but I am very sorry. Perhaps if he had left it some oppertunity would have presented soon—You will think I have quite forgot you I am affraid— Mr Brown and his Wife have been here to make me a vissit this P.M. She has got prety well again.

{June 17, 1755}
Teusday A.M.

Yesterday the Gentlemen of the Court came into Town—to day the Court sets. There has not been a Supream Court held in this County this seven years till now, and now they have business enough to hold 'em three weeks tis thought. The King has many cases some of High-Treason—I am affraid of Hanging work.

I believe I have never told you that we have a French Master in the House with us. He is lerning the scholars french and Mr Burr is lerning two. He knew somthing of it before—Mr Burr has had a mind that I should lern, but I have no time—The married women has something elce to care about besides lerning French tho' if I had

time I should be very fond of lerning, but I must give up writing
to you if I did, and I could not bare that.

{June 18, 1755}
Wednsday A.M.

I am going to Newyork on a little Business all at once, so goodby
to you, for whiles I am there I shall be hurried to death [*so*] that I
shall have no time to write one word.

{June 21, 1755}
Saturday Morn. 6. o'Clock.

On Wednsday P.M. about 4 o'Clock saild for York, no passengers
but me, and happy for me just as I was going out of the house your
No. 12. came to hand. This I read for my entertainment and comfort,
and it did me good at the heart. I was exceding glad that I had no
company—I had a very bad Voyage of it, did not get to Newyork
till 3 o'Clock in the Morning. Thursday I was on my feet from 7
in the Morn 'till 7 at Night driving about York streets like Mad.
I went to Nancy Smith and got her to go with me. I was at Cap.
Bryants, Capt Jancys, Cousen Jonne Powels, see his wife, at Mrs
Bradleys, Mrs Mercys, and Mr Hazzards.[1] I lodged at Mrs Richards.

Tis the old story at Newyork about a Minnister about Bellamy.
Mr Hazzard has been to Mr Bellamy to see how matters stand with
him and he thinks he can be obtained. I believe that they will make
one more tryal for it but the Presbytry will do nothing in it. They
must go to the Synnod about it—Mrs Donaldson and Miss Kitty
are booth very poor, they look like ghosts. Mr Donaldson is in
trouble for want of a Child. He would not fail of it for a great deal
of Money—Mrs Donaldson, Miss Kitty and Miss Nancy all spake
greatly in praise of you my dear which did me good like a Cordial
for I have been much affraid that Fickle folks had prejudiced 'em
against you.

{June 22, 1755}
Sabbath Eve.

I have been at meeting all day and heard Mr Pomroy, a gentleman
very famous in the New-light-times—he preached well but his
delivery is so slow that a bodies thoughts have time between his

---

1. "Capt Jancy" was James Jauncey. See note 30, Letter No. 9, above.

words to run throu the World and my head has ached all day and
I fear I have got no good[2]—O my dear I dont live to God as you
do! No I am *carnel, fleshly, Worldly minded,* and *Devilish.*

{June 23, 1755}

Monday—All in confusion, a taylor here and a deal of company.

{June 24, 1755}

Teusday, a most dreadfull head-ach. P.M. Mr and Mrs Brainerd
came to see me. She is a charming woman. I am sure you would
love her if you knew her, and I hope it w'not be many months before
you will. I feel much better since she came.[3]

{June 25–27, 1755}

Wednsday, and Thursday, and Fryday, all up in Arms a cleaning
House, white-washing, rubing Tables, cleaning silver, China and
Glass, etc.

And poor *I* am almost tired out of my senses.

{June 28, 1755}
Saturday P.M.

I am so worried that I am but just alive—have seen Mr and Mrs
Brainerd which has done me some good.

This Week I have heard more that people have said against me
than all that I have heard since I have been in Town. I have wondered
that they let me alone so much. Mr Burr has told me frequently
that when he was dismissed I must expect to hear, and bare a great
deal of Ill nature, and I am prety well fortifyed. I found that what
I heard made no impression upon me, nor did not make me atall
gloomy, as might have been the case now I am so fatigued.

What they say is two foolish to repeat. I wonder that they are so
much put to it to find somthing to say against me. If they knew
me half so well as I do myself they would have brought out somthing

2. Benjamin Pomeroy, son of Joseph and Hannah Seymour Pomeroy, was pastor
of the Hebron, Connecticut, Congregational church. His wife was Abigail Wheelock Pomeroy, sister of Eleazar Wheelock, founder of Dartmouth College. Benjamin
was later a Dartmouth trustee. Once called "a most thundering preacher of the
new-light order," he had twice been brought before the Connecticut Assembly
during the Great Awakening for "disorders in preaching." Dexter 1:485–88.

3. Experience Brainerd. See note 17, letter No. 9, above.

more to the purpose than this Nonsence—One thing they say is that I am very Proud but you would laugh to hear what they bring to prove it.

Eve—Tis good for us my friend to go throu evil as well as good report, and very necessary to our knowing our own hearts, and the corruptions in it. Some times such things bring such Corruptions to our sight as we never mistrusted we had there.

O how kind is God in all his dealings with his own Children! I cant but have great hopes that I shall get some good out of such trials, that I shall be brought nearer to God by 'em—And O what reason for thankfullness if it should be so! This rejoices me greatly, that whiles they are trying to pull me down they are setting up Mrs Brainerd, and she is vastly more deserving than I be I know sertainly, and they cant affront me by saying so. It is what I have hoped, and desired ever since they talked of coming into Town, that the people might like her much better than ever they have me.

{June 29, 1755}
Sabbath at meeting all day

A.M. Mr Burr preached from those words, "I am of Paul, and another saith I am of apollos." I wish you could have heard the sermon—it was exceding proppor for this place under their present circumstances—he indevoured to shew the absuredety of setting up one Minnister in oppossision to another because of there different gifts (which has been the case in this place with a number) and also to excite thankfullness that God in infinite wisdome had so ordered it, and how one was sent to *plant,* and another to *water* etc.

P.M. Mr Brainerd preached a very good sermon from those words, The Spirit and the Bride say come and whosoever will let him come and take of the water of Life freely. I hope I have got some good this day. O may God have all the glory!

{June 30, 1755}
Monday A.M.

I am charmed with your piece of Poetry—you desire Mr Burr to correct it. I wonder how any body can mend it. Tis compleat only tis not long enough, pray go on make an edition—indeed my dear you have some very beautyfull thoughts in this little piece, this for one

The Nameless he spoke fourth Creations Birth,
And strait all heaven was filled with sacred Mirth.

This is only one, but what could be more beautifull than these two lines—*say*—you cant be totally blind to all your fine thoughts.

{July 1, 1755}
Teusday Eve 9 o'Clock—July the 1.

Mr Burr is gone to Morristown to Presbytry. Mr Knox is to be ordained and Mr Burr preaches the sermon.

You tell me with a good deal of ernestness to recall what I said about your dieing or rather your not dieing—I cannot recall what I have said for I look on it to be quite right and so must you if you look a little—I have the Scriptures of my side. It is spoken of as a full proof of the wickedness of a people or person when the Righteous die and none lay it to heart—You say what good do you do—I answer that allowing what you suggest (which is very far from the truth altho I dont chuse to charge you with telling a *Fib*) to be true that you do no good to any petecular person yet you dont know how much good your praiers do—you ought to be *willing to live* that you may pray for a sinfull world that have no heart to pray for themselves. You dont know how many precious blessings you may pray down upon your friends that you love dearly, and should not this thought make you *thankfull* that your life is spared altho' it would be your unspeakable gain to be with Christ—I think my dear you felt a little *selvish* when you wrote that parragraph, tho' I believe it was *mostly humility*—It is not wishing you *ill* to wish you to live longar, for Consider my dear that the more good you do, and the experience you have in divine things here, the more Glory, hereafter, *and tis right to have some respect to the recompence of reward.*

{July 2, 1755}
Wednsday P.M. Extream hot.

I went to see Mrs Brainerd. Mrs Burnet and Miss Polly Banks were there so I could have no free conversation with her, and did not stay long but came home, and soon after I got home Mr Burr came home—Mr Knox is Ordained.

{July 3, 1755}
Thursday. Eve. Fine weather.

P.M. Rode out to see a friend under affliction. Tis good to go to the house of mourning, Nay tis better than to go the House of

Laughter—Tis our Sacrament next Sabbath—O to have an heart prepared for the solemn ordinances!

{July 4, 1755}
Fryday Fine weather.

Mr Hervies *dialogues* we got at Philadelphia, but I cant get sight at 'em since I came home, for one is pulling, and another halling. I dont expect to have em till everybody elce here has read em— Those that have read em admire em much, and some think they are not equel to his Meditations.[4]

Eve—you seem concernd about Lucy for fear she is affronted about not going to Boston but I can assure you she is not in the least— *and I am fully of opinnon* that it is best she did not go on more accounts than one[5]—I am starved to death for those private papers you have sundry times mentioned—I think you told me that they contained some other reasons for your not coming here this summer, that you did not think it best to send em by Mr Spencer—I think ⟨ . . . ⟩ is a *great Fool* to have ⟨ . . . ⟩—I believe she will find that it wont be so well always with her—I am greatly out in my guss if it dont prove so—But she must *Bake* as she has *Brewed*.[6]

I dont know wheather I could forgive you if you should throw away your self on some *good-for-nothing Fellow or other,* as you seem to suppose to be possible if you hant society—Indeed I dont concieve of it to be possible unless you are bereaved of your reason as much as any Widdow in the World.

{July 5, 1755}
Saturday

My poor little Sally has been under great affliction for some time past. She has had an extream bad sore head. The Doct says tis somthing of the scall head but tis now better and looks as if it would soon be well but she is sadly broke out all over her Body [so] that she is as sore as Job himself.[7] We cant lift her up in lap without

4. James Hervey's *Dialogues between Theron and Aspasio,* published in three volumes in 1755.

5. Lucy Edwards. See note 25, Letter No. 9, above.

6. Esther seems to be talking here about Joanna Eaton Spencer. See note 4, Letter No. 11, above.

7. Scall head was a scaling scalp disease similar to eczema. *OED.*

hurting her much—We have been obliged to Cut off her Hair which just began to grow very pretily—Mr Burr grieves about the loss of her hair for he is very fond of good hair—but how light is this affliction to what many are called to bare in Children and how light to what we may expect—O to be fitted for Gods will and pleasure!

Eve

I wish I could be willing to *be and do, and suffer,* just what God pleased without any will of my own, but I am stubborn, willfull, disobedient. How far these tempers from the Christian temper! O my dear teach me to be a Christian! How unfit am I to aproach the Lords Table!

{July 6, 1755}

Sabbath, and our Sacrament

(Mr Burr is gone to New York to keep Sabbath again.)

Mr Brainerd preached A.M. from the 8 chap of II Corinthians 9th vers, "For ye know the grace of our Lord Jesus Christ, that tho' he was Rich, yet for your sakes he became poor, that ye through his poverty might be Rich."

First he shewed how Christ might be said to be Rich—
Secondly how and in what respects he became poor—
Thirdly shewed that it was for us that he became thus poor—
Fourthly that we were greatly inriched by Christs poverty—
Fifthly shewed us the aboundant grace of our Lord and Saviour that he was willing to become thus poor for us vile sinfull man—
And then made some application, etc.

It was a very good sermon calculated to do good. P.M. Had a very bad headach so did not go out.

I was in great hoopes of meeting Chirst in some extreordinary manner at his Table, but alas God has dissappointed me! Perhaps to shew me tis not in *means,* nor *ordinances*—but I desire to be found waiting at the *Pool.*

{July 7, 1755}

Monday Eve. 10 o'Clock.

I have been to see poor Mrs Ogden. She is and has been for a long time very low—came home before Night expecting to see Mr Burr, but he is not come yet. I immagine the Rain we have had this P.M. has prevented.

O—I ha'nt told you that Sally runs alone. She began to walk the day she was 14 months old. She is backward with her feet, tho she has walked by things all over the house almost 4 months, but now [*that*] she does go, she goes very well. She will go out-doors or any where.

{*July 8, 1755*}
Teusday

After I had done writing last eve Mr Burr came home as weet as a drowned Rat—he brings a deal of news from Newyork which I shall tell you tomorrow.

{*July 9, 1755*}
Wednsday

Newyork people have voted without one dissenting voice to give a call to Mr. Bostwick.[8] If he fails then a call to Mr Edwards of Stockbridge, which I should not like atall if I thought it probabal that he would come—he will by no means do for 'em if he would come—Newyork people have given up Mr Bellamy intirely, even Mrs *Mercier* is now unwilling he should come, and sundry others that were very warm for him are *against* him now.

The remarkable, and wonderfull good news from your forces at the Eastward, sertainly calls for great thankfullness and praise.[9] O how good is God to an unthankfull, wicked, ungreatfull people! O what shall we render to the Lord for his goodness to the sinfull Children of men!

The success of our forces by sea is no less to be acknowledged with great thankfullness and praies.

8. David Bostwick, from New Milford, Connecticut, was pastor of the Jamaica, Long Island, Presbyterian church. All we can discover about his wife, who is mentioned later in the journal, is that she was probably from Southbury, Connecticut, and that her family name was Hinman. Rev. Bostwick became the pastor of New York's First Presbyterian Church, but not until 1756, after many months of negotiation. At that time, the Scottish Presbyterian faction who opposed him left to form their own New York church. William Sprague, *Annals of the American Pulpit*. . . (New York: Robert Carter & Bros., 1858), 3:131–34.

9. Esther was probably referring here to Robert Monckton's military successes in Canada (see note 29, Letter No. 10, above).

{July 10, 1755}
Thursday A.M.

It is joyfull to hear of the success of our Armies, but how much more joyfull to hear that these mercies were the means of reclaming a Backsliding people—This is an unspeakable comfort that all hearts are in the hands of the Lord, and he turns 'em just as he pleases—It is as easy with God to sanctify mercy as to bestow it—and O what a judgment is unsanctified mercies!

{July 11–12, 1755}
Fryday and Saturday—

Not well, and could get no time to say anything to my *Fidelia,* but only that I think of her.

{July 13, 1755}
Sabbath Eve.

A.M. Staied at home with a pain in my stomach—P.M. ventured out, heard Mr Brainerd from John XV. and 22, "If I had not come and spoken unto them they had not had sin," etc. the whole vers. T'was a very good discourse. He is a very good man, and seems always much ingaged for the good of souls. I hope our people w'not be so foolish as to reject such a Man, and such a preacher—but Newark people are as diffecult as Newyork, and some w'not like this or the other man because such and such persons like him, etc. You know how people can act when they have got out of temper—Mr Smiths youngest Daughter has broke her Arm, but is like to do well.

{July 14, 1755}
Monday Morn.

We have lately discovered that Sallys Neck is crooked. Her Head grows leaning upon her right sholder. Whether it is natural or come by habit we cant tell but so it is—I am under a great deal of concern about it, for if it cant be helped it will grow more so as she grows older, and will be a great deformity—Mr Burr seems much distressed about it, I think more than I am. What to do we know not, but Mr Burr thinks to go into New-England to one Doct' Porter at Wethersfield who is the most skilfull surgeon in this part of the World perhaps—but what is best God only knows. [10] He has wise

10. Dr. Ezekiel Porter, husband of Mary Belden Porter, was widely known for his surgical skill, especially for setting broken and dislocated bones. Henry Stiles, *The History of Ancient Wethersfield* (New York: Grafton Press, 1904), 2:534.

ends in view no doubt. Perhaps He foresaw that we should be two Proud of her, and so he has sent this calamaty to mortify us and her—Mr Burr says if she was a Boy he should [*not*] much care about it, but I am not sertain but he would be more concernd about it, for it does make a Man look underling and meaching—It is best to be just as God pleases, if we could but think so all would be well.

P.M. I am sure tis time to say somthing about your coming here next fall for the time comes near—As to my going to Boston I give it up for this reason. My friends at Stockbridge have let me know that they expect that if I am alive and in tollerable helth that I go there, and there is some reason that they should for if I dont go this fall I cant possibly go before we moove to Princeton—Mr Burr think I must go to Stockbridge without fail—so I give up Boston as a gone business—But pray let a body know when we may expect you here [*so*] that I may order my affairs accordingly.

{July 15, 1755}
Teusday Eve

I have been to attend the Funeral of (I may say without breach of charrity) An Old Sinner—Tis a most meloncholy thought! A most affecting sene to follow an Old gray-headed Person to the Grave! This Mans Life has been as far from relegion as any mans in these parts. He never praied in his famaly in his Life, and was not only not relegious but made a scorf, and jest of all relegion.

O it is a dreadfull thing to go into Eternity in such a condition!

{July 16, 1755}
Wedns-day Morn, 7 o'Clock.

I am of late very low spirited. I wish you was here, you would soon cure me with your inlivening conversation—but what signifies wishing? Tis as it is, and I ought to be content with the ordering of a kind God who knows what is best for *me* and *you* my dear friend.

P.M. Rode up to see Mrs Smith—she is well considering—her little Daughter is in a very hopefull way. Eve. Went to see Mrs Brainerd. She looks to be taken Ill every hour.

{July 17, 1755}
Thursday, Violent hot.

I made a vissit at Parson Browns, had an agreable time of it—Pray dont you think you can get here by the Commencement? say—

Our youngsters that are to take degrees are to appear in their Hab-
bits—we have a pattern from England to make 'em by—I am not
so sertain about going to Stockbridge for the Indians have made
thier appearrance near Stockbridge, and I dont like to be killed by
the *barbarous* retches—Mr Burr thinks I had better go (if I do go)
before Commencement for the sake of my Brothers company, who
is to go home about three weeks before the Commencement [*so*]
that he may go to Boston on some business for Mr Hawley, who is
marrying a Wife and cant go.[11] Pray say somthing about your
coming in your next.

{July 18, 1755}
Fryday P.M.—July the 18.

Last Night about 12 o'Clock Mrs Brainerd was taken in Travil,
and by a little after 2 she was dilivered of a fine daughter. Mother
and Child are both in a good way[12]—Tis *long, very long* since I have
had a Letter from you—and tis two long since I have sent to you,
but I cant hear of good oppertunitys, and I am discouraged about
sending at random, for fear my Letters should be lost, or get into
the Post-office—but I think to try it once more as I have a very
good oppertunity to send to Newyork—My Duty to your honored
parents, and Love by the Bushels to all the Sister-hood as tho' I
mentioned 'em by name.

Next Week is examinnation and I am affraid I shant get time to
send if I dont send now—I think you may determine that I sha'n't
go to Stockbridge this fall. The Indians are so thick about in the
Woods there—Now my dear to bid you *farewel* tho' I hope but for
a short time—I can tell you that I depend on your coming either
before Commencement, or soon after, as much as I do that Autumn
will come, that is if your life is spared—Mr Burr joins with me
in abundance of respects to all that I have mentioned as well as
your dear self in petecular—My paper is full—You have the praiers

11. This may have been Gideon Hawley of Stockbridge, who served under
Jonathan Edwards as a missionary. If so, he did not marry at this time. Early in
1759 he expressed an interest in marrying Lucy Edwards, but he married Lucy
Fessenden a few months later. Sibley 12:392–411.

12. This infant was Mary Brainerd, the only child of Experience and John
Brainerd to survive childhood. Field, *Genealogy of the Brainerd Family,* p. 286.

and kind wishes at all times of your most affectionate friend

Esther Burr

(My Brother and Sister send service to you.)

(No. 16.)

{July 19, 1755}
Newark. July the 19th. 1755.
Saturday P.M.

Once more to my dear friend,

Yesterday P.M. I sent to Newyork No. 15. and when the gentle-man returns that carried it I shall hope for somthing better than what he took with him. But it wont do to lot on it, so long as the world is so full of disappointments, so Ill be trying to prepare for crosses of this nature.

The Weather is extream hot, hardly the like has been known—poor little Sally seems as if she could not live long if the heat was to hold a few days more.

Eve.

O the dreadfull, Awfull News! General Braddock is killed and his Army defeated—O my dear what will, what must become of us! O our *sins,* our *sins*—they are grown up to the very heavens, and call aloud for Vengence, the Vengance that the Lord has sent—Tis just, tis right—I hant a word to say against the ordering of God—for I know I have been guilty enough to procure this judgment of heaven—I realy believe that our sins are much greater, and more aggravated then the sins of our enemies, and it would be infinitely just in the ever blessed God to deliver us into there hands and utterly reject us and cast us off forever as he has done many a time his professing people heretofore.[1]

We hear that the Army was very sick before the ingagement, which looks more like the immediate hand of God than if they had fell only by the sword of the enimies—O if the Lord be against us who can be for us!

1. On July 9, 1755, Major General Edward Braddock's army was defeated by the French and their Indian allies in a battle along the Monongahela River, eight miles from Fort Duquesne (later Pittsburgh). This defeat and Braddock's death threw the white population of the Middle Colonies into a panic. *DAB* 2:550–51.

{July 20, 1755}
Sabbath A.M. fine and cool.

Mr Burr preached a sermon suteable to the present meloncholy circumstances of our Land from Isiah LXIII. chap. and 10 vers, "But they rebelled and vexed his holy spirit: therefore he was turned to be their Enemy, and he fought against them"—First shewed how the holy spirit might be said to be *vexed,* then shewed what *rebellion against the spirit was,* in many peteculars, then applied the Whol to our present circumstances, and shew that we might expect God to fight against us, so long as we went on to grieve his spirit in such an abominable manner as we evidently had for many years, etc. I hant mentioned all the heads of the sermon but only a few, but what was said was very propor for the ocasion.

P.M. Mr Brainerd preached from the 2 chap Job, 10 vers, "Shall we receive good at the hand of God and shall we not receive evil"— A very good sermon—an uncommon solemnity has appeared on the face of our congregation this day—O what caus of thankfullness if this awfull dispensation of God might be the means of reforming a backsliding people! O that it might teach us to depend wholy on God, and not on an Arm of flesh! God is able to bring *sweetness* out of this exceding *bitterness.*

{July 21, 1755}
Monday Eve.

Mr Brainerd, Mr Burr and I have been at Elizabethtown and hearing so many different accounts about this Ohio, we went to the Governors to know what might be depended on—Another express he has had to day brings more comfortable news then the first. He says that the Genneral is not killed but has been defeated and has lost his Artillery but not his provisions—Tis bad as it is and a very great frown of heaven but not so bad as at the first—We cant hear peteculars yet and perhaps shant this week or fortnight—Mrs Spencer is about again, she calls her child Sally.

{July 22, 1755}
Teusday Morn. 6 o'Clock.

You my dear will excuse me to day because I am hurried prepareing for the Trustees who meet here to morrow for examination.

{*July 23, 1755*}
Wednesday P.M. 4 o'Clock. fine and cool

As the Gentlemen are gon upon business I have time enough to tell you the best news to me that I have heard this many a day, that is I have a Letter from *you, yes you, my dear friend!* O how refreshing is good news from such a friend—Tis a Cordial—but I must go and read a little more, and see what you have got to say now.

Eve—*So* Madam you are about business I see—Tis well you wrote me word of it—for I should have been as mad as Fury if you had popt off and not have told me of it—But stay—*did you use to like Widowers?* This is new doctrine to me, but some Widowers are better than young men, as they go *Now a day*—When I have time I'll write a deal about *it,* and everything elce.

I must tell you some of Sallys witt—Miss Suekey shews her the picture of a Face that was Black, and tells her it was a Baby, she must Buss it, and she almost got her mouth to it, when she started back and said it was Nanny (for so she calls Harry) and would not Buss it, nor have anything to do with it.[2]

{*July 24, 1755*}
Thursday Eve.

I have been this P.M. to vissit a good Old Woman, one of the best, if not the very best, Christian in Newark. The conversation turned wholy on relegion. I hant spent an afternoon so agreably this many a day—this Woman has been under affliction of late.

{*July 25, 1755*}
Fryday morn six o'Clock.

I am highly pleased with *Leonillas* conduct, I cant pick one flaw in it. Tis reasonable and very judicious, and greatly to be commended upon all accounts. Should your beha[vi]our be like it, I should be *proud* of you—indeed my [d]ear I should b[e *v*]*ery* proud.

Mr Burr has given his opinion, [on] a sertain a[ffa]ir which I shall send in the pr[ivac]ies as you desir[e.]

2. The Miss Suekey Esther was referring to here was probably not her sister Susanna, but the young servant or slave in the Burr household. See note 27, Letter. No. 9, above.

I am a good deal concernd about that soar [on] your Leg. I a[m] affraid somthing bad will be the end of it. I hope [you] will send me word as soon as you can, for I shall [be u]neasy till I hear further.

{*July 26,1755*}
Sa{tu}rday

Dreadfull, Dreadfull [n]ews we have from our Army! Some new stor[y] comes every day, but all very bad. We can depend [on] nothing we hear as yet, but so far we can deter[mi]ne that the best is *exceding* bad. I shall write no [m]ore about it till we have sertain intellegence—[I] hear Doct Shippin is about to bring his little [da]ughter to stay here this summer, but that wont cro[wd y]ou out, for Mr Burr told 'em that if they did [send] her it must be very soon because we expected [you] about the end of August.[3]

{*July 27, 1755*}
Sabbath day P.M. 1 o'Clock

Mr Brainerd preachd exceding well this A.M., but I was so dul in Body and mind that I heard as tho I heard not, and I had as good have stayed at home for all the good that I got. But for all, I think to go this afternoon and see if the Lord wont [p]leas of his mercy send so[m]e quickning and inlivening word that sh[al]l awake me ou[t] of this death.

Eve—This morn Mr Burr went to [Elizabetht]own to preach for Mr. Spencer w[h]o is absent and [to]morrow sets out for Princeton. He is always u[pon] the go.

Yesterday I was fa[vo]red with Mr [and Mrs Be]lchers and Mr Peter Smiths and wife [co]mpany to drink Tea with me. Mrs Smith has [la]tely lost her little Son, he was about six mon[t]hs old.[4] She seems quite sorrowfull—J[en]ny is in the right of it, a person may

3. Dr. Shippen's daughter was Susannah Shippen. See note 6, Letter No. 14, above.

4. Peter Smith was William Peartree Smith, son of Captain William and Catharine Harris Smith. He was a member of New York's First Presbyterian Church and a founding trustee of the College. His wife, Mary Bryant Smith, daughter of Captain William and Eleanor Bryant, was also a member of the New York church. Of the couple's ten children, only two survived to adulthood. In 1757, after Governor Belcher's death, the Smiths moved to the former Belcher mansion in Elizabethtown, and Peter became the town's mayor. Dexter 1:719–20.

tell very soon, the [tem]per of mind you was in when you wrote such and [su]ch passages—your *pen* discribes your Temper [ex]actly, and I dont think *it can Lie*. You have t[aug]ht it better manners. (Jenny is sertainly an uncommon Child.)

{July 28, 1755}
Monday

Tis much to that serta[in] G[entl]emans honour that he has declared he wont Marr[y *a*]*ny Gay Lady*. I like him much for that speach—[I hope] he will ⟨ . . . ⟩ agreable to his declareation ⟨ . . . . ⟩ I wish I could see him, I [could] tell him of some hiden excelencies, and th[. . .] the Phenix.

{July 29,1755}
July 29. Teusday. Cloudy and Rain

Mr Burr is returned from Princeton, and brings sertain News from General Braddock. He is dead. He died of a wound in three days after he was shot, and we have lost a[ll] our artellery [and] Baggage. Further peteculars you wi[ll h]ave before th[is] can get to you—Tis an awful dreadfull fr[own] of heaven upon us! But [wha]t less could [we] expect! Our sins are gro[wn] to the heave[ns and] call aloud for Vengeance.

I am [very] unwell so yo[u wi]ll excuse me from saying [any]more than [that I] am your friend, sick or Well.

{August 3, 1755}
Sabba[th] Eve, August the 3 day.

I have been silent f[or sev]eral days past. It seems to me to be a fortnight [. . .] I have only time now to tell you that I hant [for]got you, and shall give a very good reason for my [si]lence, as you may see in Private papers under G[. . .]t. I have an oppertunity to send to my Sister Dw[igh]t and Lucy to morrow, so am busied this Eve in [wri]ting to them. Miss Lucy is at Newhaven [wi]th Mrs. Noice.[5]

5. Lucy Edwards was probably staying with Abigail Pierpont Noyes, Sarah Edwards's half-sister. Abigail's husband was New Haven's Congregational minister, Joseph Noyes. Dexter 1:85–89.

{August 4, 1755}
Mo[nday]. fine and cool.

P.M. Rode to Eli[zabeth]town to make a vissit to Madam Belcher.
Had a [pleas]ant time of it.

I am surprized to [see] the World so ready to sensure General
[Braddo]cks conduct and Men of sense two seem as if they could
not be content to have him *only dead,* but they must set him in the
most disadvantageous light they possibly can, and rake up everything
that ever he did in his life that was not commendable, to distroy
his Char[ac]ter—One say[s h]e was *proud,* and would take no advise,
he [th]ought himself [abo]ve advise—Another that he was an
im[pu]dent rash Ma[n] and a third that he is *a Coward* etc., This is
no[t ge]nerous, supposing these things to [be] true, at least [some
o]f em. For my part I feel griev[ed] at my heart t[o t]hink that the
poor gentleman has [lef]t his native c[oun]try to come into this
Wilderness to [. . .]ed to our barbarous Indians—And tis an unwise
[piec]e of conduct to judge a matter before we hear it, and [. . .]
we cant make a judgment just how matters [sto]od. Perhaps we
shall see he took the most prudent [. . .] in all respects—altho'
these things are unserta[in]. This is sertain, that the hand of God
was [*shown*] in a very [rem]arkable [*manner*] in what is done and it
would be better fo[r u]s to Eye that, and not look so much at
instruments.

{August 5, 1755}
Teusday Eve

Mr Bostwick has [given?] Newyork a possitive and full denial,
and that ha[s mad]e em vastly more ingaged. Those that were
indifferent [to] him before he was applied to, are now extreamly
ingaged. Mr Hazzard for one he says he will give out of his own
pocket five £ a year rather than have him fail.

{August 6, 1755}
Wednsday fine and cool.

P.M. Made a very agreable vissit at Mrs Sergeants—She has a very
prety Baby much pretyer than Sally was at her age—Mrs Sergeant
is very hearty and well and in good spirits, not so vapory as she
used to be—This having Children does good sometimes—My Brother

and Sister talk of going home soon, but I am affraid it is not safe—
I hear that a 100 Indians are gone from Stockbridge with Mr Shirley.[6]
I wonder what Mr Edwards does with himself. I reason he seems as
if he had nothing to do.

{August 7, 1755}
Thursday, fine weather yet.

I made a vissit at Mrs Brainerds, carried Sally with me which I
have never done above two or three times since she was born. There
was a house full of people (as there always is as soon as a woman is
a Bed) and a deal of confusion, and I had not much comfort, but
wished my self at home 10 times in half an hour—Mrs Sergeant
was there. She and I got into a room by our selves a little while,
and chated with some comfort.

{August 8–9, 1755}
Fryday and Saturday.

Two gloomy to write—the [situation?] of our publick affairs are
so meloncholy that I am sunk at my heart, and go bowed down like
a Bullrush—I never was so sunk with anything in my life.

At Meeting all day and heard Mr Burr, as Mr Brainerd is again
absent—Mr Burr has given most excelent advise to such as I am,
to those that are sunk down with our present dark and gloomy
circumstances. He indevoured to lead us to God our only refuge,
and exhorted to faith and praier—O! if a praying spirit was to be
seen amongst Gods people things would look incouraging, and I
should hope mercy was yet in store for this wicked Land—You cant
conceive my dear friend what a tender Mother undergoes for her
children at such a day as this, to think of bring[ing] up Children
to be *dashed against the stones by our barbarous enemies*—or which is
worse, to be inslaved by them, and obliged to turn *Papist*—it seems
to me sometimes if I had no Child nor was likely to have any that
I should not be much distressed, but I must leve the subject—tis
two dreadful to think off.

6. Massachusetts Governor William Shirley, who had succeeded General Braddock as commander of the British forces in the colonies, was then marching toward
Niagara. *DAB* 17:120–22.

{August 11, 1755}
Monday Eve

I feel a little better to day, not so gloomy—but one thing vexes me. Mr Burr has put some Tickets into the Philadelphia Lottery, and I think we have lost enough by lotteries. We have lost about a hundred pounds York money by em, and Im not willing to loose anymore unless duty evidently calls—Mr Burr has put in a Ticket for Sally but none for me because I am against it.[7]

{August 12, 1755}
Teusday.

I have been to see a poor Woman that is a Widow, has a Child a dieing with the bloody Flux, poor Woman.[8] She seems much sunk. I feel greatly grieved for her—What a differance God is pleased to put between this poor Widow and me! And all of free grace, and mere mercy. I am sure I deserve nothing but infinite evils from this God who is so mercifull and kind to me—I indevoured whiles I sat and looked of the poor dieing Child to immagine my dear Sally in his case—but the thought was two dreadfull to be long indulged.

{August 13, 1755}
Wednsday—Augt 13.

The Governor and Lady came up to see us just at Night, and Caps Bryant with em to see about a Minnister. The old story, and the same party concernd. There is the *Scotch party and Hazzard*—The *Gentlemen,* and Mr *Vanhorn* and *Loyer Smith*—all go on in the same way, and the Old Cap' sputters as thick as ever—Next Week there is to be a Presbytry on Mr Bostwicks affair about removeng to Newyork—they dont mind his denial one jot, but have him they must or they are ruined as much as when Mr Bellamy was on the Carpet.[9]

7. Lotteries were a method of raising public revenues.
8. Bloody flux was a common term for dysentery. *OED.*
9. The First Presbyterian Church of New York was still in disarray, almost as divided over calling David Bostwick as it was over Joseph Bellamy. The "Scotch party" was the Scotch Presbyterian Society, who had opposed replacing the Scottish psalms with Isaac Watts's version, and who formed their own church when Bostwick was finally called. "The Gentlemen" were a group of wealthy and influential church members who seem to have opposed evangelical ministers (including Joseph Bellamy). Mr. Vanhorn was David Van Horne, one of the elders of the church and apparently one of the most active participants in its various controversies. Captain Bryant was William Bryant. Webster, pp. 628–50; Charles A. Briggs, *American Presbyterianism: Its Origin and Early History* (New York: Charles Scribner's Sons, 1885), pp. 278–83.

{*August 19, 1755*}
Teusday P.M. August 19.

I have been quite silent for several days past.

Mr Burr has been very Ill indeed. The Doct supposed his disorder to be the intermiting Fever, but I hope tis like to be carried off with sweating and useing some simples. He mist his fit last Night, and seems very comfortable to day, [*so*] that I am in great hopes he may soon recover his usual helth.[10]

Yesterday I was agreably surprized [by] Mr Oliver and his Lady who came and spent the P.M. with me—Mrs Belcher came with em—I think Mrs Oliver a very prety Woman. Indeed I thought so when I saw her in Boston but I guss she will bare acquaintance as well as any of her sex—excepting your Ladyship—Mr Oliver delivered me your pacquit which I have not had time thoroughly to peruse yet—because I am Nurs but I am very impatient and ketch it up and read a word now and then.[11]

{*August 20, 1755*}
Wednsday. A.M.

I take it very kindly of you that you have took the freedome to send my Love to Mr Whitefield. I wish you would everytime you wrote or as often as you think proppor.

Mr Burr thinks himself well enough to go and see Mr and Mrs Oliver, so this P.M we desighn to spend in their company, and I doubt not but we shall be highly pleased.

{*August 21, 1755*}
Thursday A.M.

According to our purpose we went to the Governors to wait on Mr and Mrs Oliver. They are very agreable persons indeed. They have appointed to go to vissit the two [Cuylars] famalies and see their fire Engine to throe Water out of the Mines which it will do in very great quantities. Ill tell you more about it when I have seene it, for Mr Burr and I am to go with em.

10. *Intermittent fever* was a commonly used term for malaria. Peter Wood, *Black Majority* (New York: W. W. Norton, 1974), p. 70.
11. Possibly Andrew and Mary Sanford Oliver. See note 3, Letter No. 12, above.

Eve. I desighned to have wrote a deal to day but I had company all P.M. and now Mr Burr is taken very bad again.

{August 23, 1755}
Saturday Morn.

I shall be obliged to send this paquet before I can say all I want to say in reply to your last—but I'll say as much as I can and be as short as I can not from choice but of nesesity because of Mr Burrs Illness—Mr Burr desires me to add for him that he thinks a sertain person will make a kind and affectionate husband and he has and always has had ⟨ . . . . ⟩

I thought I had told you that Mr Brainerd was invited here by the people of this Congregation to preach on probation and tis likely they will give him a call to settle as their minnister. I hear of nobody that dislikes him.

You charge me with being two severe on a sertain Gentleman—but pray recollect what you have said your self and you'll find you have been much before me—I thought I might follow an example set me by such a Lady as Miss Prince. To be sure I did not expect a reproof from her for it—but when persons get *in Love*, they themselves may talk against the object beloved as much as they pleas, but if any body elce says a Naughty word, but only in jest, tis Treason—This I have known to be the case sundry times—So you may expect as long as you hold so severe your self, I shall follow you, for I cant help thinking all you say or do is right.

These poor fettered folks you seem to pity so much I look upon as the happest part of the world, and if I was to wish you any Ill for your severity on us, it should be that you might never be married, but such a friend as I am cant wish you a very great Ill nor any Ill—We are not obliged to you for your seeming Pity, for in the first place we dont want it, and in the second place you dont pity us, but Envy us for our happy lot. *Say* dont you?

The Old saying is, you may know who is shot by their fluttering. Now nothing is more common than for persons to run out against the married state, and say they never intend to be married, etc. when they are just upon the point of determining to except of the first offer. Hant you observed this?

{*August 24, 1755*}
Sabbath day A.M.

Mr Burr has had a very bad night indeed, much the worst that he has had since his illness.

I am greatly distressed about what may be the Isue. The best I expect is that he will be confined this Month—I think there is great dainger of his fevers turning to a Nervous or Hectick.[12] If this should be the case there will be no hopes of recovery—but I indevour to think and hope the best for my heart is ready to sink as it is—If God shou[ld] (as he may justly) remove Mr Burr, I of all perso[ns] am the most Misrable.

{*August 25, 1755*}
Monday Morn.

I watched with Mr Burr last Night, and a most dreadfull night he had—he took a Vomit yesterday P.M. and it had the strangest effect on him that ever I saw in my Life. I expected for half an hour every minute he would *die*, but God of his infinite mercy has spared him to this morn, and how much longer he may live God only knows, but this is sertain that if he hant spedy help he cant live long—I am perswaded by the symptoms he was under last night that he has the Nervous Fever—O my friend pity and pray for me! God is about to try every reighn of my soul! I cant be resighned to the Will of God if it is to bereave me of all that is *near and dear* at one stroke! I can see it infinitely just, but I [c]ant be willing that justice should take place—O my heart is full, but I can say no more for this paquet must go directly, and I am Mr Burrs Nurse, and will be as long as I can crawl.

Mr Burr desires me to add and say, that he never expects to see you in this world but he hopes to meet you in heaven—his advice is to make it the business of life to prepare for heaven.

Mr Burr think much more darkly of his case than any body elce does—I am far from determining that you will never see the *dear* Man again, altho' his case is undoubtedly very daingerous—O dear Miss Prince pray for me!

O pray for that I may have a right temper of mind towards the

12. Nervous or hectic fevers were those accompanying consumption and similarly debilitating diseases. *OED*.

ever blessed God! O pray my dear for every grace for your affectionate, and greatly afflicted Friend,

Esther Burr
August 25, 1755

{August 30, 1755}
Saturday Augt

P.S. to No 16.

As Mr Oliver does not go forward till the beginning of next week I shall send your Lottery account, and desire you would send my accounts by the first opportunity, for they have lain much two long already and have got jumbled—Your loss in the Female company is £4″ 8″ 2″ 1/2 and how Mr Burr settled those other two Tickets when he was in Boston he has forgot, and can find no accounts any thing about it, and so desires you would send him that account with mine, that we may know how affairs stand between us.

Mr Burr is much better than when I sent away my paquit. He has been down stairs and desighns to Ride out some time to day—little Sally is somthing better.

Yesterday P.M. my Brother and Sister set forward for Stockbridge [so] that I seem quite lonesome.

We have received a Letter from Mr Edwards, and he says he shall be here at the Commincement and I wish we could be sure of seeing Miss Prince as soon, but I fear—Tho' I will hope as long as I can.

I should not have sent your Lottery account if we had any sertainty of your coming, but it depends so much on so many circumstances, that I look on it somthing doubtfull—I will if I can keep my self from lotting on it so much as I did last spring.

I shall with this inclose a sermon of Mr Knox's, the gentleman that is gone to the *Island of Saba*—I think it is an ingenious discourse for a young man. [13]

Pleas to give my Duty to your honored parents and Love to *Julia*

13. The sermon Esther enclosed was Hugh Knox's own ordination sermon, *The Dignity and Importance of the Gospel Ministry, Displayed in a Sermon Preached . . . on the Day of His Ordination, before the Presbytery of New-York* (New York, 1755). McLachlan, pp. 101–05.

and all the Sister-hood as tho' named.

From my dear, Your affectionate friend

E.B.

(No. 17.)

{*September 5, 1755*}

Newark Sept. 5. 1755.

Fryday Eve.

To my ever dear Friend.

Altho' I write yet I expect you will come for the Letter your self, and I dont intend to send it by any body short of your own dear person, so dont let me be disappointed.

I am sorry my Letters are like to get to you no soonner. I have given 'em to Mr Oliver or I would send em another way, but I dare'n't ask for em.

They are not gone, nor like to go before Commencement I believe. They with the Governor and Lady drank Tea here this P.M., and Next Week are to go and see our *Woonderfull Falls*—Mr Burr and I am to go with em.[1]

{*September 6, 1755*}

Saturday—Sept. 6.

Very busy puting up Beds and no body to help me and it is a good deal of work to pin up two beds.

{*September 7, 1755*}

Sabbath at Night

At meeting all day. Heard Mr Brainerd from those words, Except ye repent ye shall all likewise pirish. He made two good practical discourses—he is not a man that can with ease desend into deep doctrines of divinnity, and maintain an argument with clearness as some can—but there is much to be said in excuse for him, as he has never had opportunity to study much since he has been in the minnistry—Mr Brainerd is an excellent good Man, and has his heart much on doing good without any by ends of his own to serve—but

1. Probably what today are called the Great Falls, located on the Passaic River in Paterson. In the 1750s they would have been about half a day's ride from Newark.

there is a considerable number of our good people that cant like his preaching so well as they intended to, and I am affraid the consequence will be that he will not settle here.

{September 8, 1755}
Monday. Morn.

Our house is to be turned up-side-down to day to clean, so shant be able to say much to you, but you may be sure of some of my thoughts.

{September 9, 1755}
Teusday Eve. very hot

Tis Court in Town this week and a time of great confusion. My head runs round like a top. I tired my self yesterday a good deal, and so consequently low spirited to day—This World is nothing but one continued sene of confusion and trouble—and *happy, happy* are those that have got throu it, and are arrived safe to their heavenly fathers house.

Mr Oliver and Lady are to be here to morrow and lodge here to morrow Night. I lot much on it, for every time I see them I like them better and better—I thought Mrs Oliver very plain when I first saw her, but she grows quite handsome. If she stays much longer I shall think her a beauty.

{September 10, 1755}
Wednsday 5 o'Clock P.M.

Mr Oliver and Lady not yet come and I am affraid will not come atall, and if they do I dont know whether I can go with em to the falls I am so Ill. The Weather is as hot as it has been any time this summer and if it dont alter, it will be enough to kill us and our horses to go to the Falls and back again in a day.

{September 12, 1755}
Fryday 1 o'Clock P.M.
Violent hot.

Wednsday eve about 7 o'Clock Mr and Mrs Oliver came almost sick with the heat, and were determind not to go unless it was cooler in the Morn.

Yesterday Morn we found the heat a little abated so concluded to set out, which we did and went as far as Mr Courtlands and there stopt to consider of the matter for we found it very warm. Finally concluded to Ride a mile or two farther and see how it would feel, and if no wind would be so good as to blow to refresh us. Mr Smith who was with us said he thought it would do, he felt some wind, and Mrs Oliver and I said (she and I Rode togather, and Mr Burr and Mr Oliver) we felt the wind and Mrs Oliver was almost cold enough to bare a Cloak. Mr Burr said he wished we would be so generous as to spare them a little of it for he found no Air for his share—Well upon this they kept along prety contentedly till we had got about half way, and then it grew so violent hot, that Mr Oliver proposed turning back. Mr Burr said he chose to leve it to the Ladies and desired to know what we thought. Mrs Oliver spoke and said *that when they had put their hands to the Plough they should not look back*—upon that they drove on without puting me to speak my mind for they saw Mrs Oliver had a mind to go forward—Was not it quite merry that we should go on without knowing what to do for so long a time—We got to the falls about 11 o'Clock and found the River so very low that it was no curiossity atall compared to what it is in the spring. We might have gone quite across the River just above the falls on the stones without wetting our feet. The bottom of the River under the falls was quite dry in many places, but Mr Oliver and his Lady were much entertained with the sight and did not begrudge their pains. Just at sun set we came home very much tired, Mrs Oliver and I sick with the head-ach, but got a dish of coffe as soon as we could and felt much refreshed by it—this Morn Mrs Oliver seemd quite well, but poor I have a very bad head-ach yet.

About 9 o'Clock this A.M. Mr Burr set out with Mr and Mrs Oliver for the Governors. Mr Burr desighns to go to Newyork and spend the next Sabbath there if they have no other supply—Mr Oliver expects to sail next Monday if the wind favours.

It hurt me to take leve of 'em. We seem as if we had been acquainted this year or two, and I shall always remember them with respect.

By the way Madam Belcher did not go with us. She was affraid the heat would kill her Horses and that would have been as bad as if one of the company had fell and broke their necks.

{September 13, 1755}
Saturday Eve. Still very hot.

P.M. Went to hear a preparritory sermon to our sacriment. The Text was Sanctify your selves to day, for to morrow the Lord will do Wonders, a good practical discourse as Mr Brainerds sermons all are, but I want [*was not*] in a good frame to hear. It was so very hot in our close meeting-house that I could not attend, or at least I did'n't to my shame, tho' I heard enough to know it was a very good sermon.

I am much disappointed by my fathers not coming to day as I fully expected. I fear he or some of the famaly are sick.

{September 14, 1755}
Sabbath. Eve, the hottest Sabbath we have had

At Meeting all day, and am almost over come with the dreadfull weather—Mr Brainerd preached in the A.M. and adminnistered the sacriment—P.M. One Mr Johnson from Newengland preached a very good sermon.[2] I think the word and ordinance have stired me up a little. I have felt some ingagedness this P.M. and Eve. Blessed be God for it.

{September 15, 1755}
Monday. Still hot.

Mr Burr came home by noon and brings joyfull news from our forces at Crownpoint—O that we may ascribe praise to him, to whom it belongs![3]

2. We think this was Jacob Johnson, son of Rebecca and Jacob Johnson of Plainfield, Connecticut, and husband of Mary Giddings Johnson, originally from Preston, Connecticut. At this time he was pastor of the North Society in Groton, Connecticut, which later became the town of Ledyard. Another possibility is Stephen Johnson, minister of the Congregational church in Lyme (now Old Lyme), Connecticut. Originally from Newark, he was the son of Nathaniel and Sarah Ogden Johnson and the husband of Elizabeth Diodate Johnson, from New Haven. Dexter 1:649–51, 738–40.

3. On September 8, 1755, colonial and Indian forces, under the command of General William Johnson, fought their French and Indian adversaries in a brief battle at the head of Lake George. Although they did not drive the French from Crown Point as planned, or even get near it, Johnson's men did shatter their opponents' forces, capture the French commander, and establish both Fort Edward and Fort William Henry on Lake George as English frontier outposts, thereby providing some measure of protection for white settlements to the south and east.

Tis a most signal deliverance, and the hand of a kind God evidently in it.

Mr Burr brings news that Parson Pemberton and Wife are expected at Newyork this week, and shall have Letters by 'em—I hope you will soon have my pacquit. Mr Oliver and Lady sat out last Saturday.

{September 16, 1755}
Teusday Morn

Tis *hurry,* and *Fly,* and will be so till Commencement is over— I am but poorly able to bare [. . .] now I am so over come with the heat of the weather, but I have always been supported yet and I trust I shall still be so far as is best.

{September 18, 1755}
Thursday Eve. fine and cool.

The Governor and Lady rode up this P.M. and made us a vissit, and the good gentleman as usual directs me what I shall get for his dinner, in jest—He says he must have a Pudding and a Roast Chicken—When they came I was at the Oven baking little Caks for Commencement. I brought them some of em, for the Governor loves such things. He and Madam Eat and commended em as good.

After they went away I received your Letter No. 15. It came as I expected by Mr Pemberton. I cant hear wheather he has brought his *Charmer* or not.

{September 19, 1755}
Fry-day

The nearer to Commencement the more hurry—a great deal of Company to day and a Relation of Mr Burrs from Fairfield is come to stay with us till after Commencement[4]—I hant got time to read half your dear Letter—tho' I have the private billit, and am well sattisfied that you remain *your own,* as well as mine.

After Braddock's defeat on the Monongahela, this was joyful news for English-speaking colonists.

4. This was twenty-nine-year-old Elizabeth (Betty) Burr, daughter of Aaron's cousin, Colonel Andrew Burr, and Sarah Sturges Burr. Elizabeth later married Daniel Osborne, also of Fairfield. Charles Burr Todd, *A General History of the Burr Family* . . . (New York: Knickerbocker Press, 1902), p. 146.

{September 20, 1755}
Saturday A.M. Sepr. 20.

What—not come this fall nither? I give you up—you will never come again—Tis realy a soar dissappointment—I am grievously dissappointed every way—nobody from Stockbridge—nobody from Boston.

P.M. I am affraid I ha'nt received all your privacies that I aught to have had with this Letter. I had only one quarter of a sheet of paper wrote down one side, which you desired me to read in the first place, the whole of which was about *Jesuit* except a caution or two about Mr Pemberton.[5] Page (287) you mention an Errand sent you by Jenny which vexed you, and direct me to the private papers for further intelligence. Nothing of this is to be found—Tis possible Mr Burr droped it, for he first opened the Letter, for it was given to him, and he is eager as well as I am.

{September 26, 1755}
Fryday Sepr. 26.

Well Commencement is over and all our company gone off except My Father and a Cousen of Mr Burrs from Fairfield who you saw at Mr Thaddeus Burrs when you was there. On Teusday A.M. Mr Pemberton and Peter Smith came here. They lodged here till yesterday. Teusday Night about 12. o'Clock my father came very unexpectedly. He is well and left all well at home. I had a Letter from Lucy. She is at Newhaven, and well.

There was but little company in Town compaired to what there was last year tho' I had as much as ever I had since I have been here—I am called off and can write no more yet.

{September 27, 1755}
Saturday P.M.

This morn Mr Burr with my father sat out for Philadelphia, and now I have time to think how I feel—I find my self much worried, feel dragged out of my senses, can hardly keep off the Bed.

Mr Pemberton said not one word to me about you no more than if there had been no such person. Mr Burr says he asked if you did

5. For "Jesuit," see note 12, Letter No. 14, above.

not write by him to Mr Burr and he told him that Letter was to me, and that was all.

Now Mr Burr is gone to Philadelphia. He cant go to Boston tho his and my inclination was to have him go that way rather than this on many accounts, but chiefly on yours. But the Minnisters thought it his duty to go to Synood as some affairs of great importance are to be brought before 'em at this setting, in petecular the affair of removing Mr Bostwick—by the way he is sick here in Town of the Intermitting Fever, was taken the day after Commencement— I am so low spirited I can write no more.

{September 28, 1755}
Sabbath Eve.

I must send this Letter away as it is or miss of sending by Mr Pemberton—Pleas to give my very kind regards to all our friends as if I named em—My duty to your Father and Mother.

I do hope and will hope that you will come here before winter— only think my dear how lonesome I shall be all alone this winter. I have been trying to perswade this young woman from Fairfield to stay but she is obliged to go back to keep house for Thaddy.

Do try hard my dear. You cant think how glad I shall be to see you once more—I wish I could write to the bottom but tis late and the Letter must go to Night or not atall ⟨ . . . ⟩ *day, day*—I am and I hope throu the goodness of God ever shall be your true friend.

Esther Burr

(I this moment heard that Mrs Smith is in Travil.)

(No. 18.)

{September 29, 1755}
Newark Sept 29. 1755.
Monday.

Last night I sent a Letter to you to go by Mr Pemberton, but I hope you will be on your journey hether before he gets to Boston— you see I hope yet, altho' my hopes have all proved vain as yet—I am so vapory that I can write nothing but nonsense as you see—I hardly know what I write, but this I know, that I wish you was here.

P.M. Rode out with my Cousen, made some vissits, came home and felt much better and was able to eat a hearty supper.[1]

{September 30, 1755}
Teusday, fine day.

My Cousen and I walked as far as Mrs Sergeants and made a very pleasant vissit. She is very hearty and in good spirits, quite free from her vapory disorders tho' at times she says she has somthing of 'em—her having a Child has done her a deal of good.

Mrs Sergeant is a good woman and loves to speak of relegion to those she is acquainted with. Conversation took this turn some of the time, which was treuly delightfull—Mrs Smith is delivered of her fourth Daughter, is well and the Child well.

{October 1, 1755}
Wednsday Morn.

Court sets in Town this week and there is a deal of Roguery to be looked into and amongst the rest our poor Chair Horse has been most sadly Cut on his Back [*so*] that we expected he would die with it, but he seems to be in a fair way to recover. One of the jury have been to me about it to know if Mr Burr left any orders about the matter or any names that he would have called over. But I told 'em that he had not, and desired em to let it alone till he came home, for I perceive I am like to be called before the jury as an evidence of some insults we received a night or two before the horse was abused, and I shall be frighted out of my Wits, for I never was called before a Court in my Life, or so much as sworn. I dont know but I should faint if they call me to speak, for I am very bashfull in such cases.

{October 2, 1755}
Thursday

Fine weather invites to ride. Rode out with my Cousen, made several vissits and did a deal of business, such as speak for Butter, buy syder and Apples; and now I am as tired as if I had been heard at work all day. Indeed vissiting is the heardest work that I do. I have made a business of it this week. My Cousen has a large acquaintance in Town and must look of 'em all before she goes home,

---

1. Esther's cousin was Elizabeth Burr. See note 4, Letter No. 17, above.

and we thought best to improve this week now My Father and Mr Burr are gone, and next week we shall hope for their company— We have been out every day this week as you may observe and I am realy tired of it. I believe I shall stay at home to morrow.

I have been deceived about Mr Pembertons going home. I thought he went the beginning of this week but I perceive he dont go till next Teusday, so I might have kept my journal one week longar. But I believe tis no loss, for I can write nothing but *a mess of stuff nobody knows what*—[If] I dont do a little better soon I shall give out—but I am almost discouraged with myself. I dont know what ails me, it did not use to be quite so bad—I have no spirits, nor life. I feel like an *old dead horse,* and shall stink in the nostrils of every body soon, if I dont come to life. I had rather draw flours than write such nonsense and this is folly.

{*October 4, 1755*}
Saturday P.M.

My Father and Mr Burr are come home, both of em sick. Mr Edwards tired himself sick, and Mr Burr sick of a cold. I got somthing for their refreshment and have put 'em both to Bed— Synod is not broke up so we have no news about York affairs.

{*October 5, 1755*}
Sabbath Eve.

Mr Edwards preached all day two charming sermons from those words, "When a wicked man dieth his expectations perrish, and the hope of unjust men perrisheth."

My Father seems much better to day but Mr Burr is very ill yet tho' he went out all day.

{*October 6, 1755*}
Monday Morn.

Mr Edwards is determined to go to Newyork to morrow, and I have a deal to do to get him and Mr Burr and my self ready (for we are all going in a bunch) because tis sooner then we first proposed. Mr Burr is much better today then yesterday—Your kindness will excuse me for the present when I assure you that my heart is with you whether my pen is imployed for you or not.

{*October 7, 1755*}
Teusday Eve.

We had a fine passage to Newyork, saild about 11 o'Clock in morn and came to York by 3 in afternoon, came to Cap' Richerds (for here I lodge since Mr Cumming is mooved) and found her well, and seemd glad to see us.

Mr Burr gets well very fast, and proposes to go from hence to Fairfield to see his friends there.

{*October 8, 1755*}
Wednsday Eve, and a fine day we have had.

This mornning Mr Burr and I went to Mr Hazzards to see how my father did after his voyage, and here we meet strange news from the Synod. That is this, they have contrary to former votes, repeatedly two, Voted that the Scotch Psalms be sung in the meeting in Newyork one half of the time, which Mr Burr was as much surprized at he said, as if they had voted to burn down their meting-house.

The Synod have also appointed a large committee of their own body to go to Jamaca and consider of the affair of Mr Bostwicks removal there because his people objected that they had not had time to consider of the matter. But Mr Bostwick says what signifies Committees as long as such a diffeculty attends the Church of New-york as they lay under about the psalms, for singing two sorts of Psalms tends only to keep up the contention that has so long subsisted among them.

P.M. I went to see Peter Smiths wife which I never did before, and she treated me very well, but is extreemly offended with what the Synod have done, and declares that if they ever set the Scotch psalms in their meeting she will leve it and go to the French Church, for she will not go to the Church of England if she stays at home— This after-noon Mr Burr is gone forward on his journey—Towards night I went to Mrs Bradleys, found em all well, and Mrs Donaldson in such a way as they all wish—and now I am tired at the heart— so good night.

{*October 9, 1755*}
Thursday Eve.

I went to see Mr Edwards erly this morn expecting to go out of Town but the wind was so high that I did not—and he tells me that he dined at Loyer Smiths yesterday and he never saw a man in such a Rage as he is about the Psalms. He is quite beyond reason or anything but passion, and declares that if my father or any other Minnister in the Country should offer to set the Scotch Psalms he will get up immediately and go out of the house, and order all his famaly out, and will never again set his foot into that Meeting. My Father said he indevoured to reason calmly with him and would have him consider if that method would be the most prudent that could be taken, but *he* would not hear him talk, and told him that it did not signify for him or any body elce to talk with him, for he was resolutely fixed, *and would not be moved.*

{*October 11, 1755*}
Saturday—very cold.

Yesterday about half after 3 o'Clock in the morn I went on board and came home by 11 in the A.M.—but down sick with the cold, for I suffered a vast deal, and I am so poorly now that I can hardly hold up my head.

My Father expected to sail yesterday or today, but I am affraid that he is not gone because the wind is contrary.

{*October 12, 1755*}
Sabbath Eve—very cold yet.

Somthing better, so well that I was out all day, but yet I dont feel right, I could not attend so well as usual. My head seems confused, and I feel draged out—I believe Mr Brainerd preached well but I was not in a frame to hear.

{*October 13, 1755*}
Monday.

Rain all day, and so dark that we could hardly see to work, and propor for the times, I have my old raggs about me, trying to make one new Gound out of two old ones—This dark dull weather makes one feel very badly. I dont think persons so fit to serve either God or Man as when the weather is fine and clear.

I have some privacies to write that I will take time for as soon as I can, and send em when this goes.

{*October 14, 1755*}
Teusday. Cloudy and dull.

My Cousen and I took it into our heads to go a vissiting, for I am grown such a Gossip you must know that I cant bare to stay at home two days going. So rain or shine, out we were resolved to go, and try [to] see what that would do, for tis so dull at home now Mr Burr is gone that we are tired of it—Well, we went to see the Widow Ogden and quite unexpectedly to us, we found her alone and had a very pleasant time of it, but I am weary now Night is come.

{October 15, 1755}
Wednsday P.M. Cold.

A.M. Taken up in doing business and this P.M. I propose to stay at home and look for Mr Burr and I shall be quite discouraged if he dont come.

{October 16, 1755}
Thursday A.M.

Mr Burr is not yet come home, and I dont wonder at it for the Wind was two high to come over the ferry I suppose, but to day tis prety pleasant and I shall look very hard.

P.M. 3 o'Clock. My Cousen gone out a vissiting and I all alone and have a very bad head-ach, not able to write or do any thing elce but lay on the Bed, and I should sertainly go to Bed if I did not look for Mr Burr home. I hate he should come and find me on the bed sick.

Eve. Mr Burr came home about 4 o'Clock this afternoon, is well and all friends are well at Fairfield. He Says that Mr Hubbard is about courting Miss Eunice Denny which will be odd enough, for *he is above fifty, and she but 24* and there is Cousin Thady two, designs to make tryal and he is several years younger than she. *I Phantsy it will look very comcal to see a Man of 50 or 60, and a man of 20 Fighting for a Lady of 24,* wont it? I should not begrudg to go to Fairfield this Winter on purpose to see such a *Battle.*[2]

{October 17, 1755}
Fryday.

Made a visit at Parsons Browns with my Cousen and Mr Burr. We had a very pleasant time of it—Mrs Brown inquired after you— Rode and called just to see Mrs Serjeant. She is well.

2. Eunice Dennie married Thaddeus Burr in 1759 (see note 15, Letter No. 11, above).

{October 18, 1755}
Saturday.

Very busy Ironing and mending and prepareing for another Touer—
Mr Burr tells me that he has appointed to go to Princeton the
beginning of next week, and Peter Smith and his Wife are to be
over and go with us, and I have a deal to do before I can go, so
good-by.

{October 19, 1755}
Sabbath

Bad headach all day, but went out for all. Mr Burr preached both
parts of the day (as Mr Brainerd is absent) upon Christs being the
Sun of Righteousness, two very good sermons, but I have great
reason to complain of deadness and coldness under the precens of
grace.

{October 20, 1755}
Monday the 20.

Dark bad weather for our journey, and it looks as if we should
be obliged to adjourn our ride for a day or two, but if it clears off
we shall set forward erly to morrow morn.

{October 21, 1755}
Teusday.

As fine a morning as one could wish, and as we proposed Mr
Riggs with Cousin Betty and Mr Burr with me, we sat out, came
to Elizabethtown and found Mr Smith and Wife all ready to get
into the Chair. We also met an invitation from the *Doct and Lady*
to dine with 'em at Brunswick. We came forward and found the
Doct at the Ferry ready to receive us and conduct us to his house—
Went, found *Her* well and seemd very glad to see us—Dinner was
ready upon Table and down we sat with good stomachs, Eat hearty,
it being late, and what was prepared very good—We had no time
for chat, for as soon as dinner was over we were obliged to be going
or we could not reach Princeton before Night. We just said *goodby*
and came forward[3]—Came to Princeton a little before Night prety

3. The Doctor and Lady were Alexander and Eunice Cumming. See note 5,
Letter No. 9, above.

much tired. Mr Smith and Lady, Mr Burr and I take lodgings at a very good Tavern, and have things very comfortable.

{October 22, 1755}
Wednsday Night.

We have spent this day in Viewing all the Raireties In and about this Princely Town and we have seen *Wonders* to be sure—In the Morn we went to see the College. We went to the Top of it, and it affoards a very fine prospect the finest in the Province. Then we Rode out to see a very Rich Mine lately discovered about seven miles from the College. The Ore appears to be very Rich. One may see streaks of Gold and Silver very plainly and I was surprized to take a small bit of it in my hand and see how weighty it was. The Master workman tells us that some times they find bits of gold in the sand as bigg as the top of ones finger. There is enough of this Ore now above ground to load two large Vessels. There is a great number of people imployed about these Mines, some digging, others in prepareing the Ore for shipping. The Ore is judged in England to be the Richest this side of Peru. Our Loyer Ogden has one or two rights in it, and all the owners are such rich men that dont Want it, but God knows how to Dispose of this Worlds goods, and he is able to give em hearts to use what he has given em to his Glory, tho' to appearance it must be nothing short of the power of a God to influence 'em so to do—We came back to our lodgings, dined, and in the P.M. I went to Vissiting. Mr Smith and Wife and Mr Burr walked out to see some land that Mr Smith has a notion of purchasing—Eve all came to our lodgings. Some people came in to see us. We spent the Eve very pleasantly and propose to set homeward very erly to morrow.

{October 23, 1755}
Thursday Eve—At Mr Woodruffs.

It raind this morn [*so*] that we did not set out till 9 o'Clock, so was obliged to drive forward as fast as possible. We could not stay to call at the Doct but went straight throu Brunswick, and came to Elizabeth Town, sun about half an hour high, and proposed to go home this eve. But the Governor would not let us go unless we would ingage to come down and dine with him to morrow, which we could not do, so to my great mortifycation I am to stay here this Night—I want to see Little Sally. I know she is calling Mamma, Mamma, as loud as ever she can—Mamma hears you, you little Puss, but cant come to Night.

{October 24, 1755}
Fryday.

Came home this morn, found all well—O my dear what reason of thankfullness! How often has God carried me out and brought me back in safty, and preserved my famaly in my absence? Such favours should not be forgot by me—but Alas how soon do I forget Gods mercies! O my ungreatfullness, Ingratitude, to the best of beings! Just would it be in this infinite good being to deprive me of every comfort, and make me everlastingly missarable as I am ungratefull.

{October 25, 1755}
Saturday

Sally is very Ill. I cant tell what is the matter with her but I think she will have a fit of sickness—I pray God to prepare me for whatever he is about to bring upon me.

{October 30, 1755}
Thursday P.M.

Since Saturday last I have gone throu' a vast deal of [exercise] both of body and mind. My dear Sally has been a very sick Child indeed. Her disorder has been *Worms,* which you know are very daingerous. She is now I hope upon the recovery, to be sure. She is better for the present, God grant that it may continue.

Added to all, Mr Burr was obliged to go to *Jamaca* on the affair of Mr Bostwicks removal. Tho' on Teusday morn when he sat out the Child seemd alittle better, but soon after he went away, she grew worse than ever she had been, and I was affraid he would never see her again.

{October 31, 1755}
Fryday P.M.

My little Sally aparently mends. She has not Vomited since yes-terday, and her purge abates. She has been followed with both ever since she was taken Ill.

Now Sally is better I begin to feel that I am almost Worried out for she will go to nobody but me—I expect to see Mr Burr every minute. I should have looked for him yesterday but it was a very stormy day.

{*November 1, 1755*}
Saturday P.M. 4 o'Clock. Novbr. 1.

Not till this afternoon about 2 o'Clock did Mr Burr come home—the Committe were much devided in their sentiments about the removal of Mr Bostwick and they would do nothing but refer the matter till the setting of the synod next spring, and so Newyork affairs are *hung up to smoak till warm weather makes an alteration*—Sally has got upon her feet again, and could get out of my lap and run to her Papa, and make her honours *and say papa and kiss him*—but poor *I* am down sick.

{*November 2, 1755*}
Sabbath Eve.

I have been able to go out all day to day and heard Mr Brainerd. He preachd well, tho' in the afternoon he indevoured to discribe true *Humility,* and I thought he was a little confused, but on the whole he did well—I wish our people might settle him.

{*November 4, 1755*}
Teusday Eve.

Yesterday we was so stuffed and crowded with vissitors that we could get time for nothing but to wait of em—but today my Cousen and I have been to see a good Woman that has lately lost a Brother, and he has left em without hope, and the poor woman seems as if she could not live under the tryal. Sertainly my dear it must be one of the greatest tryals that flesh and blood are called to. You and I have never been called to tryals of this kind, and I hope never may.

{*November 5, 1755*}
Wednsday Eve.

Cousen Betty and I have been to see Madm Belcher (this pen will not say one word) and we had a very pleasant time of it, but only we heard a most dismal account of the cruelty of the French and Indians to the back inhabitants of our southern Provinces. We also heard that there had been 15 hundred French and Indians discovered just on the berders of this Province, [*so*] that we are surrounded by our Enemies on every side, and unless the God of Armies undertakes for us we are lost, for our people seem to know nothing what to do more than a parsle of Children would in such a case, nor half so much as Newengland Children would.

{November 6, 1755}
Thursday.

A.M. My Cousen left me to go home. It hurt me to part with her, for she is a Clever creture as you will see in a hundred, a pious discreet person about 29. years of age. I was very urgent with her to stay with me this Winter as I was like to be alone, but her friends could or would not spare her, so her Brother came for her.

P.M. Miss Hannah Sergeant and I went up to see Mrs Smith.[4] She is very well and her little one is as fat as a Pig. I am prety much tired so I wish you a good Night.

{November 7, 1755}
Fryday. Morn.

I have at last received a little good Letter from the best friend I have in Boston. I have been wondering, and hopeing, and expecting this long time—you are very good to take such pains to let me know that you hant forgot me. I am very sorry to hear that Mr Prince is so Ill. I hope he may recover and live to be a blessing to you, to me, and the World a great many years yet.

I am concernd to know what rude treatment my last paquit met with. I hope it was not serched—I shall be affraid to send by water again and how I shall send I cant tell—I hope Parson Pemberton delivered what he had safe.

{November 8, 1755}
Saturday.

It is a very cold day but I was obliged to ride three miles on some urgent business, and now I feel but poorly. This P.M. Mr Burr is gone to Elizabeth Town to see if somthing cant be done for the

4. Hannah Sergeant of Newark was Mrs. (Martha) Smith's step-niece and the daughter of Jonathan Sergeant and his first wife, Hannah Nutman Sergeant. In about 1759 she married John Ewing, who was a tutor at the College from 1754 until 1758. Later in the journal Esther described a confrontation she had with Hannah's future husband over his attitudes about women. McLachlan, pp. 95–98.

defence of our frontiers—I wish our Province had the spirit of New-england. We should soon drive off this five hundred that are on our borders—I feel very gloomy.

{November 9, 1755}
Sabbath Eve

A cold day but I have been out allday. It was our Sacriment. I felt somthing better than I did yesterday, but did not feel alive in Gods service. O to live always near to God! This might be called life—But I am dead whiles I live! O how I long to see you! Do pray come soon in the spring—I cant be dissappointed any more—I am already quite impatient about it—As for my going to Boston I give it up—and if you dont come here I dont think I shall ever see you in this World.

{November 10–11, 1755}
Monday and Teusday.

So busy about some Tayloring that I must beg to be excused. You must know that I am the Taylor. I'm altering old Cloths which is very hard work.

{November 12, 1775}
Wednsday P.M.

Tis general Training at Elizabeth Town and everybody gone but I, so I think to go a vissiting—tis fine pleasant weather as ever I knew at this time of the year.

Eve—I have made a pleasant vissit at Mrs Ogdens—poor Woman has been confined by illness ever since last May but is recovering slowly—I wonder where this good paquet is. I would fain fancy that it is coming, is just at Newyork, but I suppose I shall be disappointed. I wish some good Capt' would be so good to me for this once as to set out and bring your very good Letter—Come Capt Wimble wont you? I'll love you this Twelvemonth if you will.

{November 13, 1755}
Thurs-day Eve.

Mrs Brainerd spent this afternoon with me—this is the first time she has been here since she layin. Poor woman has been kept down with one disorder or other continually—she has been troubled with very greivous sore Eyes—her spirits are very low. I never saw her so down and low in my life except when she was once in a melancholy way, and I am much affraid she is getting into such a way again.

{*November 14, 1755*}
Fryday.

Very busy about some household affairs, and almost down sick with a bad cold I got a going out on Wednsday.

{*November 15, 1755*}
Saturday P.M. 5 o'Clock—fine weather.

Mr Burr and I am just returnd from a Ride, and comical enough we were turnd over as sure as rates—You remember what a good obedient Chair-horse ours use to be, but he is grown very Naught, so that I hant dared to go out with out Mr Burr with me for some time past. He has a nasty trick of going Tail first if his Lordship hant a mind to go any farther—so now he sets up his *hinder*—and run us back on a side hill and over we went as slick as could be. Mr Burr sprung out and held the Horse or I must have been Torn to pieces, for I could not fall out, our carriage being a Chaise, but I fell in such a manner, up one corner of the Chaise, that I could not get out without some time for it, and if he had run, as he had set out to do, I must have remained where I was till the Top of the Chaise was torn off and I thrown out—I could not help laughing at first, but I think that this deliverance calls for thankfullness, for I was in the utmost dainger of loosing som one of my Limbs at least, as well as being frighted, which might have been of fatal consequence.[5]

{*November 17, 1755*}
Monday Eve—fine weather yet

I am almost down sick with this cold, but I went out all day yesterday and heard Mr Brainerd. I think I never heard him preach so well in my life. His discourse was exceding well adapted to the circumstances of this people, and this Land—This Congregation are about to have a meeting to see what their minds are with respect to calling Mr Brainerd to be their settled Pastor—I wish they may be united in him for I dont think they will ever do better. Mr Brainerd is an Excelent Man, and a Charming Minnister, tho' I dont

5. Esther was six months pregnant at this time.

think he is equel to some others in the Pulpit, yet as to other
minnistereal gifts he's very extreordinary.

{*November 18, 1755*}
Teusday Morn 7 o'Clock—
a fine morn

We have been surprizengly shocked by an Erthquake this morn
between 4 and 5 o'Clock. It continued the longest that ever any has
done in this Country. Mr Burr says he thinks it continued near 3
munits. For my part, I could not think the time less than 4 munits,
but I was so surprized that I was not capable of makeng a just
judgment, for to be sure nothing in Nature that ever I met with
in my life seemd so awfull and dreadfull. I trembled for some time
after it was over so that the Bed shook under me.[6]

P.M. 2 o'Clock—I just now received your kind dear No. 17. but
where are Nos 15. and 16? I have had nithe[r] of 'em, unless that
little line that had dated October 13 be one of them, and that is
not Numbered. There is missing from Page 274 to Page 314. I was
overjoyed to have a Letter from you once more. It quite removes all
that gloom that this awfull Erthquake had left upon my Mind, but
to see so much missing and two Numbers two, gives me a great
deal of uneasiness—you mention one Letter gone to Stockbridge. I
hope to have that in time, but I hant heard from there since my
Father came down. I am affraid that will be lost, for we loose Letters
between there and here very often. I shant be easy untill I have all.

Eve. I am distressed about sending by water. I am affraid all will
be opened and exposed, and if I dont send by Conklin I shant send
till next spring, or rather next never[7]—What in the World does
any Villins want to see our Letters for. They will do no body any
good but our selves—they are unintelligable to any but the Free-
mason Club—I like the Name you have given us prodigiously. You
are a Comical Girl—you are a quear creature that is sertain—how

6. This earthquake shook the whole east coast of the continent that morning.
7. This may have been Benjamin Conklin, who graduated from the College
that year and went on to become pastor of the Leicester, Massachusetts, Congregational church in 1763. Once in Leicester, he married widow Lucretia Lawton.
McLachlan, pp. 139–40.

did you think of freemasons for us? (I was forced to leve off to laugh to my self.)[8]

{November 19, 1755}
Wednsday. P.M.

We have dreadfull news from our Army at Lake-George and have reason to expect worse. An express is come to Newyork with intelligence that there is about Ten Thousands French and Indians within a few miles of the Fort at that place, and what is our Army to such a great Number?

O things look dreadfull dark! I am almost sunk into the Eerth with gloom—I am two melancholy to write.

Eve. More bad news—Mr Davenport came here this eve and brings tidings that my Unckle Hopkins of Springfield is dead. He dies of a Lethargy. This adds to my gloom.[9]

{November 20, 1755}
Thursday Morn 8 o'Clock.

I did not expect to sleep any last night but these words of the holy Psalmest quieted me in some good measure—*The Lord Reigns, let the Erth rejoice*—This is an exceding comforting consideration, that God does Rule and order all things, and he will have his glory out of this Wicked World, and I think I do rejoice that it is so, and this comforts me—and it is enough to still the greatest tumults that ever any Poor soul was tossed by.

8. Freemasons were a convivial fraternal order with secret signs and rituals, devoted to mutual help and brotherly feelings. Sarah Prince may have chosen to call her friends "female freemasons" because of the secrecy and dedication that characterized the male order.

9. James Davenport, great-grandson of New Haven's founder John Davenport, and husband of Parnel Davenport, was at this time serving as minister to the Presbyterian congregation in what is now Pennington, New Jersey. Although he had redeemed himself with evangelicals over the years, during the Great Awakening he had made numerous enemies among both New and Old Light preachers with his revival "excesses"—with his attacks on "unconverted" ministers and with his attempt to establish a separatist church in New London, which was accompanied by his well-known book-burning ceremony. Samuel Hopkins, the son of Hannah and John Hopkins and minister of a congregation in what is now West Springfield, Massachusetts, had been married to Esther's aunt, Esther Edwards Hopkins. Dexter 1:184–87, 447–50.

{November 21, 1755}

Fry-day—Company to dine and drink Tea, and a deal of company to sup.

{November 22, 1755}

Saturday—Very rainy dull weather, and I feel just like it.

{November 23, 1755}

Sabbath Eve—Rain all day

I was out all day, but did not feel so much ingagedness as I wished for. 'Twas a stranger that preached, he preachd very well. He took notice of the late Erthquake and the voice of God in it— there was another small shock felt again last night about 9 o'Clock— I am greatly concernd for fear there will be an eruption soon, where God only knows, perhaps some of us may be swallowed up alive— We have just now sertain news that this report of an Army of French and Indians being near our Army is false, which gives me great eas in my mind—I *think*—I dont know what *to think*—but I *think* I will send this Letter by Concklin. I wish I could have your advice to night in the affair. Why want [*weren't*] we made so that we could *fly?* Tho' tis so cold to night I dont know wheather I could bare to Fly 300. miles. I believe I should grow benumbd and drop by the way—Let's see—I must say all I have to say soon for this must go to morrow or next day—You sent my Love to Mr Whtefield—That is a good girl, and I love you for it. You must do so every Letter you write.

{November 24, 1755}

Monday.

You did not do quite fair that you did not tell me what that thing was that Constancia thought there was nothing in. It may be I should be convinced if I heard and heard her reasons (I mean about Jesuits affair) but in the main she thinks I was right—it makes me a little proudish I assure you.

I highly approve of your treatment of the Jesuit. If he will go on in such a way tis good enough for him—but at the same time I pety you. You are under many diffeculties, and if it lay in my power to help you, you would soon be reliefed—but this is my, and I trust your comfort, that there is one that is *able* as well as willing to help and reliefe you under all your tryals.

P.M. I cant contrive who Cats-paw is—He is an impudent fellow be he who he will. Pray give me his name in your next—That was a quear notion about the advertisement. Was that Widower Jesuit? I guss not tho'.

Eve—I am going to trouble you about business now—I want to know how a body may have some sorts of Household stuff—What is the price of a Mehogane [*mahogany*] Case of Drawers 〈 . . . 〉 in Boston, and also a Bulow Table and Tea Table and plain Chairs with Leather bottoms and a Couch covered with stamped Camblet or China, all of that wood.[10]

I should be glad to know what is most fashionable—wheather to have looking Glasses or sconcers for a Paylor, [*parlor*] and what for a Chamber.[11] Pleas to send me word by the first oppertunity, for tis time I was looking out for tis but about 10 months and we moove.

{*November 25, 1755*}
Teusday A.M.

Last night late came Doct Shippin and his Daughter. She is to winter here. She is a little Miss of but Twelve years old, and quite a Child for she is the Baby. To morrow is our Thanksgiving, and I in [some] hast.

{*November 26, 1755*}
Wednsday, our thanksgiving.

I had a very Ill turn last night but feel better than I could expect to day. P.M. Went out and heard Mr Burr from those words of David, *I will sing of mercy and of judgment*—A very propor text for the present day. I am so poorly I can write no more.

{*November 27, 1755*}
Thursday.

Very poorly, and a deal of company all day. P.M. 5 minnisters to drink Tea. One of em tarries over nigh[t.]

---

10. Stamped camblet or camlet was an embroidered or watermarked cloth. *OED*.

11. Sconces were brass or iron bracket-candlesticks, which held one or more candles and were fastened to a wall. *OED*.

{*November 28, 1755*}
Fryday Morn.

I just now heard of an oppertunity to send to Boston by land, so have concluded not to send by Concklin—the person going to Boston is Mr Cleverly, a lame man. I suppose you know him[12]—I am but poorly today with the headach, and Sally is not well.

Pleas to give my duty to Mr Prince and your Mamma. My kindest regards to all the female Freemasons, and Julia, in all which Mr Burr joyns me. I want to write to the bottom but am not able. I hope my dear friend you wont forget me at the Throne of grace, as I dont nor never can forget you when I have an heart to remember my self.

From, my dear, your most affectionate friend,

E. Burr

P.S. Mr Clark has been here this week and inquires with a great deal of concern when *Sister Nabby* will be here again.

November 28. 1755.

(No. 19.)

{*November 29, 1755*}
Saturday. A.M. Newark Novbr 29. 1755.

Nothing discourages me so much about our public affairs as the growing divisions between the Provinces. They seem to have a jellous Eye over one another for fear one should share more than their part in the honnour (when indeed I see no honnour to share in). Divisions are growing amoungst our cheif officers. Our Assemblies this way are extreamly divided and set against their Governors. You will see the speach ⟨ . . . ⟩ our *Honnourabl* assembly have made our good Governor, and how they will comply with none of his desires, nor nothing that is reasonable—That Letter of Coles from our Army at Lake-Gorge, tends only to raise a party spirit throu the Land, and has done it effectually here and at Newyork. That I conclude you

---

12. Possibly John Cleverly of Morristown, New Jersey, son of John and Hannah Savil Cleverly of the section of Braintree, Massachusetts, that is now Quincy. For at least part of his adult life he had been a preacher. There is no record of his ever marrying. Sibley 6:79–80.

have seen in the Newyork Mercury—such a pack of horrid lies I suppose were never put togather before in this Country.[1]

P.M. I have at last received your dear Letter Number 16. Sent to Stockbridge, and now I am easy for I set my self to look for No. 15 which I was sure I must hav[e] had, and I found it under some papers very safe, so I have all now—Eve. A deal of bad news two. [. . .] [are?] in this Province, and one in Pensilvania. [I am?] such a fool that I have forgot both page and No. of my last. I mistook about [. . .] Sat it down before I sent it away, but I [. . .] to take notice, but I [. . .] No. 18. and about p. 146—[. . .] shall go on accordingly.

{November 30, 1755}
Sabbath

God seems to be come out in a way of awfull judgment against this whole Land. O that the people migh[t] lern righteousness! But insted of lerning righteousn[ess] they lern Wickedness apace—Gods awfull judgments seem to have no other effect on us here but to harden us and make us more secure both in a Temporal as well as a spiritual sense.

Eve. Mr Burr is just returnd from Elizabeth-Town and Mr Spencer with him—this morn Loyer Ogden desired Mr Burr to go with him to the Governors to perswade him to call our Assembly (on [hearing?] [. . .]) and try em once more, for if ever they will do any thing tis now. And so he has concluded to do, and if they dont do somthing for the defence of this Province he will desolve 'em immediately, and see if we cant chuse a better one.

{December 1, 1755}

Monday   company all day   Decm the 1.

{December 2, 1775}
Teusday Eve.

Last night Mr Tennent came here with another gentleman from Freehold, and Mr Spencer, and Mr Brainerd, and *Brother Clark,* all

---

1. The "divisions between the Provinces" were disagreements about who should take responsibility for fighting off the French and their Indian allies. Massachusetts and Connecticut had at this time taken most of the initiative, while New York, New Jersey, and Pennsylvania, which were much more directly affected, had done very little.

awake about our affairs and ingaged to do somthing[2]—Mr Tennent brought with him an Indian from the forks of Delaware who with his famaly and three others, had fled to Mr Brainerds Indians, and this account he gives; two days before this place belonging to the moravians was destroied, there came an Indian to him and those other famalies of Indians, and told him that the Indians all had concluded to joyn with the French, and that a large company of them was gone down to Pensilvenia and another great company was gone to destroy Minisink, and that the rest were to Burn this moravian place that Night.[3] But they had concluded to put it off two days longer [so] that he and those other famalies might have time to joyn with em, and added that if they did not joyn they were to be killed as the Eng[li]sh were. And if any one of them should discover their desighns to the white people they were to be cut in pieces whiles alive and be made to eat their own flesh, and if they refused to Eat it they would ram it down their Throa[ts] till they died—he further says that as soon as the messenger was gone he set his Wife and two Children on his horse and bid em flee, whiles he went to tell these poor Moravians what they might expect. And accordingly he wen[t] to Justice Horsfield their cheif and told him all he knew, but the Justice would not belive him but told him that it was an Indian story, and he an Indian and so not worth regarding. Then he went all along the back settlements and told em what to expect—The Indian is one that Mr Brainerd is well aquainted with and one that may be depended upon. He speaks English very handsomely and can read well, and is a sober well behaved Man, and seems to have more sense than common—he says also that we hant one Indian that is a friend to us but those that came with him (I mean the Delawares) that he knows they took up the hatchet sometime this fall past at a Treaty they had with the french. This Indian with Mr Tennant is gone to the Governor and Council who are now sitting—Mr Burr is gone to York.

2. Brother Clark was probably John Clark. See note 4, Letter No. 13, above.

3. The Moravians (the Renewed Church of the United Brethren) were pietistic Protestants who had established religious communities and Indian missions in Bethlehem and Nazareth, Pennsylvania, not far from the New Jersey border. Minisink was located just across the New Jersey boundary in New York.

{December 3, 1755}
Wednsday.

You would laugh to see what quear work we make of War here. I am sure I could not help laughing heartily to see our people 3 days getting ready to go about 50. miles, and when they were ready wait a whole day for the Colonel who was affraid and wanted the Indians to get out of the way before he went—Tis high time that we had felt the sword. Newjersy has had a [p]eaceable time of it ever since it was settled, whiles [the]ir poor Neighbours have been [killed!]

{December 4, 1755}
Thursday.

You justly observe of Mr *Heardy* that he is a New *Broom* and so of consequence will be [applauded?]. So much is undoubtedly true of him, that he is a gentleman of good sense and Lerning, and *a Gentleman* in the strictest sense of the word, and one that seems much ingaged for the good of this Country. (Mr Burr thinks that I have said two much of Mr Heardy. He says he is not so sertain of his Lerning nor sense nither tho on the whole he thinks he will make a good Governor.)[4]

Eve. Mr Burr came home says all friends at Newyork are well— but they are in a sad jumble yet and he is affraid always will be— Mr Bostwick was appointed to supply em the Three Winter months, so according to order he is there—Mr Peter Smith was so good as to invite him to take lodging at his House and he excepted and that has put some of the Congregation quite out of Temper, and they think nothing will do but Mr Bostwick must hire lodgings as unable as he is to affoard it.

{December 5, 1755}
Fryday.

Our people are returnd from Minisink, and all comes to no more than a poor old shop by accident got on fire and burnt down to

4. Esther was talking here about Sir Charles Hardy, who was made royal governor of New York in 1755. He was the son of Sir Charles and Lady Elizabeth Burchett Hardy and the brother of Josiah Hardy, who became New Jersey's governor in 1761. John W. Raimo, *Biographical Directory of American Colonial and Revolutionary Governors, 1607–1789* (Westport, Conn.: Meckler Books, 1980), p. 266.

Ashes before our 5 hundred Men got there to put it out—Such things do a deal of hurt. Besides the expence such things harden people.

{*December 6, 1755*}
Saturday

I have received a paquet from Stockbridge. I suppose it came with yours but was not sent over at the same time. They are all in usual helth. My youngest Sister continues poorly, I fear she is not long for this world[5]—The money that you desire me to send to my Mother I believe I shall not send, for I know of no oppertunity that will do to send mony by till next spring, and I conclud you will have got the Rideing hood before that time—I am sorry that you hant sent me my account, for Life you know is very unsertain and it appears so in a specual manner to me. I should have been glad to have had all such matters settled before next March.[6]

{*December 7, 1755*}
Sabbath Eve.

Alone, all gone to meeting.

This Sabbath has in many respects been a good day to me—tho' I have been unable to go out this P.M. and Eve. God has ennabled me to trust in him and rely upon him—and tis my comfort and joy that he will be glorifyed what ever becomes of me, and I feel willing to be and do and suffer anything that is for his glory—O my dear this is an unspeakable comfort that he never left any to be confounded that put their trust in him.

{*December 8, 1755*}
Monday. preparing for Wood frollick tommorrow.

{*December 10, 1755*}
Wednsday

Yesterday we had our Wood brought with less confusion than ever we had before—People are much more Kind to us than we expected they would be after Mr Burrs dismission.

5. This was Elizabeth Edwards (see note 5, Letter No. 14, above) who was *not* long for this world. She died in 1762 at the age of fourteen. *Edwards Genealogy*, p. 16.
6. Esther's second child was due in March, and she feared that she might die in childbirth.

Eve. As it was a day of hurry and work to get things in order again, Mr Burr perswaded me to go this P.M. to Elizabeth Town with him, for he said if he went and left me at home I should work myself to death. So I set all to their propor business and went to make a vissit to Mrs Spencer, then to the Governors, and he with Madm and his Son from Hallifax were come up to our house[7]—we had a very pleasant Ride of it for the Weather is more like the beginning of May than December. As we returnd stoped and yoked a coupple of honest steady persons that I hope will indevour to make it set as easy as possible on each other.

{December 11, 1755}

Thursday. Busy all day in writing Letters.

{December 12, 1755}

Fryday—very stormy dull Weather.

A strange gloom has possessed my mind for some weeks past, but God in infinite mercy has for some days removed it, and innabled me to trust in him and to rest sattisfied that he should order all things as he pleases.

{December 13, 1755}

Saturday Eve.

I think God has been Near to me this eve—O how good tis to get near the Lord! I long to live near him always—nor is it living unless I do—No tis *death*—Worse than *death*—I feel excedingly affraid of being left to distrust God as I have done for some weeks past—Nothing but the mighty power of God can keep me from it—I feel my self infinitely weak and unable to do the least thing of my self—And God appears all Sufficient—I have the Headach all day to day.

7. Governor Belcher's son (by his first wife, Mary Partridge Belcher) was Jonathan Belcher, Jr., who was then chief justice of the Supreme Court in Nova Scotia and later that colony's lieutenant governor. A bachelor at this time, he married Abigail Allen in April 1756. She was the daughter of Abigail Waldo and Jeremiah Allen of Boston. Sibley 8:343–64.

{December 14, 1755}
Sabbath Eve.

Not well, but out allday—and I hope got some good but O how little! I am amazed at my barrenness under such advantages! Why does not God deprive me of every means of grace and cut me off and send me down to the dark Regions of Dispare where many are that have never sind against such light as I have.

I have been taking some pains with Sukey Shippen. She is a poor ignorant stupid Girl in matters of relegion, tho' not so ignorant as I feard I should have found her[8]—she has an old Aunt that lives in the house that has taken some pains with her—she says her Aunt is a very good Wom[a]n and I believe she is by all I have heard—and I dont know but they think she is good enough for all the House.

{December 15, 1755}
Monday. Fine warm weather.

P.M. Vissited Loyer Ogdens Wife who has lately lain in with a dead Child. Had as pleasant a time of it as could be expected—I am in good spirits, feel better than I have for some time.

{December 16, 1755}
Teus-day

Dreadful Rainy, blustering bad weather, but the News more *Dreadfull.* We have most *meloncholy* accounts from our frontiers, and no body stirs no more than if it was impossible—tomorrow our Assembly sets and Mr Burr with some others are going down to see if they cant influence em to do somthing for the defence of this Province.

Eve—*Most shoking news*—That 17. Men of War are Landed in Cabritton [*Cape Breton*]—see nothing but *distruction* before us— *Universal distruction*—And *Wo* to them that are *with Child,* and to them that give suck in these days! But after all we are in Gods hands and this comforts me, and he will be Gloryfied by us and off us. This is realy a comfort that God will loose none of his glory, whatever becomes of me or mine.

---

8. Susannah Shippen. See note 6, Letter No. 14, above.

{December 17–18, 1755}

Wednsday and Thursday. Sick with the Head-ach and sunk in spirits.

{December 19, 1755}
Fryday.

Mr Burr is gone to Elizabeth Town again and so of consequence these *other* cretures ant so thick about, and I'm for improving the oppertunity about some *little Matters*—I think it seems as bad as it did before and rather worse if any thing.

{December 20, 1755}
Saturday.

I wish I could help troubling you with my troubles that can do nither you nor me any good, but I am perplexed about our publick affairs. The Men say (tho' not Mr Burr he is not one of that sort) that Women have no business to concern themselves about em but trust to those that know better and be content to be destroyed because that they did all for the best—Indeed if I was convinced that our great men did act as they realy thought was for the Glory of God and the good of the Country it would go a great ways to meke me easy.

{December 21, 1755}
Sabbath Eve

Last Eve I had a very comfortable season of it. I trust God was near to my soul and helped me to trust in him—I have been out all day and it is extream cold and I am almost over come.

{December 22, 1755}
Monday.

Some of the coldest sort of weather that ever we have in this part of the Country.

{December 23–25, 1755}
Teusday. Wednsday. Thursday.

Extream cold and all the Ink in the House froze up—and with all a good deal of company, [*so*] that I have had time for nothing heardly.

{December 26, 1755}
Fryday Eve. The weather a little warmer.
P.M. Made a vissit to Mrs Brainerd. Mr Brainerd is gone a journey and she is quite alone—she is yet but poorly and I am affraid will be all Winter.

{December 27, 1755}
Saturday.
All in the Clutters about business for we have done none this week and Minnisters one and another must come *pop* in. I wish folks would [*not*] always come when they are least desired.

{December 28, 1755}
Sabbath Eve.
Out all day tho' I had a very Ill turn last Night. I overdid my self bustling about as I did yesterday—Mr Burr Preachd from those Words of our Saviour, *What think ye of Christ*—and I suppose you will conclude that I thought the sermons good without my saying so.

{December 29, 1755}
Monday.
Eve—this P.M. we were favoured with the company of Governor Belcher and Madm and their Son the cheif justice and another Gentleman—Sally to be sure must make sport for us. Madm could not perswade her to go to her or say anything to her, but the slut would go to Justice Belcher and kiss him—I was almost vexed with her—The Presbytry are to set here on Wednsday this week—so good by for to Night.

{December 30, 1755}
Teusday Eve.
Most Awfull news we have from some parts of Europe. L[isbon] wholey distroyed besides a vast deal of other damage done by an Erthquake—Why was not it our portion to be distroyed as well as they—I am sure no people could deserve such a judgment more—but God is infinite in mercy and does not deal with us according to our sins but according to his sovereign *good* pleasure—I wish this instance of goodness might so affect us as to bring us to repentance—

God is trying all methods with us and nothing serves to reclame but I fear only to harden.

{December 31, 1755}
Wednsday. P.M.

My company have dined and are gone to Meeting so I have a minutes lasure and but a minute, and besides I am prety well tired— Now I want to ask your advise. Madm Belcher is very urgent to have me go to Princeton with her this week or the first good day we have. Now I want you to tell me if I had not better stay at home *all things considered*—The cheif justice and my Mr Burr make up the company—I dont much like this gossiping about just now, but Madm is a good deal ingaged about it. She invited me last summer but I could not go then for Mr Burr was sick—I wish I could send this and have an answer by to morrow.[9]

{January 1, 1756}
Thursday. Eve—January the first—1756

This P.M. all our company left us, and altho' the company of Minnisters is very agreable yet I am so tired that I was not sorry when they left the House—Yesterday just as I had done writing Madm Belcher rode up to the door and has answered the question that I asked you. She says tis two cold for any Body to go this week, so I am in hopes that we shant go atall. (I forgot to wish you a happy New Year which I do from the bottom of my heart wish you a great many.)

{January 2, 1756}
Fryday P.M.

I have been to vissit a person under sore affliction by the Loss of a Son at sea. The Vessel was cast away. This must be an exceding great tryal. I dont know how I could support under the like— somebody comes in and pesters me.

{January 3, 1756}
Saturday.

According to appointment Mr Burr and I went to the Governors to dine and suffered much with the cold and I have got sick.

9. Here again Esther was referring to the late stages of her pregnancy.

{January 4, 1756}
Sabbath Eve

Very poorly all day but out in the A.M. Heard a sermon from those words of our Saviour to Peter, *But who say ye that I the Son of man am.* I am quite poorly, unable to write any more.

{January 5, 1756}

Monday. A very stormy Cold day.

{January 6, 1756}
Teusday Eve.

I provided I may say a prety genteel dinner to day for Madm Belcher, and Justice and his Gentleman, but they sadly disappointed me for they did not come, altho the day was very fine and warm, the finest we have had this many a day—I dont like it to be served so tho tis by a Governors Lady—tis not write, is it?

{January 7, 1756}
Wednsday A Fast throu-out our Presbytry.

This day that I lotted on has in great measure been lost to me— I was out in the forenoon but t'was very imprudent for I have been obliged to lay a Bed this afternoon to pay for it—I have had as bad a pain in my Head and stomach as almost ever I had in my life— tho throu mercy I am now a little better or I should not be writing.

I think our circumstances never called louder for fasting and humiliation than now—but I fear they are not kept to the Lord— I fear the Almigh[ty] will say, *that your sollemn Assemblies I cannot away with*—It will not do for me to think of our dark circumstances—I was going to enlarge but tis not best now I am so poorly to say or think anything about 'em—We are in Gods hands—And that aught to be enough.

{January 8–10 1756}
Thursday, Fryday and Saturday

Confined with the Hysterick-Cholick.[10]

---

10. This may have been a term for a physical and/or emotional problem related to pregnancy, since the word *hysteric* was still associated with the womb in the mid-eighteenth century. *OED.*

{January 11, 1756}
Sabbath

Altho I have been so very Ill all the week past yet I have been able to attend Public worship all day—A.M. Mr Burr preached from those words, *He is the Cheifest amongst Ten-Thousands*—The execelency of Christ is a most glorious theme—then attended the holy ordinance of the Lords Supper—but Alas! I have reason to lament a cold dead heart.

P.M. Heard a Young preacher—he did very well. I hope he may be a Blessing in the Church of God.

{January 12, 1756}
Monday

Mr Burr gone to Newyork and I as busy as a Bee.

{January 13, 1756}
Teusday-Eve.

This eve Miss Sukey began with me about her souls concerns, and I find she has had a great many very serious thoughts since she has been here. She is full of her inquireis, what she must do to be good. She tells me she trys to pray from her Heart but finds she cant, and she seems to have some sense of sin—you cant think how my heart is rejoiced—O that God would give us this one soul! I seem as if I could not be denied my request that God would perfect the good work that seems to be begun in her whiles in this house— O how great a blessing upon us—I hope God has heard some of my poor praiers for her—and I hope for a heart to pray more ernestly for her than ever—What a comfort to see those under our care inclineng to the ways of Relegion and True virtue.

{January 14, 1756}
Wednsday a very stormy day.

I find a great deal of pleasure in instructing this Miss I have with me, for she seems to have both Ears open when ever I say any thing by way of instruction—she is a very judicious Child for one of Twelve years old—she grows quite Womanly lately—I shall be very prowd if I can make a Clever Girl of her, for she was realy a Baby when she came here—she grows very notable. She has Worked one Chair for me in about three weeks—Did you ever see so many *Shes*, without one *He* before—I think this weather makes a Fool of me (Hant I *cunning* with all my *folly* to lay it to the Weather.)

{January 15, 1756}
Thursday. Eve 10. O'Clock.

I have had Parson Brown and Lady to see me this P.M. Mrs Brown is as clever as ever. The good woman inquired after you very kindly and desired me the next time I wrote to you to send her kindest regards to you—she said the *next time I wrote*—she does not know our method of corresponding—I would have told her, for I know her friendly heart would be pleased with it, but I was affraid she would tell her MAN of it, and *he* knows so much better about matters than *she* that he would sertainly make some Ill-natured remarks or other, and so these *Hes* shall know nothing about our affairs *untill they are grown as wise as you and I are*—O I wonder where this Mr Burr is. He has made me look all day for him for nothing— good Nighty.

{January 16, 1756}
Fryday—fine weather.

Eve—Mr Burr got home at last. He carried over with him a subscription that the Trustees have lately set forward in this Country, and he shewed it to General Shirley who readily set his name to it with £50 at the end of it, and our Governor Pownall 50£.[11]

{January 17, 1756}
Saturday.

Mr Burr got about 200 Pounds in Newyork which I think is prety well for the first tryal and only four days time.

Now my dear think once more and in ernest two about coming to Newark, for Mr Burr tells me he is determined to see Boston next spring by the beginning of May, and If you ant *Married* do pray come with him, and if you be, pray come with your *Husband*— How does that Word sound?

---

11. "Governor" Pownall was New Jersey's lieutenant governor Thomas Pownall, son of William and Sara Burniston Pownall. In 1757 he replaced William Shirley as governor of Massachusetts. Raimo, *Biographical Directory*, pp. 144–45.

{January 18, 1756}
Sabbath. Eve.

Imployed in writing home.

{January 19, 1756}
Monday

I am half determined to send this Letter to go by General Shirley—but Mr Burr says he does not know whether I had best send till I hear from you, for he says perhaps I shant direct the Letter right, and if I send it to Miss Sally Prince it will never find you—but I dont Prophesy such hurry about Matters tho' he is a Widower.

{January 20, 1756}
Teusday—Eve.

We have had a most fine day of it so I took it into my head to Walk out and am come home tired as you [. . .]

{January 21, 1756}
Wednsday

A very fine Rain allday, which Is a great mercy indeed, for it seems as if we should not have water for Man or Beast much longer by reason of the drought—the like has been never known for so long a time, not in these parts—We have been obliged to run almost all over Town for water ever since about Commincement time.

{January 22, 1756}
Thursday A.M. Janry the 22. 1756.

I am determined to send what I have wrote to day so must bid you farewel—It looks very unlikely to me whether ever I shall see you again in this world, but I hope to meet you in a better where we shall never part.

Pleas to give my most Respectfull regards to your Honored Papa and Mamma. And my kindest regards to all the Sisterhood—I will mention their names because it may be the last oppertunity I may ever have to do it—First *Marina* because she is married—*Constancia* who I love as one of your best friends—*Confidenta* as another—*Laura* as a good Christian and a friend to all such—*Simpathia* for her name tho' I dont know her—*Leomira* as a promising young Lady and has many amiable quallities—and *Julia* I love for two many things to be mentioned in a Letter—You my friend I shall Love for-ever—

pray for me till you hear again—pray ernestly for your   Esther
B[urr.]

(Mr Burr desires his Regards to you and Mr Prince and Mrs Prince.)

(No. 20)

{January 23, 1756}
Janry 23. 1756.

Once more to my dear Fidelia
   Nothing is more refreshing to the soul (except communication
with God himself) then the company and society of a friend—One
that has the spirit off, and relish for, true friendship—this is becoming [*to*] the rational soul—this is God-like.
   Yester-day, after I had sent away No. 19. I made a vissit at Mr
Smiths. She [*Mrs. Smith*] has a friendly heart and much of it appeared, more than usual, which give me more of a sense of the
privilage and blessing of friendship than I have had for some time—
Tis my dear a great mercy that we have any friends—What would
this World be with out 'em—A person who looks upon himself
to be friendless must of all Cretures be missarable in this Life—Tis
the Life of Life—but I can make no new observations on this head
to you.

{January 24, 1756}
Saturday

   Yesterday P.M. went to see Mrs Brainerd—poor Woman is yet
kept under the bonds of affliction. I pity her from my heart, I know
what it is to be a stranger and amongst all strangers when sick—
but I am most of all concernd to find out that she is not pleased
with being here, and is not willing that Mr Brainerd should settle
here, and more than all that our people have found it out. I wish
this mant [*may not*] do much towards preventing Mr Brainerds
settling here.

{January 25, 1756}
Sabbath Eve

   At meeting all day tho' prety cold—I have been uncommonly
troubled with wandering thoughts to day whiles at meeting and the

word preaching—O how far am I from what I ought to be! What a wicked heart!

{January 26, 1756}
Monday

Very busy about setting the House a little in order, for I have been obliged to neglect it two much of late by reason of the bad weather, which has been either extream cold or very muddy—Loyer Ogden has a Child at the point of death, and they in their distress sent for Mr Burr to come and pray with it, which I look on very remarkable, for the Loyer is *a very great Biggot to the Mother Church.*[1]

{January 27, 1756}
Teusday Eve.

Mr Burr gone to Presbytry—I have just now finnished Working the bottom of a great Chair. I have done it at odd times when I could spare the time. I recon if I could have sat stedy at it I could have done it easily in five days.[2]

{January 28, 1756}
Wednsday Eve.

Mr Burr returnd and brought company with him, one lodger—just now Miss Sukey has finished me another Chair bottom which she has done in a fortnight, and that is very notable for such a Miss, ant it? I shall be very prowd if I can make her a nottable Girl—for she was a mear trifler when she first came.

{January 29, 1756}
Thursday A.M.

Loyer Ogdens Child is like to recover from the sides of the Grave—it was given over by every body for several days—I wish that Mrs Ogden might be suitable affected with the Mercy, as she has been extreamly anctious for the Life of the Child.[3]

1. David Ogden was an Anglican. See note 3, Letter No. 11, above).
2. Working the bottom of a chair may have been making a needlepoint cover for the cushion.
3. Gertrude Gouverneur Ogden. See note 3, Letter No. 11, above.

{January 30, 1756}
Fryday Eve.

I have been to take a Ride this P.M. but the weather proved very bad and it has made me sick so I wish you a good night hopeing to be better able to write tomorrow.

{January 31, 1756}
Saturday

Very sick all day with an extream Headach.

{February 1, 1756}
Sabbath Febry the 1. 1756. N.S.

Altho' so very ill yesterday yet I was able to go out all day, and heard two very affecting sermons on the relegious improvement we aught to make of Earthquaks—The Text was those words of our Saviour, 25 Matthew, "And Earthquakes in divers places"—The Assembly appeared very attentive and some were affected—I heard lately that Mr Prince has somthing in print on the late earthquakes. I wish you would be so good as to send it to me as soon as you can, or if anything elce has been printed on that subject I should be exceding glad to see it.[4]

{February 2, 1756}

Monday Poorly and very busy two.

{February 3, 1756}

Teusday—somthing better—Letters of business to write.

{February 4, 1756}
Wednsday

This Morn Mr Burr set out upon his journey to Philadelphia with Justice Belcher.

P.M. Mother Sergeant was so good as to send her Chair for me and one of her Daughters to wait of me to her House, and I very gladly went and spent the whole afternoon with her, and a very agreable one it was.

---

4. Thomas Prince's sermon was entitled *An Improvement of the Doctrine of Earthquakes, Being the Works of God, and Tokens of His Just Displeasure. Containing an Historical Summary of the Most Remarkable Earthquakes in New England . . .* (Boston, 1755).

I propose to vissit as much as I can whiles Mr Burr is gone to keep my spirits up, for it never seemd so lonesome to have him go from home—but he was obliged to go. He could not get excused handsomly, for the Governor was set about it, and the good gentleman is grown a Child.

{February 5, 1756}
Thursday Eve.

P.M. Made a vissit at Mrs Ogdens, and she has been Worrying of me to go with her to morrow to make a Wedding Vissit. I said that women in my circumstances had no business to go sticking themselves up at Weddings. Well she would leve it to the company (for there was a number of young Women by) and they said I was right, so Mrs Ogden left off at last.

{February 6, 1756}
Fryday morn. Very poorly, not able to write—Febry. the 6 day.

{March 26, 1756}
I am my dear Fidelia yet alive and allowed to tell you so—I have been able to write nothing from the time of my confinement till now which is the 26. day of March and 7 weeks since I was delivered of a Son.[5]

I have but a short time to write and but little strength, tho' I have good will enough to write a quire of paper. I shall endevour to say as much as I can in as few words as possible for reasons that I shall give—I conclude you have received long since a Letter from Mr Burr informing you that I was unexpectedly delivered of a Son the sixth of Febry. Had a fine time altho' it pleased God in infinite wisdome so to order it that Mr Burr was from home as you will see by looking back to the last page.

It seemd very gloomy when I found I was actually in Labour to think that I was, as it were, destitute of Earthly friends—No Mother—No Husband and none of my petecular friends that belong to this Town, they happening to be out of Town—but O my dear God was all these relations and more then all to me in the Hour of my distre[ss]. Those words in Psalms were my support and comfort

---

5. Her son, of course, was Aaron Burr, Jr.

thro' the whole. *They that trust in the Lord shall be as Mount Zion that cannot be mooved but abideth for ever*—and these also, *As the Mountains are found about Jerusalem so is the Lord to them that put their trust in him,* or words to that purpose—I had a very quick and good time—A very good layingin till about 3 weeks, then I had the Canker very bad, and before I had recovered of that my little Aaron (for so we call him) was taken very sick so that for some days we did not expect his life—he has never been so well since tho' he is comfortable at present.[6]

I have my self got a very bad Cold and very soar Eyes which makes it very diffecult for me to write atall. Some times I am almost blind.

For my comfort and refreshment I received your No. 18. not long since. I think I never was so glad to have a Letter from you in my life. It did me good like a medicen. O that the Lord would reward you for all your kindness of this nature to me an unworthy Worm of the dust—With your Letter I received Mr Imries printed one, for which I am much obliged, but cant now tell my thoughts but only this that I wish and pray that he may prove a True Prophet.[7] O how comfortable is the thought that the glorious day is so near—O my friend this puts new life into me, altho' perhaps *you and I* may loose our lives in the cause—O that we may be fitted for the fiery Tryal and come forth as gold seven times tryed—I can write no [more] now for I am almost blind and have not time. I must lay down my pen a little while to recover my sight.

I wrote you word in my last which I sent away abut the 23 of Janry that Mr Burr was determined to see Boston this spring, but their is a meeting of the Trustees at the time he intended to set out so he is undetermined at present whether he can go or not, but I shall do all in my Power to remove all objections that seem to be in the way. If Mr Burr does go he will be at Boston by the latter

6. The canker were sores, often found in the mouth, but in women, also on their breasts. *OED*.

7. David Imrie's printed letter was *A Letter from the Reverend Mr. David Imrie, Minister of the Gospel at St. Mungo, in Annandale. To a Gentleman in the City of Edinburgh, Predicting the Speedy Accomplishment of the Great, Awful and Glorious Events Which the Scriptures Say Are To Be Brought to Pass in the Latter Times . . .* (Edinburgh, 1755).

end of April, and I hope, and beg, and pray that you will not fail to return with him. He depends upon it as I do fully.

I have seen Mr Prentices's sermon on the Earthquake and am greatly pleased with it—I want to know if Mr Prince has printed any thing on the same subject—I have also just seen Mr Byles's Poems. I think they are the best that ever he printed.[8]

I am greatly rejoiced to hear that the spirit of God is mooving amongst you and at the Eastward of you. I have no such good News to tell you, for never did People this way so give them selves up to wickedness. Sin has grown aparently within a year in this place— what our young people are coming to God only knows, but it seems as if nothing but swift distruction was in reserve for them—I can add no more—you have my heart is all I can say—Pleas to give my Duty to your honoured parents, and kind Love to all the Sisterhood and Miss Jenny.

> I am, my dear friend, your most
> affectionate Friend and Sister
> Esther Burr

Mr Burr sends Duty
and Love etc.

(No. 21)

{April 3, 1756}
Newark April 3. 1756.
Saturday.

Dear, very dear Friend

Not long since I sent you No. 20. by a cupple of schollars that belong to Newberry.[1] It was a broken business but the best and most I could send for reasons I have given you in it.

I have not been able to write since till now by reason of soar Eyes

8. The title of Thomas Prentice's sermon was *Observations Moral and Religious, on the Late Terrible Night of the Earthquake. A Sermon Preached at the Thursday Lecture, in Boston, January 1st, 1756* . . . (Boston, 1756). Poet and minister Mather Byles published a book of poems on natural disasters, *Poems. The Conflagration, Applied to That Grand Period or Catastrophe of Our World, When the Face of Nature is to Be Changed By a Deluge of Fire, As Formerly It Was By That of Water. The God of Tempest and Earthquake* (Boston, 1755).

1. These were students from Newbury, Massachusetts.

and a Presbytry that have been setting here this week—I am thro' the goodness of God on the recovery tho' tis by slow degrees—My little Son has got to be quite hearty—Ah—I thought it would be so if I began to write. Here comes somebody to *Pester* and to *Hinder.*

{April 4, 1756}
Sabbath.

Out A.M. Heard a stranger (Mr Burr and Mr Brainerd are both gone, Mr Burr is at Princeton) from those words of the Prophet Isiah, *Who hath believed our report,* and to whom has the Arm of the Lord been revealed—a good discourse. I am unwell so could not go out P.M.

{April 5, 1756}
Monday

Extreamly ingaged—what with prepareng for my spining frolick, and what with fixing out Sukey Shippen I am almost crazy. Mr Burr is just come home and has brought Doct Shippen with him for his Daughter, so goodby.

{April 6–9, 1756}

Teusday, Wednsday, Thursday and Fryday all devoted to spinning folks.

{April 10, 1756}
Saturday

I am almost wore up to the hub with so much spinning frolick, and poor Mr Burr for his part is quite sick with a bad cold and soar Eyes. Tis a general distemper throu the Town—I cant write I feel so quere—P.M. Governor and Lady made us a vissit.

{April 11, 1756}
Sabbath

A.M. Mr Burr preached to our young People. P.M. Mr Brainerd preached from those Words in Proverbs, *And thou mourn at the last saying how have I hated instruction etc.,* a very propor subject to inforce what was said in the forenoon—but Alas for me I feel dead under all.

Monday.

Here are these Newbury scholars come back again and are not a going this 10 day. I would not care if you had my scrawls, and what is worse then all is they have left em at York locket up in a Chest, and I cant send it till they go.

Today Mr Burr is to set out for Princeton to the synod and Trustee-meeting and whether he is to go to Boston or not is quite unsertain till his return, and then if he does go he will set out the day after he comes home.

{April 13, 1756}
Teusday Night

I thought to have said a deal to you to day but behold the Court sets in Town, and I have had company from erly in the Morn till late in the Eve, and now I write with the Son at the Brest—When I had but one Child my hands were tied, but now I am tied hand and foot. (How I shall get along when I have got 1/2 dzn. or 10 Children I cant devise.) I have no help in the House except what is in our Ketchin and you know what that is—our young women are all Ladies and its beneath them to go out.

{April 14, 1756}
Wednsday Eve

I had just seated my self for writing this P.M. and company comes in—Tis *vacancy,* and I thought to have had a Vacancy as well as the scholars, but no such good luck for me. All I do say to you must be before Mr Burr comes home for he will be in such a hurry about geting away that I shall have hardly time to Breath—I cant help looking for you a little with Mr Potter and his Wife, but tis with fear and trembling[2]—If you dont come this spring I shall dispare of ever seeing you in these parts, for if you M-a-r-r-y as I think you will before a nother spring I suppose we shall see no more of you in our world—Well tis a mighty strang piece of conduct of that sertain Gentleman—I wonder what ails him—I surspect he is bash-

2. Nathaniel and Hannah Potter lived in Brookline, Massachusetts, where Nathaniel was then pastor of the Congregational church. He was the son of Phebe Bunnell and Noadiah Potter; she was the daughter of Hannah Brown and Samuel Livermore. McLachlan, pp. 56–59, 80–82, 156–57.

full. You must e'ne do the business for him—Tackle up your Chair and go a Courting, and bring the matter to an Issue, [so] that a body may know what to depend on—Its vastly uncomfortable to be hung up between the Heavens and Earth as it were Gibbeted—if Mr Burr goes to Boston he will do somthing in the affair you may be sertain, for you know he loves to be poking about matches.

(As I stept out of the Room Miss Sally gets this and has rumpled it [so] that tis not fit to send but you will excuse it—I scolded at her but she said she was a going to write.)

If Mr Burr goes I shall trouble you with some business. The things I want I will put on a piece of paper by it self—As for privacies I hant many and I guss I shant have time to write em so I will let 'em alone till you come.

What you mention about the Doctor Shippen Mr Burr had found out by some means or other and had wrote to Mr Whitefield in the strongest manner to prevent his doing anything in the affair. The little Man is the most averse to Titles of honnour of anybody I ever saw or heard of. He says no money would tempt him to be willing to have such an attempt sucseeded, so good Mr Whitefield may set his kind heart at rest about it.

I have very lately heard good news from Long Island that their is an awakning in some parts their—O what a happy people should we be if God's Providences should Rouse us out of the deep sleep we seem to be fallen into. I cant but hope Mr Imrie is in the right. O how reviveing the thought—I long to see what he has Published. I am almost impatient about it.

{April 15, 1756}
Thursday-Eve.

Very affecting is Mr Alexanders death. He died very suddenly— he was you know a profesed Deiest and so he died, and now he knows how much he was out of the way[3]—tis a remarkable time for sudden deaths. A Man at Elizabeth Town droped down in the

3. James Alexander, born in Scotland in 1691, had been a lawyer and politician in New Jersey and New York. He is best known for serving as counsel (along with William Smith) to Peter Zenger, the publisher and printer who was tried in a celebrated libel case in New York in 1735. Alexander died on April 2, 1756. *DAB* 1:167–68.

street and expired in about an hour after. The sorrowfull accident that happened in York bay you saw in the news—their is Three persons in this place that lay upon the point of death and the Doc's cant tell what ails them, tho one of them seems to have the numb-palsy.[4]

I have had company to dine with me to day and company at Tea—O I had almost forgot to tell you that Nancy Smith is married to Mr Hait. She will [be] a nigh neighbour to us at Princeton[5]— *Cousen Joney Powel* her Brother is (I hear) very jellous of his Wife— just like the Man ant it? My Eyes are so very weak that I cant see to write any more so a good-nights rest to you.

{April 16, 1756}
Fryday Morn

I have heard from the synod that their is not a quorum of the Trustees so I guss Mr Burr will not go to Boston which will be a very great desappointment to me—I never had such a desire to have Mr Burr go anywhere in my life as I have to have him go to Boston this spring—You will never come here again if he dont go soon I am persuaded—but for all I'll hope for the best till he comes home which will be today if the weather dont prevent which is not very good.

I saw Mrs Brown, Parson Browns Wife, and she desired her kind regards to you. She is a good creture, is often inquiring about you and speaking in your Praise.

11. o'Clock received No. 19 by Mrs Potter—I have read the Private papers and hant patience to read any more till I vent a little by writing—I never was so near being angry at you in my life. If you was her[e] I should sertainly Cuff you—Indeed my dear I think you are a little Proud—I have incouraged you in it two under a notion of *nobleness of mind, and greatness of soul* but to be plain you have carried matter of this sort two far. *You have stood upon points two much, and two long,* and I should have told you so before if I knew as much as I do now. (You must pardon my severity for I am two warm about it but I cant bare to see you *murder your self*—it would have been better that Cats-paw had done it of the two.) Why

4. Numb palsy was paralysis. *OED*.
5. For Benjamin Hait, see note 15, Letter No. 10, above.

you would not have the Man act like a fool would you? Well why
will you oblige him to either become a fool or give up the affair,
and without desighn in you two for you dont chuse nither—I am
almost two vext to write—I wonder in the name of honesty what
business you had to run a way time after time when you knew he
was a coming—You may repent it when it is two late—for I dont
know of such another match on all accounts not on all our shore.

You should consider my dear that he does not, nor cant know
the reasons of your conduct—tis most likly that he thinks that you
dislike him, or elce that you are a Mortal proud creture, which must
sink you in his opinnion, and may lay a foundation for unhapyness
all your days after Marriage for my dear no man likes a woman the
better for being shy when she means the very thing she pretends to
be shy off—not that you have ronged anybody this way but I think
you are in a fair way to rong your self in such a way and can never
be retrieved—Why should you cheat your self out of happynes all
your days for the sake of a few nonsencical points—but I have done
enough and two much. Tis time to tell what I think you should do
for tis not right to blame and not tell how to amend, and hear I
shall wait for Mr Burr[s] return and if he concludes not to go, shall
consult togather and give you the best advice we can. If he goes I
shall have no time to write any more but he [can] say all better
then I can write.

P.M. 4 o'Clock

Now my zeal is a little coold I feel as I do after whping Sally
prety hard, and am affraid I have whiped her more then was needfull.

I have read all you was so good as to send me except the sermon
of Mr Princes for which I am much obliged.[6]

Every Letter I have from you raises my esteem of you and increases
my love to you—their is the very soul of a friend in all you write—
You cant think how those private papers make me long to see you.
Tis impossible for one that has no better faculty of communicating
then I have, to give you any Idea how full of those *petecular matters* I feel. I am like working Liquor, Bottled up that will sertainly
burst unless it has vent soon, but I'll try to keep in till Mr Burr
comes home.

6. See note 4, Letter No. 20, above.

With pleasure I have read the two Letters you sent me. They have raised the Ladies in my esteem greatly. They are handsomly wrote and what is more the spirit of a friend may be seen plainly— I hope Mrs Donaldson is happy in her Husband. She is a deserving Lady and I think if I am any judge she has more of a turn for friendship then Miss Kitty altho Kitty is a friendly creture.

Sally can speak quite plain—and Little Aaron begins to smile and play. He is a fine quiet Child—I never before knew you had such an aversion to marrying a Minnister. Well all helps along the main thing—I feel like a natural Fool. I cant gather my thoughts no more then I can gather the Wind that now blows. I am swallowed up in that same affair—the little Boy crys and I must mind him for all matrymony.

{April 17, 1756}
Saturday Morn

Mr Burr came home last night and today is to set out for Boston, preaches at Newyork tomorrow so hant time for anything but just to desire my kind Love to the freemasons—Mr Burr will say and do all about a sertain affair that is propor—To my great grief you tell me not to expect you this spring so I give you up for this World, but hope to meet you in a better. Till then I remain your most affectionat and sincere Friend, and as a token of it send you my best friend for a time, and hope after he has done you some good turns (this good turn is to see you married) you will return him to his and your

Esther Burr

April the 17. 1756.

Pleas to procure for me the following things—
6 Fann Mounts—Two good ones for Ivory [sticks?].
To Black and Wh[i]te—and two Wh[i]te ones.
¼ lb. of Gumarrabick and one large Pencil and one small.[7]
One Dz of Short Cake-pans.
My Milk-pot altered to some shape or other.
A pair of Correl Beeds.

7. Gum arabic is a substance that comes from certain acacia trees and has many uses. Given the context of Esther's entry, she may have used it as glue. *OED*.

Some Codfish.
Patterns of Caps not your airy caps for [Beaus?]
Send me word how to cut Ruffles and handkercheifs.
Send word how they make Gounds.

(No. 22.)

{April 19, 1756}
Monday April the 19. 1756.

To my ever beloved Fidelia

This morning by six O'Clock ⟨ . . . ⟩ I sent away my best beloved (in this World) to make you a vissit, yes you my Fidelia and I wish both he and you may take a great deal of sattisfaction the short time you are togather—the Rain prevented his setting out on Saturday as he intended. I need not tell you how lonesome the House and every thing about it appears, nor could [I] if I would, but you may if you Marry know by experience. Little Sally observing m[y] gloom about Mr Burrs leveing me sets herself [v]ery pretily *as I think* to comfort me. She immagined I was [sic]k—*She says Mamma poor Mamma is sick. Dont be sick Mamma—Papa ant gone*—upon this I smiled, the little cretures Eyes sparkled for joy and she says in a [. . .] part *Mamma ant sick—dear Mamma* etc. Theirs a Mother for you—but you cant accuse me of troubling you in this sort very often so you will excuse it. I am affraid of giving you two large a dose of Husband and child.

{April 20, 1756}
Teusday.

All in confusion setting the House a little in order for it hant been done to any purpose since I Layin.

{April 21, 1756}
Wednsday.

I am much worried with Yesterdays bout but not two much so to think a vast deal of you my Friend and your diffeculties—I pity you from the bottom of my soul—Perhaps Mr Burr may be some comfort to you in adviseing both you and sombody elce. I cant but hope and trust that all will turn out for the best and your comfort in this Life two—I do indevour to commit you to God the Wise disposer of all things—Mr Badger according to Mr Burrs desire mooves into the House today to keep off the Pokers.

{April 22, 1756}
Thur[s]day a fast in this Province.
I was at meeting all day and I think I never heard Mr Brainerd pray and Preach so well. I believe he had much of the presence of God with him. He is a most excellent Man, happy for this people if they settle him—But alas for us! What signifies our fasts without a reformation? Will God be pleased with Thousands of Rams, or Ten Thousands of Rivers of Oil? No verily tis the sacrifise of a broken heart and a contrite spirit, a universal turning to the Lord that he requires—some part of Mr Brainerds sermon was reviewing the sins of our Nation and especually of this land, and truly our sins are many and exceding great and call aloud for Vengence— Another head of his sermon was to consider the judgments that impended over us—Gods judgments are abrod in the Earth in an awfull manner and tis of infinite Mercy that we are not utterly consumed as some of our fellow Cretures have been by the tirrable Earthquake.

{April 23, 1756}
Fry[d]ay—a fine day
P.M. Madm Belcher, Mrs Woodruff, Mrs Ogden, all from Elizabeth Town came to vissit me. Mrs Belcher is very good about vissiting *the Widdows* and afflicted, etc. I think I never had half so much company any vacancy as this. For about a Month past there has not been above 4 or 5 nights except on the Sabbath but I have had Travellers to Lodge.

{April 24, 1756}
Saturday.
Charming fine weather for Traveling. Tis a favour ant it my dear— I quite forgot to tell you yesterday that Nancy Smith *that was* and her Husband came to see me in their way to her new home—they seem to be quite pleased with one another. I hope it may hold tho Nancys temper is a little out of the common road, but Mr Hait is a very good Tempered man—It requires a good store of prudence to live and behave in the married state as we aught but many, very

many poor young thoughtless cretures think nothing of this is need-full after marriage, but vainly immagine that happiness comes of consequence, but I w[ould] humbly ask such persons if ever they injoyed any [gr]eat good without taking any pains for it, and I wou[ld] further ask if the pains has not in some degree [. . .] proportion to the happiness sought—Doct Watts verily beautifully observes upon this set of young cretures—

If there be Bliss without desighn,
Ivies and Oaks may grow and twine
And be as blest as they.

{April 25, 1756}
Sabbath Night—a fine day

(This day I immagine Mr Burr spent at Road Island). Out all day—Mr Brainerd sertainly preaches better and better—I wish I grew better under such means. Tis an argument of great hardness when such excellent means dont move the persons that set under them—this day I suppose Mr Burr kept at Road Island.

{April 26, 1756}
Monday Morn.

This day Mr Burr gets to Mr Olivers at Middleborough.[1]

A most charming day—What a charming place this world would be if it was not for the inhabitants—O I long for the blessed and glorious times when this World shall become a Mountain of Holiness and [an] habitation of Righteousness.

P.M. Company.

{April 27, 1756}
Teusday Morn, a lovly day again.

All nature is in its Glory. Newark looks like a Garden. You remember how it looked the spring you was here—tis so pleasant

1. This would be Peter Oliver, brother of Andrew Oliver (note 3, Letter No. 12 above). He was the son of Jonathan Belcher's sister, Elizabeth Belcher Oliver, and her husband, Daniel Oliver, and the husband of Mary Clarke Oliver. Most remembered as a Loyalist judge in Massachusetts for several years prior to the Revolution, he was at this time judge of the Inferior Court of Common Pleas in Plymouth County. Sibley 8:737–63.

I cant stay at home all day. I must walk out and see the beauty of Nature a little, so I think to go and see *Mother Sergeant.*

P.M. spent very pleasantly at Mrs Sergeants. Eve. Heard that my Brother and one of my Sisters are to be here next week. (By this time Mr Burr has got to your house—O how glad you are to see him, and he as glad to see you, and I wish I was there two.)

{*April 28, 1756*}
Wednsday Eve.

A.M. very busy and not well—P.M. felt better, went to see Mrs Riggs in her Widdowed state. These Widdows should be kind to each other—Mr Riggs is gone into the Army, Captain of a company of Batoos.[2] This eve comes in Mr Woodbridges Daughter from Stockbridge and has brought me Letters and news that all are well[3]— My sore Eyes are returnd upon me very bad [*so*] that I cant see to write any more.

{*April 29, 1756*}
Thursday—this day is your fast I think.

A.M. Company—and company to dine—P.M. Went to Mrs Brownes spining-frollick. Came home and found company—Eve, two minnisters to lodge—My Eyes very bad and a very sore Throat.

{*April 30, 1756*}
Fryday

A very Rainny day so my good Minnisters staied to dinner with me then sat out yesterday. Mrs Brown inquired very kindly about you and desired I would give her kind regards to you the next time I wrote. She dont know that I am always writing and I dare not tell her for fear she will tell her *MAN* and everybody hant such a Man as I have about those things.

2. Batoos may have been batons. *OED.*
3. Probably Mabel Woodbridge, daughter of Joseph and Elizabeth Merrick Barnard Woodbridge. Her brother Jahleel, who later married Esther's sister Lucy (see note 25, Letter No. 9, above), was entering the College's grammar school about this time. She later married Josiah Jones, son of Josiah and Anna Brown Jones, also from Stockbridge. McLachlan, pp. 365–66; Electa F. Jones, *Stockbridge, Past and Present . . .* (Springfield, Mass.: Samuel Bowles and Co., 1854), pp. 137–38, 148–49.

{May 1, 1756}
Saturday May the first
Very rainy—very sore Eyes—and company to keep Sabbath with us. I cant add because of my Eyes.

{May 2, 1756}
Sabbath.
A fine day, my Eyes as they were but yet out all day. Heard two good sermons.

{May 3, 1756}
May 3. Monday Eve.
This morn Mr Burr sets out for the Eastward. P.M. I made a vissit to Miss Betsy Williàms of Stockbridge who is here[4]—also saw Mrs Brown, Mrs Sergeant, and a good many other friends, Eyes a little better (company to lodge).

{May 4, 1756}
Teusday
Mr Potter and Wife came to dine with me and spent the P.M. with me. A great deal of other company, a Who[le] Room full—I was full, so could not ask Mr Potter to lodge here for I have three young Ladies to sleep there this night, 2 of them from Stockbridge old aquaintance.
Eve—spent very pleasantly with my young friends.

{May 5, 1756}
Wednsday Morn.
I cant say any thing about Mrs Potter in this Letter for reasons you may easily guss but I will tell you my opinnion in a private paquit by the first good opp[ertunity.] A.M. A deal of company, strangers and just as we were setting down to dinner more company came to dine.
P.M. Mr Smith and Wife drank Tea with me. Eve as it happens

4. Elizabeth (Betsy) Williams was the daughter of Colonel Ephraim and Abigail Jones Williams. Her brother Elijah graduated from the College in 1753, and her half-brother, Ephraim, who had died in battle in 1755, was the founder of the school that later became Williams College. Elizabeth's future husband was minister Stephen West, who succeeded Jonathan Edwards in the Stockbridge parsonage in 1758. McLachlan, pp. 87–88; Dexter 2:388–94.

no body to lodge and I am glad of it for I am almost down sick tho' my Eyes are much better.

{*May 6, 1756*}
Thursday Eve

A.M. Some company—P.M. Rode down to Elizabeth Town on business and made a vissit at the Governors. Saw young Mrs Belcher, returnd found Travilers to lodge—and now I am almost down sick[5]— The oddest affair happenned to day that ever was—I shall tell you all about it in my Privacies—but never did I hear the like—this I shant send by Mrs Potter I assure you, no I would not do it on any account. I shall contrive up somthing or other to send by her, for I had before asked her to take the trouble of a Letter to you, and she will think [*it*] very strange if I dont send one by her and will make a strange use of it that is sertain.

{*May 7, 1756*}

Fryday Eve—Last night about two o'Clock came my Brother and Sister Eunice.[6] I was obliged to be up all night almost, and have had company to Breakfast, dine and a whole heap at Tea and I down sick.

{*May 8, 1756*}
Saturday P.M. 3 o'Clock.

I have this afternoon received a long Letter from my best self. He was well as far as Middleborough—O What a mercy! I feel quite like another creture since this good long Letter came. I was down sick and meloncholly and I dont know what all before but now well and all life and spirit—I am very proud I assure you for the good Man has followed our example and has wrote journal-wise from day to day just as we do to each other.

{*May 9, 1756*}
Sabbath morn 6 o'Clock

O that the Lord would be near to me this day and give me some sense of his glory and beauty as he is revealed in the gospel of his

5. Young Mrs. Belcher was Abigail Allen Belcher, new wife of Jonathan Belcher, Jr. See note 7, Letter No. 19, above.

6. Eunice Edwards was almost thirteen years old. When she grew up, she married Thomas Pollock of North Carolina. *Edwards Genealogy*, p. 16.

dear Son! I feel as dead as a stone—I have no zeal for God or his service—O why ant I sent down to the dark regions of dispare before this day? Why ant I deprived of all advantages for relegion for my horred abuse of them—tis of Gods mear good pleasure and infinite condesention that I be not now lifting up my Eyes in Eternal Torments insted of beholding one of the blessed days of the Son [. . .] Man.

Eve. Out all day. The two Tutors performd exceding well (Mr Brainerd is gone a journey). Mr Ewing Preached and Mr Badger praied and he is very gifted in prayer.[7]

{*May 10, 1756*}
Monday

A.M. Very busy about household affairs. P.M. made a very pleasant vissit at Mrs Brainerds—I feel somthing gloomy—God knows what his desighns are altho' they look dark to me—Company to Lodge.

{*May 11, 1756*}
Teusday Eve. May 11.

A.M. Company. P.M. made a vissit at one of my honest Neighbours—and now I feel very poorly. My Eyes are much worse and very painfull. Company to Lodge.

{*May 16, 1756*}
Sabbath-day. May 16.

I cant express how much I have undergone since last Teusday with my Eyes. Wednsday Morn I was so bad that I could hardly bare the least gleem of light in the Room. I sent for the Doct. He has given me somthing that has helped me alittle and but a very little for I cant bare to look outdoors for my Life. It seems as if the light would knock me down. I am now going to lay a Blister on the back of my Neck, which I hope may help me.[8] I cant add I am almost blind and faint, for I have a good deal of fever.

{*May 18, 1756*}
Teusday P.M.

I have a very fine Blister that has helped my Eyes much but tis extreamly tedious and makes it very difficult for me to do any-

7. For John Ewing, see note 4, Letter No. 18, above.
8. A blister was any substance applied to raise a blister. *OED.*

thing—I made shift Yesterday to write one or two short Letters home, and in the afternoon had company. One was a Lady from York.

Mr Potter and Wife set out for Boston this week. I suppose they are gone, and you will be sadly disappointed when you find that I have sent no Letter, and will wonder at the reason—I should have wrote a short Letter, one contrived that I could trust with em if I had been able—but I am the less concernd as your Mrs Belcher sets out Next Monday and will be there near as soon as Mr Potter will for they will travil very slow and she quite fast. I am affraid I shant be able to write all my privacies but I will now go about 'em and do as much as I can.

I am not ashamed to own to you that since my Illness I think the time very long since Mr Burr left me.

{*May 19, 1756*}
Wednsday P.M.

Just now came one of Mrs Potters Brothers with her complements and desires to know if I have any commands to Boston so she is not gone, and I think to set down and write a formal Letter to your Ladyship, and how to begin I cant think for tis so long since I have used formallitys with you that my Letter will have nither Head nor Tail, but no matter how great a monster it is for I shall write it more for Mr Potter then for you[9]—I know sertainly that he will see the inside of it. He is used of old to such things. Madm Belcher and her Daughter were here just now as they were going to Mr Cuylors, and she says she will take very good care of a Letter for me.

{*May 21, 1756*}
Fryday

To my unspeakable surprize and joy Mr Burr arrived safe about 4 o'Clock P.M. yesterday—O Lord help me to be suitable thankfull for so great a mercy—He is pretty well tho' has taken some little cold in his return.

9. Hannah Potter had two brothers who were students at the College at this time—Isaac Livermore, who became a minister, and William Livermore, who became a lawyer. Both men died in the 1760s. McLachlan, pp. 156–57.

I cant express how much gratitude I feel for your extream kind treatment of my dear gentleman. He is full of it I assure you—he says you are so kind and friendly that it makes him quite ashamed of himself when he thinks how unworthy he is of such favours and friendship as yours and he has no way to recompence but by good wishes and prayers and a heart full of friendship.

{May 22, 1756}

Saturday—Extreamly busy and cant write.

{May 23, 1756}
Sabbath

Out all day altho' very poorly, more fit to be a bed—Mr Brainerd preached very well but I could not attend, and to my shame I doubt I got no good. As my Blister drys I find my Eyes grow worse and I grow more poorly, have a constant Fever and very low spirited— and to tell the truth I am in a bad way. I am affraid I shall fall into some of my former weaknesses.

{May 24, 1756}
Monday Eve

Saturday just at Night Potter sends me a Letter, the most *Insolent* of anything I ever saw or heard off—He did not know that Mr Burr was come home. If he had he never would have wrote it—I will send you a true coppy of it if my eyes will allow me to write so much. If not I dont know but I may spare the Original (tho' tis very choice) upon condision you return it the first good oppertun-ity—Mrs Belcher was here this P.M. and intends to go on Wednsday so I must send this down tomorrow. Mr Burr thinks tis not best to send anything in the shape of a Letter by Potter, and then there will be no occasion for Mrs Belcher will get to Boston before them for they are waiting for a Vessel and dont know when they shall go—Just now Mr Burr receives a letter from Potter in answer to one Mr Burr wrote in answer to that intollerable Letter he sent me— tis the same strain yet, tho not quite so high to Mr Burr as to me. Mr Burr would have you keep the privacies containing the said affair and not burn em for ever so much, that you may be able to detect him in his lies, for he dont stick at the truth one Morsel—I have found him out in several lies to day to my surprize.

If he should say nothing you may be quite silent. I believe tis best for he is now a Minnister and a body would not scandalize such an one unless there was a real need. [10]

I feel the highest gratitude for your exceding kindness to me and I love you more and more every day I live and so does Mr Burr.

The Buttons I kindly thank you for and have put em into Sallys sleves as you desire—Sally says in her Language—*O Mit Pint give Tally fine Buttons, that a Dood Mit Pint, Tally love Mit Pint*—Now I must interpret it or you will never find it out—O Miss Prince give Sally fine Buttons, that a good Miss Prince, Sally love Miss Prince.

{*May 26, 1756*}
Wednesday Morn

I am going now to coppy Potters Letter so shant have time to say much more to you now—My Duty to your honored Parents and Love to all the Sisterhood and Miss Jenny From Dear, Dear friend your

Fidelia

(Your Lottery account I will send the next oppertunity.)
(Mr Burr sends his Most Respectfull, Most affectionate, Most Humble regards to Mr Prince and Lady and the Charming Daughter.)

(**No. 23**)

{*June 2, 1756*}

To My Dear Fidelia

After a whole weeks silence I have found time enough to say that I Love you altho' I hant wrote for so long a time.

This day week which is Wednsday I carried No. 22 to Mrs Belcher, made a pleasant vissit at the Governors, and since that I hant had a moments vacancy, for I have no help in my Famaly but Harry and in a poor state of helth myself [*so*] that tis very diffecult for me to get along in any shape, as you may guss, having two young Children on my hands—Yesterday Mr Burr went to Princeton. His vissits to me are but short tho' this has been pretty long,

10. For more on Nathaniel Potter's unsavory character, see McLachlan, pp. 80–82.

above a week—I must get time to write to Philadelphia to day but I cant conceive how.

{*June 3, 1756*}
Thursday Eve

Mr Burr is come home and brings news that Mr Brainerd had determined to leve Newark and go again with his Indians, and what will become of poor Newark I cant think nor contrive—Mr Brainerd would have done exceding well in this place, and I can think of no body that is like to suit them so well.

{*June 4, 1756*}
Fryday Eve.

Made a vissit at Loyer Ogdens. Mrs Ogden has Broke her Legg by only turning her foot a little aside.

{*June 5, 1756*}
Saturday

All in the hurries with a great Ironing so cant get time to say any thing but that I think of you if I dont talk to you.

{*June 6, 1756*}
Sabbath Eve.

Out all day but very unwell, dead in spirit and almost dead in Body. I dont know but I should think of a journey for my helth if it was a season propor for it.

{*June 7, 1756*}
Monday Eve.

P.M. I thought best to try vissiting [*to*] see if that would not do me good so I went to see the Widdow Ogden and Mrs Brown. There I heard that Mr Brown is desighning a journey to Boston, sets out next week. I shall send what little I have wrote and shall hope for a great deal from you by him.

{*June 8, 1756*}
Teusday Eve.

Today I have been to Elizabeth Town to the Governors and Mr Woodruffs and sundry other places—Mrs Woodruff tells us that when Mr Potter was at their house last he received Mr Burrs last Letter and was very angry and displeased that Mr Burr should express a concern for his Carracter and said he did not want Mr Burr to be concernd for his Carracter but would have him take care of his own and that he had more reason to be concernd for himself then for him or words to the same efect but I think those were the very words.

Wednsday

Tarried at home and excedingly taken up in the affairs of my Famaly—it greives me to the heart that I cant spare more time for you—you cant conceive how my time is taken up. Some times I never set down a Wholeday unless to Vittles—and *good By* as they say here.

Thursday Eve

P.M. Made a vissit to Poor Mrs Ogden that has been confined above a year and mostly to her Bed—I think she is better then when I saw her last but still keeps her Bed wholy. I think she will never recover.

Fryday

A.M. Received your kind dear No. 21. Tis full of Love to a poor undeserving Retch—O that I might be truly thankfull for such a friend! And may you continue favours of this sort—I feel (I hope) thankfull that Mr Burrs vissit has been any comfort to you. Tis next to comforting you my self.

I am much obliged to you for the Book you sent me—P.M. Made a vissit, had an agreable time of it.

Saturday all in the hurries—I hate these hurries of a Saturday. I would never have it so if I could help it.

Sabbath Eve.

A.M. Very poorly, tarried at home.

P.M. Made shift to go to meeting, heard Mr Brainerd preach his farewel sermon to this people, for he has concluded to return and settle with his Indians—I am greatly concernd for poor Newark. What they will do I cant think nor contrive, but I expect they will break all to pieces—there is some talk of sending for Mr Duffield but tis doubtfull whether he can come or not. Tis supposed he is ingaged.[1] (Cake pans came safe)

{June 15, 1756}
Teusday A.M.

Yesterday I could not get one vacant moment for my Life—and at last went to bed sick and feel poorly to day—Mrs Housemans Diary is a most charming thing. I hope the Lord will be pleased to make it a blessing to me.[2]

P.M. Company and Rode out—Mr Burr remembers the Chaise but has forgot the owner, and we are out of our Witts to know who he is—We like the Chaise and the fortune, and should be highly pleased to see you here in that same Chaise, but the Gentleman we can say nothing about till we know who he is—if you dont send his name the next opportunity I shall be quite vext at you.

{June 16, 1756}
Wednsday Morn.

Mr Tennent came to Breakfast with us and we look every minute for Mr Bostwick—I am called.

{June 17, 1756}
Thursday P.M.

Company here and my Letter called for. Mr Brown goes erly tomorrow morn so I have left em to bid you farewell—give my Duty to Mr and Mrs Prince. Love to *Julia* and all the Sisterhood for whom I feel a great friendship altho' some of 'em are unknown to me by sight—My Complements to Mrs Bromfield and her famaly

1. George Duffield, son of Margaret and George Duffield of Pequea, Pennsylvania, graduated from the College in 1752 and served as a tutor there from 1754 to 1756. He was licensed to preach in New Castle, Delaware, in March 1756, just three days after he married Elizabeth Blair, daughter of Samuel Blair of Fagg's Manor, Pennsylvania. Elizabeth, who is mentioned later in the journal, died in childbirth in 1757. McLachlan, pp. 51–53.

2. *The Power and Pleasure of the Divine Life; Exemplify'd in the Late Mrs.* [Hannah Pearsall] *Housman, of Kidderminster, Worcestershire, As Extracted from Her Own Papers,* ed. Rev. Mr. Richard Pearsall (London, 1744; reprinted in Boston, 1755).

and tell em that I heartily simpathize with em under their greivous loss.[3]

I hant time to add but that I Love you sincearely (and I fear two much) and I hope always shall, for I find it daily increasing—Mr Burr joyns in respect and kindness to my dear Fidelia and all her friends and mine—

Esther Burr

June 17. 1756.

(No. 24)

{June 28, 1756}
June 28. 1756.
Monday P.M.

I have to my great greife been silent almost two weeks—tis such a hurried life I live as you cant conceive of I am sure, for I could not have thought I could have lived thro' so much business as I do daily—I am obliged to leve off as I supposed I should when I sat down, for this is the first time I have sat down today unless to suckle my Son or to Eat, and tis now near 5 o'Clock P.M.

6 O'Clock—One moments time more for *my dear Fidelia*—since I wrote last which was by Parson Brown I have made several neserssary vissits, one to Mrs Smith of the Mountains. Poor Woman has been confined to her Room this six weeks with a Broken Breast. She is extreamly sunk in spirit and I am so low that I could not do much to comfort her—there was the last Week the most Tirrable Whirlwind that was ever known this side of the West Indies at the Mountains the effects of which we rode out to see and twas truly an awfull sight, a Number of Houses torn to pieces, a vast many dammaged, Whole Orchards torn up by the roots, not a Tree lef standing, 5 Buildings, some of em quite new, torn [*so*] that there is not one stick left on another but parts of them blown several rods. Vast large Trees that were a foot and a ½ and two foot over

---

3. Probably Abigail Coney Bromfield, a member of Boston's Old South Church. Her husband Edward Bromfield had recently died, and some of the couple's several children and their spouses were also members of the Boston church. Hamilton Hill, *History of the Old South Church* (Cambridge, Mass.: Houghton, Mifflin and Co., 1890), 1:319; 2:23–25.

twisted off in the strongest part, others blown up by the roots and many stript of their limbs and the Body left standing—whole fields left without a fence.

But aboundent Mercy in the middest of all for their was not one Life lost tho' some wounded but not mortally—twas the most affecting sight I ever saw of the kind. Mr Burr was so affected with it that he concluded to preach somthing to the purpose and accordingly yesterday he preached all day from those words in the first of Nahum the 3rd verse—pleas to look [at] it and you will see the propriety of the subject.

{June 29, 1756}
Teusday

Very poorly—but just at night rode out, and now feel a little better.

{June 30, 1756}
Wednsday Eve.

A bad Head-ach and some fever, and worried to death with company. All the P.M. making Tea till the Bell Rang for College praiers.

{July 1, 1756}
July 1. Thursday-Eve.

Fever again and Pain in my Breast and all my joints—I feel extream low-spirited. Tis my opinnion that I am like to have a fit of sickness. O to be prepaired for all God has in infinite Wisdom to lay upon me!

{July 2–4, 1756}

Fryday, Saturday and Sabbathday, the Fever at the same time a day. It begins to rise about 10 O'Clock in the Morn, and holds till 4 or 5 P.M.—then I feel prety well, but weak.

Sabbath—unable to go to meeting.

{July 5–6, 1756}
Monday and Teusday.

Yesterday Mr Burr carried me as far as Second River, and it was of great service. I hant felt so well as today not this month. P.M. Rode out again, called at two or three places—I long to hear from you, but I shant till Mr Brown comes I suppose—Why you might be dead and buried before I could hear anything of it.

{*July 7, 1756*}
Wednsday Eve. exeding hot—
This P.M. made a vissit at Mrs Browns, a very agreable Lady she is—she tells me she expects her Husband next week. I shall think the time almost as long as she will for I do long to hear from you *most desparately*—Another Tirrable Whirlwind back in the Country, the peteculars I hant yet heard but by what I have heard twas more dreadfull then that at our Mountains.

{*July 8, 1756*}
Thursday Morn still extream hot.
An agreable Breakfast, this morning *your paquit*—I hardly know whether I am most rejoiced or most sorrowfull—but I think I have most cause for joy and thanks to a good and kind God who has brought my dear friend from the sides of the grave—I was quite overcome with reading the peteculars of your late Illness so that I was obliged to break off several times in the middest of reading to give vent to my Passions—I would call upon my soul and all that is within me to praise the Lord for his goodness to you, to me, to all the Sisterhood, and to the publick—altho' our loss would have been your gain—but my dear you must wait a little longer for this unspeakable gain—no my dear your work is not done, and I hope the World will long be Blessed with em, and you late, *very late* receive an abundant reward for all your good deeds, done in the Body—I feel thankfull that I did not hear of your Illness till you had in some measure recovered, for I beleive it would have been two hard for me under my present disorders and low spiritedness.

I look upon you as a new friend given me, as it were taken from me for my unthankfullness, and lent to me agin to see if I would make a better improvment of such an excellent enjoyment.

{*July 27, 1756*}
Teusday July 27.
It is now more than a fortnight since I have wrote one word—could you know what a life I live you would not wonder—as I have a few moments to spare from the great hurry of my affairs I will

indevour to recollect what remarkable has passed since the 8 of this month which was the last I wrote and the day that I received your kind Letter—since which time I have been crowded with company from different parts, from Philadelphia, from LongIsland, and NewEngland and no soul to help me but Harry and my young sister that is with me (These vissiters broke our Chaise all to [splinders?] for us)—we have done our utmost to get good help but to no purpose—I could not have thought it so very diffecult had not I tried throughly—you may think I hant found much time to vissit. I rode once to Elizibath Town and once to see Mrs Smith and that is all—last Thursday Lord Lowdin arrived at Newyork and yesterday set out for Albany[1]—I am heartily sorry to hear it confermd that poor Boston is bereaved of their Governor and that Mr Pownel is appointed in his stead whom I am perswaded will be very disgusfull as he has been one means of geting Shirley removed—but all things are ordered of a wise God so all must be for the best.[2]

This Morn we had a Letter from Sister Lucy. She arrived safe at my fathers the 3d of July—we had not heard one word from Stockbridge till now since the beginning of May last and know not one word of Lucys going to Boston but by yours.

This day the Presbytry sets at our House. I expect the Minnisters every moment. Tomorrow is the exammineation—perhaps you may wonder that I can find time to write now and not for a fortnight past but here is the mistry. I have got an exceding good Wench to help me till Fryday, one that I can trust and I am resolved to chetch every vacant moment for you—I am impatient for Mr Browns return home. He has been looked for above a fortnight.

{July 28, 1756}

Wednsday 5 O'Clock. All my company gone, and I quite sick, so am going to see if I cant get a little sleep to rest me.

1. In March 1756, John Campbell, Earl of Loudoun, had been appointed commander-in-chief of the British forces in the colonies. He was on his way to Albany to assume his command. *DNB* 3:828.

2. Thomas Pownall was replacing William Shirley as governor of Massachusetts. He had been in England since February 1756, where he had been appointed Lord Loudoun's "Secretary Extraordinary." He did not return to begin his administration until August 1757.

{July 29, 1756}
Thursday.

Mr Burr tells me that I must go to Princeton next Week. He has promised that I shall go with Mr Peter Smith and Lady so I rode out to see if I could get a good carefull Nurse to take the Son two or three days and was succeded and have got the best Woman in Town for that purpose to late it and suckle it[3]—You may juss [*guess*] I am Head and Ears in hurry till this journey is over. I would not consent to go but I am in hopes it may be of service to my helth.

This day a most awfull instance of death has happened in this place—A young Man about 18. Well in helth about 10 O'Clock in the Morn and buried by 6 P.M. He was in a Horse Cart in the middle of the Town by the Church, plain as a Housefloor. The Horse set a running (what frighted him nobody knows). The young man standing in the Cart pulled hard to stop the Horse, the Reigns broke, he fell back and was so stund that he knew not anything but went to get up and fell with his head in between the Cart and Whele and tore his scull off and scattered his Branes along the street for several rods—It has made me quite sick—I wish it might put me and all in mind of Death and Eternity.

{July 30–31, and August 1, 1756}
Fryday—Saturday and Sabbath.

Friday. Got time to make one vissit of duty.

Saturday. Hurried two death. At Night heard Mr Smith and Lady would be hear to keep Sabbath which fluttered me a good deal for I did not expect 'em and was no ways prepared for them but before I went to Bed got quite easy and resigned.

Sabbath. My turn to tarry at home as I did all day—got along with Mr Smith and Lady better then I expected.

{August 2, 1756}
Monday. August 2 day.

Last eve rode down to Elizabeth Town that it might be the easier for us today—this morn arose very early, sat out with Mr Smith

---

3. Colonial women sometimes hired other women to breastfeed their children. To late an infant meant to put it out to nurse.

and Wife and three single Horses in company, went 10 miles then took Breakfast. P.M. Came to Mr Symmons's about 11 o'Clock and it was so extream hot concluded to tarry till dinner was over (did not go to Mr Cummings as that is somthing out of the way). About 3 o'Clock it seemd a little cooler so set forward came safe to Princeton before sun set then walked to take a little view of the College for we had not patience to tarry till morning—Just looked at the Presidents House which is under cover—then returnd to our Lodgings, eat supper and tired almost to Death we were glad to go to Bed.

{August 3, 1756}
Teusday Morn, up very erly.

Soon after Breakfast went up to College to take a more petecular view of that and our House—the College is a Famous building I assure you and the most commodious of any of the Colleges as well as much the largest of any upon the Continent. There is somthing very striking in it and a grandure and yet a simpliscity that cant well be expressed—I am well pleased with the House they have begun for us—you have a room in it.

P.M. 4 o'Clock set out for Brunswick (I might have told you that Mr Smith and Wife are quite charmd with the College. He says all he wants is to live in it.) Came to Doctor Cummings. They were very glad to see us and she almost over joyed. Soon after I came in she inquired after you and when I told her that you had been on the borders of Eternity she seemd quite distressed and shewed a great deal of tenderness—that Woman sertainly Loves *my Fidelia.* Only once she was affraid *that sombody elce* loved her two much or she would not have conducted as she did—I never saw Mrs Cummings in so good spirits and seem so free from trouble in my life. She seems as happy as is propor for any one to be in this life—poor Woman has meet with a deal of trouble in her day.

{August 4, 1756}
Wednsday

Erly in the morn set forward, came to Elizabeth Town and dined at the Governors—drank Tea at Mr Woodruffs, came home found all well—O my dear What a mercy to go and return in safety and find all well—why was not it my portion to find my Children sick or dead.

{August 5, 1756}
Thursday.

Found company from York (Mrs Mercier and her Son) when I came home last night so cant get time to write today.[4]

{August 6, 1756}
Fryday—A.M.

Received Letters from Stockbridge, all well and extreamly urgent to have me make em a vissit before I go to Princeton, and I have taken it into consideration altho' it seems impossible for me to go—
P.M. A deal of Company as I always have.

{August 7, 1756}

Saturday, Busy, Busy—*hurry, Fly—Run.*

{August 8, 1756}
Sabbath Eve.

Out all day—felt some desires and that all—O how dead to everything that is good! How little do I Love God! How cold my service—Why does he suffer me to sin away any more such precious seasons?

{August 9, 1756}
Monday Eve.

P.M. A whole Room full of vissitors—Topick of conversation two trifling—how tired I am of this poor dark World! O how good to leve it for a better.

{August 16, 1756}
Monday P.M. August 16.

Tis a Week this day since I have conversed with my dear Fidelia, but she has had a large share of my thoughts in that time—I just now heard Capt Wimble is to sail in a day or two, so I think to send these broken, confused, jumbled thoughts, without so much as looking back on what I have scrabled—If you knew with what difficulty I wrote you would be surprized that I wrote atall—but

---

4. Ann Mercier's son was John Dyer Mercier, who became a student at the College and graduated in 1762. After receiving his degree, he became a merchant and lived for many years in Quebec, apparently never marrying. McLachlan, pp. 395–97.

to be short I expect to set out for Stockbridge the latterend of this Week or the beginning of next. I carry my little Son with me—I have indevoured to know duty and think I am doing of it—I suppose I shall be gone from home six Weeks or near that time—Mr Burr sends with this a Letter for Mr Parsons and desires you would take special care of it that it go quick and safe—I shall continue my scrabbling for I shall have more time then I now have.

Mr Burr joyns me in the kindest regards to the best of Friends in our esteem—Once more I am your most affectionate friend *till death I hope and after*

Esther Burr

(Duty to Mr and Mrs Prince. Love to all and everybody that loves you.)

(No. 25)

On Board the sloop about
20 miles from Newyork
{August 26, 1756}
Thursday A.M.

To my dear Fidelia

On Saturday last (viz. Aug 21) we set out for Newyork but did not get there till Sunday Morn, and found the sloop not going in some days and then they were obliged to carry some of the forces that lately arrived, and no oppertunity to be had. By night I was quite sick for the Weather is extream hot and being out all the Night before with my little Son I was worried to death.

Monday Eve Mr Burr came over to see if he could not get us off, and accordingly found an oppertunity that would set out on Wednsday—Teusday Morn Mr Burr returnd home. I dined with Mrs Bostwick, drank Tea with Mrs Donaldson, then made a vissit at Mr Hazzards—Wednsday Morn, busy in geting ready for our passage—A.M. Wrote to Mr Burr. P.M. Received a Letter from him and wrote an answer.

Eve. About dark came on board with two of Mrs P. V. Levingstons Sisters, one a young Widdow, the other a young Miss. They seem sociable and tollarable agreable. The Widdow has a young child with her. The rest of the company are Mr Levingstons Son of the Manor who has lived with us all summer, and my Brother and Sister and two waiters—Levingston has a Voial [*viola*] and Flute and can play exceding well, and at present we sail prety fast.[1]

{*August 27, 1756*}

27 Fryday P.M. 4 o'Clock.

Just as I had done writing yesterday, a sudden gust of wind came and tore away our main sail [*so*] that we could not stir till that was mended and that was about 5 o'clock P.M. Then could go no faster then the Tide would carry us. Last night and this Morn till about 11 o'Clock it rained and it came in upon us, for our deck is very poor. Since noon the weather is fine and we have a fine Gentle breese. I suppose we are now about 70 miles from Newyork, and about 90 from Newark but tis as easy for my heart to run there as if it was but one mile and you may guss tis there often enough.

{*August 29, 1756*}

29 Aug Sabbath Morn (about 12 miles from Levingstons Manor) at a Dutch house in the Woods. Yesterday about 3 in the P.M. we arrived at Levingstons Manor, tarried just to drink Tea and then Mr Levingston was so good as to let me have a Waggon and servant to carry us to Stockbridge, and we thought it best to come to this place that we might have the easier days ride on Monday. But this morn before day our servant gives us the slip and goes home, so what we shall do God only knows—This is a very inconvenient place to spend a Sabbath. The whole house is but one room, and a large famaly and no relegion, but I desire to be thankfull tis a pleasant day [*so*] that one may walk out into the Woods and be retired—and O my dear I find God is here as well as in his house and among his people—Yes my Dear God is everywhere and does not forget his, be they where they will—as soon as Breakfast was

1. Mary Alexander Livingston, wife of Peter Van Brugh Livingston (see note 4, Letter No. 14, above) and daughter of James Alexander (see note 3, Letter No. 21, above), had several sisters and sisters-in-law. It is not clear which of them Esther was discussing here. The "Son of the Manor" was Peter R. Livingston, a student at the College at this time. He was the son of Maria Thong and Robert Livingston. In 1758 Peter married a cousin, Margaret Livingston. McLachlan, pp. 229–31.

over I took an English Bible (which is rare among the Dutch) and walked about a quarter of a mile with some longing desires that I might meet God, and I hope I found him. O how good is God to an unworthy Worm that has forsook him to meet me this Morn— I said surely God is in this place, and I hope I shall never forget it—truly my dear I hant found such freedom and delight in Gods servise for many weeks past—God does not want for means nor place—I have been long seeking God in this and the other duty and ordinance—but it has pleased him to hide his face and disappoint me in my hopes and expecttations when I was ready to think him near—but how little did I think of meeting him here—last Sabbath I lost and I greived at the loos and I was affraid I should lose this— O what shall I render to the Lord for his goodness to me? I can render nothing but myself, my poor wicked sinfull self.

Eve—50 soldiers to sup at this House and lodge which surprzed me much, but they behaved better then I expected considering they came from Road-Island—they are going for recrutes—how many difficulties one meets with in a journey, just so with our journy throu' this life.

{August 30, 1756}
Monday—30

Morn—before sun rise, set out in a Waggon for Stockbridge, was threttened with rain but cleared up and was pleasant, the road very bad but got along finely—when we had got within abot 10 miles of Stockbridge it set a raining very hard. We stoped as soon as we could find a convenient house which was abut 6 miles from my Fathers. I could not bare to stop for all night, and our waggonner was urgent to go along so we set out wet to the skin as we were and had not got far before it Raind as fast as ever I saw it in my life, and in a half an hour I had not a dry thread abot me, but kept along and just as we got to my Fathers it left raining (so some good came [*from*] bad *luck* as the vulgar say—) We came in and surprized em almost out of their witts. Lucy and Sueky were almost overcome. I need not tell you how glad they were to see us but the meloncholy news that I brought fild the house with gloom. I mean the news of Oswego's being taken which was not confermd here till I brought the dreadfull tidings[2]—the first thing I did was to strip from Top to Toe—found my self very stiff and worried, so went to bed soon but could not sleep for fear of the Enemy.

{August 31, 1756}
Aug 31

Teusday—dark dull weather—feel very poorly hardly able to set up.

{September 1, 1756}
Wednsday—Septr-1

Mrs Dwight had a letter from the Colonel giving an account how Oswego was taken which was by Treachery—O how dark do things look! I fear I shall not be able to take any comfort in my friends nor they in me.

{September 2–3, 1756}
Thursday and Fryday—2 and 3

Almost overcome with fear. Last night and Thursday night we had a watch at this fort and most of the Indians come to lodge here—Some thought that they heard the enemy last night—O how distressing to live in fear every moment—This day had several friends come to see me.

{September 4, 1756}
Saturday 4

A very busy day with us for my Brother sets out for the Jersyes on Monday and on Teusday My Mother sets out for Northampton. My Sister Dwight is near her time, so I never said one Word against it altho' I am come 150 Miles to see my friends and am apt to think I shall not come again in many years if ever[3]—I proposed when I came from home to tarry here till the second week in October but beleive I shall shorten my vissit since things are so ordered and I am so distracted with fears.

2. On August 14, 1756, the French Army under General Montcalm captured the British forts at Oswego on Lake Ontario.

3. Mary Edwards Dwight delivered her third child, Erastus Dwight, on September 13, 1756. Dwight, *The History of the Descendants of John Dwight* 1:140.

{*September 5, 1756*}
Sabbath-5

Out all day. Heard 4 excellent sermons tho so Ill for want of sleep that I am hardly my self—I hant had a nights sleep since I left Newyork—Since I have been here I may say I have had none.

{*September 6, 1756*}
Monday very hot-6

My brother set out for Newark and I had the pleasure of writing to Mr Burr, but Indeed I had nothing very pleasing to say, I am so poorly, and scared out of my Witts about the Enemy—a deal of company.

{*September 7, 1756*}
7 Teusday extream hot—

This Morn my mother set out for Northampton and hopes to return in about a month, but alas for me I shall not be able to wait her return, for I grow worse and worse, more affraid than ever—if I happen to drowse I am frighted to death with dreams. As for sleep tis gone, and I shall go two if things dont alter—My Mother gone! It adds double gloom to everything.

P.M. expected company but had none.

{*September 8, 1756*}
8 Wednsday still as hot as ever

O how dreadfully does this World look! Happy—thrice happy are those that have a sure title to a better—It looks to me that this Land is to be given into the hands of our enemies to be scurged and that severly—I am looking for persecution—but alas I fear, I fear, I am not able to stand the firery tryal! And O what an awful dreadfull thing to be left to deny Christ and loose our souls forever!

P.M. This place is in a very defenceless condicion—not a soldier in it, the fighting Indians all except a very few gone into the Army, many of the white people also, and this is a place that the enemy can easily get at, and if they do we cant defend our selves. 10. Indians might with all ease distroy us intirely. There has been a number seen at about 30 miles distance from this place.

I have had company and there has been a tirrable Thunder storm as ever I knew.

{*September 9, 1756*}
Thursday-9

I am full of news about Oswego and our Army and the Treachery of some officers at Oswego—but you will hear all sooner then by this Letter so I shant trouble you with it.

P.M. Vissitors a great many. I am sick for want of sleep.

{*September 10, 1756*}
Fryday Morn-10

I want to be made willing to die in any way God pleases, but I am not willing to be Buchered by a barbarous enemy nor cant make my self willing—I slept a little better last night then usual—but feel no easier this morn—*The Lord Reighns,* and why ant I sattisfied, he will order all for the best for the publick and for me, and he will be glorified let all the powers of Earth and Hell do their worst—I am to spend this day at my sister Parsonses.

{*September 11, 1756*}
Saturday-11

Last night 17 soldiers came to Town to our assistance. The number is two small by much to defend three Forts. Some of em are to lodge here. Hope I shant be so much affraid as before tho' they are but little better than none—P.M. heard from my Mother and Sister Dwight. All well as yet.

{*September 12, 1756*}
Sabbath Eve-12

We have been entertained today with a discours[e] from those words, Amos 8 chapter and 11 vers, "Behold I send a Famin in the Land, not a famin of Bread nor a Thirst for water, but of hearing of the words of the Lord"—a very proppor subject for this day—It looks to me that God is about to deprive this Land of his word and ordinances for their shamefull abuse of them, and just and right will he be in so doing—some times today I have felt oprest with the dark aspect of our Publick affairs, but at night when retired felt calmed with the thought that God would be Glorified—and O my dear this is refreshing that the ever blessed God will loose none of his glory lett men or Devils do their worst.

{September 13, 1756}
Monday—A.M. 13

Proposed to my Father to set out for home next week but he is
not willing to hear one word about it, so I must tarry the proposed
time and if the Indians get me, they get me, that is all I can say,
but tis my duty to make my self as easy as I can—I am realy ashamed
to tell how much I long to see my dear Mr Burr and Little Sally—
to tell the truth I am almost homesick—It seems a little Age since
I left Home and the time is not half gone yet—You cant conceive
how every thing alters upon my Mothers going away—All is Dark
as Egypt.

P.M. Vissited, all very pleasant and extream glad to see me.

{September 14, 1756}
Teusday 14

P.M. Vissited again, kindly treated, heard from Northampton.
My mother got down comfortably—the person that brought word
from her says that my Sister Dwight was just taken in Travil—I
feel very ancious for her, poor Woman, but I hope all is well over
long before this—She was taken about 10 o'Clock Monday Morn—
last Night I slept prety comfortably, which is the first comfortable
Night I have had since I have been here.

{September 15, 1756}
Wednsday-15

Afternoon vissited at two places.

{September 16, 1756}
Thursday 16

P.M. Vissited at two places as yesterday—tho' not atall well. Had
a poor night last night, in the morn a very bad headach. By noon
better or I W[ould] not have gone out this P.M.

Eve. Feel very poorly, my spirits sunk with our publick affairs
and being worried out with fear and want of sleep I am almost
homesick.

{September 17, 1756}
Fryday Morn. 17

Poor Night, but able to help Lucy about the famaly affairs a little.
Poor Girl has her Head, hands, and Heart full now my Mother
is gone.

P.M. A great many Vissitters all very pleasant. Just at Night I was surprized by one of Mr Burrs schollars coming in (he came to bring my Brother's horse). My Heart was at my Mouth for fear of somthing bad—the first thing I said was that I hoped Mr Burr was well. He replied that all were well. O what a Mercy! This is the first [lisp?] I have heard from home since I left Newyork. I have a long affectionate Letter from Mr Burr. He desires I would indev[our] to reach home by the end of Commenceme[nt] Week—that the affairs of our famaly are such that tis not prudent for us both to be absent at once so cant come for me, but thinks of a journey to Albany after my return, and to take this place in his way. Some business of importance requires his being at Albany if he goes any where.

This good news from home has made me quite well.

{September 18, 1756}
Saturday—18

Sat up till One o'Clock last night to write to Mr Burr. This young man says he can send it to him next week. Am affraid I shant be able to see home till the Week after Commencement—Mr Burr says he expects Mr Oliver and Lady to be in the Jersies next week, and I expect a Letter without fail—I shall begrudge every moment that it lays at Newark—Pray why cant you take it in your Good Head and heart to come with em, just to see me if tis no more. You cant wish for a better oppertunity—do think of it—and as Mr Burr says *Consider the matter a little*—I find I shall hope a little—but am affraid.

{September 19, 1756}
Sabbath—19

Last eve I had some free discourse with My Father on the great things that concern my best intrest—I opend my diffeculties to him very freely and he as freely advised and directed. The conversation has removed some distressing doubts that discouraged me much in my Christian warfare—He gave me some excellent directions to be observed in secret that tend to keep the soul near to God, as well as others to be observed in a more publick way—What a mercy that I have such a Father! Such a Guide!

{September 20, 1756}
Sept 20 Monday A.M.

Vissit amongst the poor Indians, which excites in me a great concern for the poor cretures best intrest.

P.M. Vissited an old aquaintance—Eve. Heard from the Waggoner and he insists on going on Wednsday so I must set out afternoon on Wednsday.

{September 21, 1756}

Teusday P.M. Vissited again, and now all my vissiting is over. Eve Perswaded Mr Woodbridge to let one of his Daughters go with him for company [for] me and now [feel] eas[ier].[4]

{September 22, 1756}
Wednsday A.M. 22

Very busy in geting my things togather—just before noon heard Mr Woodbridge is taken very ill with a Vomiting and Purging so cant think of going at present—I was at a loss what to do but upon consideration and advise concluded to go when the Waggon came, for perhaps I may loose the oppertunity of Mr Fondas sloop which is the only one that I am sertain is going down—My Father went to Mr Woodbridge and found him a little better and hopes to be able to go before the sloop sails.

P.M. 5 o'Clock set out in the Waggon after an affectionate parting with all my friends except Lucy. She rode as far as Sheffeild and will tarry all Night with me.

{September 23, 1756}
23 Thursday Morn very Erly

Parted with Lucy and set forward with my honest Dutchman only. It seemd very lonesome to go quite alone and could have no conversation not much more then with the Horses, but found I could convers with my God and did not think my self alone for he was present, and has brought me to Mr Fondas more comfortably then I could expect—[tho?] weary as you may think.

{September 24, 1756}
Sept 24 Fryday Morn 9. o'Clock
at Clavarack.

Mr Fonda says he cant go to Newyork till next Week on Teusday or Wednsday—this very discourageing—What, lay here amongst

4. Probably Joseph Woodbridge (see note 3, Letter No. 22, above). It is unclear which of his several daughters Esther was discussing.

a parsle of dumb Dutch people a whole week? Tis trying I assure you my dear—tho' the people are very sivel (but not like English) and I have reason to be thankfull they are so—All is sertainly for the best, however dark and cross it may seem—I hope I am in some degree thankfull that I am in the hands of God. I would not have the ordering of my Voyage for the world—I think it will be my duty to seek some other conveyance then by Mr Fonda—several of the Albany sloops are about to sail and many of their Masters I am acquainted with and could trust—My Son is awake so must leve you.

{September 25, 1756}
Saturday—25

Yesterday about noon came Mr Woodbridge and Daughter very unexpectedly—you see providence is kind in sending me good company when I had no reason to expect any—Many have been Gods mer[cies.]

P.M. All for the best that we are not gone yet, for tis very cold and Rainy as well as head-wind—We are such short sighted cretures we know not when a thing is for us nor when against us, but we must lern to trust *him* that does know all things and will order all for the best—5 O'Clock, there is a sloop in sight and we are about to send to her to see whether she will drop ancor till the Morn and then take us in. Eve. Find the supposed sloop to be only a Boat with men sick of the Camp distemper—so must wait.

{September 26, 1756}
Sabbath—26

Must spend another Sabbath amongst the Dutch. O tis a tryal! But I will call to mind the Sabbath I spent at a Dutch house in the Woods as I went to Stockbridge (see page 150. and 151.) a Sabbath to be remembred—then God taught me and made me feel that he was every where, and that he could bless without the ordinary means of grace—O! just and righteous art thou O Lord in depriveing me of such precious means as I have been favoured with heretofore—for my shamefull abuse off them and unthankfullness for them—O that I might spend my Sabbaths better hereafter if God should grant me them—P.M. A deel of company—The Sabbath here is no more then a play day—I wonder what they think.

{September 27, 1756}
Monday—P.M. 27

Soon this morn a fine North Wind blew up and several Albany sloops appeared. We set out in a Boat and got on Board of one of them that has no passengers, so we have the Cabbin to our selves— and sail very finely—Eve. The wind gone and we are obliged to throw Ancor and lay till morn.

{September 28, 1756}
Teusday Morn—28

A fine wind but such a thick fog that we cant see three yerds from the sloop, so obliged to lay till about 10 o'Clock and then our tide will be almost spent—P.M. We came finely throu the Highlands, but then lost our Wind as is common in this place, the Mountains being so vastly high that no wind can find us that comes from the East, West, or North, so must wait for the tide in hopes that that will carry us out of the reach of these Mountains—Eve. Came prety fast with the tide and a small west breese within a mile of Dobbs's Ferry which is about 30 miles from Newyork and here forced to lay for Morn Tide, the Wind being gone.

{September 29, 1756}
Wednsday Morn—Sept 29

7 O'Clock set sail with the Tide but soon meet a strong south wind as much ahead as could blow but with tacking and going about 5 miles to gain one we made out to get half way between the ferry and York then lost our tide and wait the motion of the Waters and Wind.

Tis very crossing to lay here all day but tis all best—Wisely ordered—Mr Woodbridge went ashore and got some fruit and other things for our comfort and we made our selves as content as we could considering for our greatest comfort that God orders all— towards night set sail with a very violent head Wind, got along but very slowly but hoped to get in to york—8 o'Clock the Wind blew so extream hard which made such a tirrable sea that we could not sail for we had not ballast—so lay all night abot 3 miles from Newyork. This was trying.

{*September 30, 1756*}
Thursday Morn—Sept 30

7 O'Clock landed safe at Newyork. What a Mercy! O how good
is God to an Ill deserving creature! Called for Breakfast at an Inn,
then got sombody to carry my little Son and went up to Mrs Merciers
where I now am waiting for an oppertunity to go to Newark—here
I have the pleasure to hear from Mr Burr and Sally that they are
well—I am quite impatient to see them as you may guss, tho I shall
find em all in confusion. Commencement is over, yet the synnod
sets.

{*October 8, 1756*}
Fryday October 8. 1756.

Much I have passed throu since I wrote last (which was yesterday
Week). We know not what a day may bring fourth—My little Son
has been on the borders of Eternity almost ever since I came home
tho now it has pleased God to give us hope concerning his recoverry.
I will give you as short an account and as petecular as I can how
the dear little babe has been.

Last week Thursday P.M. 4.o'Clock I saild from Newyork towards
Newark, my Son as well as ever he had been in his life to all
appearance (except that he had been more tensome then useual for
a few days) and so continued till between one and two in the Morn.
About an hour before we landed at Newark as he was a sleep in the
Cabbin covered Warm, he was suddenly taken extream hoarse—
could hardly breath, which surprized me greatly. I awaked him but
twas all the same, yet the Child seemd perfectly well, would play
and smile.

When I got home put him to bed warm (thinking it might be
a sudden cold) upon which he seemd to breath better and so continued till about 11 A.M. when a violent Fever seized him and the
hoarsness increased—I was much frighted thinking it was the Throat
distemper, and sent for the Doct who was at a loss to conclude what
the disorder was but ordered to the best of his skill but to no
purpose.[5]

Eve the Doct said he was affraid the Child would not live till

5. The throat distemper was diphtheria. *OED.*

morn, and Saturday Eve told us plainly that he did not think it was possible for the Child [to live through the] Night—here was the greatest tryal that ever I meet with in my life—I may compare the struggles with my self to the *Agonies of Death*—but O God made me submit! He made me say the Lord gave, and the Lord may *take*, and I will bless his name—He shewed me that he had the first right, that the Child was not mine he was only lent, and I could freely return him and say Lord do as seemeth good in thy sight— In the Morn I sent the Doct Word that the Child was alive and somthing revived. He immediately came and told me he was almost astonished to hear that the Child was alive, and when he came to look of it said the fever was abated but the Child was inclining to fitts, but hoped that might be prevented—I asked if he thought it was possible for him to live another Night. He said twas very doubtfull but he thought he stood a rather better chance for his life tonight then last Night, which was a little incouraging—When Night came the Fever returnd but not quite so violent—Monday morn he seemd wonderfully better which gave great hopes.

Teusday grew worse and the case looked very doubtfull so that Mr Burr put by a journey to Princeton altho' of importance— Wednsday, better and so has continued ever since tho he mends very slowly—O my dear help us to bless the Lord for his great mercies. I look on the Child as one given to me from the dead— What obligations are we laid under to bring up this Child in a pecular manner for God? Company comes in.

{October 10, 1756}
Sabbath Eve—10

P.M. went out, heard Mr Duffield preach and a fine discourse I assure you. This people have invited him here and are in great hopes he will settle. I think him a very propor person for the place—the Child still recovering so a goodnight.

{October 11, 1756}
Monday, Trooping and Training

A deal of company at our house.

Teusday—the child so well Mr Burr set out for Princeton. Mr Duffield and Wife tarry with me for company. She is a prety

Woman[6]—Wednsday excedingly crouded with company all day. P.M. Madm Belcher brought Mrs Stevens to see me. As soon as was decent I asked for a Letter from you but alas she had none. I wonder at it but I doubt not there is a sufficient reason. Perhaps you did not know of her coming—she says she saw you at Meeting the day before she set out so you are alive, and I hope alive like to be.

{October 14, 1756}
Thursday Company

I have not told you how my own helth was. My thoughts and all my faculties have been imployed about my Little Son, but now begin to come to my feeling—before I saild from Clavarack I took an extream cold and it has been increasing ever since, and now it is settled in to my Lungs. I think I never had so bad a Cough and all I can take avails nothing. Madm Belcher seemd much concernd and said I was much altered in my countinance. Perhaps tis the will of God to take the Mother in the Sons sted—the Will of the Lord be done in this also. If my Worke is done I disire to tarry no longer.

{October 15, 1756}

Fryday 15—Last Night Mr Burr came home and this Morn is gone to Newyork on urgent busyness—P.M. A Room full of vissitors—I am so poorly that I can write no more.

{October 16, 1756}
Saturday Morn. Oct 16

I must now send this to Mrs Stevens for she goes on Monday—I am more poorly to day then I have been heretofore. What will be the consequence God only knows—We are to be at Princeton the 10 of next month if my helth will admit, so you will direct your Letters accordingly—Pleas to give my duty to your honored Parents and kind Love to Miss Jenny and all the Sisterhood—I wish you could have seen it your duty to have come with Mrs Stevens. I fear I shall never see you more in this Life—My Babe is almost as well as before his sickness. I am unable to add but that I desire you would not forget me [*so*] that I may be fitted for all that God has for me to go throu.

6. Mrs. Duffield was Elizabeth Blair Duffield. See note 1, Letter No. 23, above.

From my dear, dear Friend your tenderly affectionated Friend
E. Burr

(No. 26)

{October 17, 1756}
Sabbath P.M. Oct. 17

To my dear affectionate Fidelia

Yesterday P.M. your dear paquit No. 25. came by Mr Burr—I am so distressed for you in your perplexed situation that I cant tarry till the Sabbath is over before I tell you I Pity you from the Bottom of my soul, and have after my poor cold manner many times this day prayed for you, that you may be Directed, that you may be inclined to do what shall be most for the glory of God and your own good and comfort boath for time and Eternity—Once I was the subject of much such perplexities. One case in petecular was very similar to yours. Then I have reason to think God was my director and trust he will be yours—dont sink. All is Wisely Ordered and best—I doubt not but duty will be made plain—When did you ever commit any case to the Lord but he directed your paths— When the Sabbath is over I shall consult Mr Burr and send you our best thoughts. Mine are but poor at best and now worse then [ever] by reason of bodyly disorder.

{October 18, 1756}
Monday

Very poorly and crouded with company, but you my dear and your case was the cheif subject of my thoughts amddest all my company and care.

{October 19, 1756}
Teusday somthing better.

All day prepairing work for some young Women that have offered to come and sew for me.

Eve. Company—Mr Burr think to deliver his own thoughts to you in a Letter about a sertain affair—Good luck has sent Mr Stevens and Lady to Philadelphia so they dont set out for Boston till next Monday—this gives us time to think.

{October 20, 1756}
Wednsday

Company all day and to dine as well as Tea.

As to the first objection you make I think it rather an Inducement. Tis best they should be Boys. They wont make you half the trouble that Girls might, be sure, if you should have Children of your own—Boys want the same principles of relegion and Virtue instilled into them as Girls, and I cant see why you hant an oppertunity of doing as much good. As they are young—you will have quite the assendent over them.

{October 21, 1756}
Thursday P.M. Mr Burr from home.

3rd Objection in my opinnon has more weight in it then all the rest—that you dont think you can esteem him enough—if you cant, tis a sufficient objection—for *Let the Wife see that she Reverence her Husband*—if you cant esteem you cant reverence—so there it must end—but I immagine you are mistaken. You cant help esteeming a person of so many good quallifycations as are under the head of Inducements—The second I dont mention because if he has as much sense as Jesuit tis enough, for you did make that no objection against him. Objection 4th—that you cant expect relegious conversation from him—*How knowest thou O Woman but thou mayest gain thy Husband.* I think there is a good deal of reson to hope it as he has such a desire to have a relegious Wife.

I know it to be the opinnion of my Honored Parents that a person aught not to make concience of this matter. They said that some other things were more nesesary to happyness in a Married state, (which things you have mentioned of him) but when Relegion meets those other things it Crowns all—tis proporly the Crown, but my dear this alone will not do—look around, you will soon see that tis not every good Man that you could live happily with in that state—one of my honnest neighbours comes in to see me.

{October 22, 1756}
Fryday

I dont think it needfull to consider the other objections petecularly, for there is not much weight in them—it would be absurd to the last degree to refuse good Circumstances for fear we should

not make a good improvment of them—a Woman at Work for the
Children to fit em for their journey.

{October 23, 1756}
Saturday—
Upon the Whole—The important point must turn here. If upon
mature deliberation and serious consideration you find you cant think
of spending your days with that Gentleman with Complaciency and
delight, *say No*—but if on the contarary, I think you may venture
to answer in the affermative—This must turn the point so you only
can determine for your self.

Madam—
I designed to have done my self the Honor of writing you a Letter
but being much hurried in transcribing a Discourse for the P.M. I
must defer it, till I write a Letter of Congratulation etc—I approve
of what Mrs Burr has wrote on a *certain subject* on the whole I like
it rather better than Jesuit—you did not say whether he was of your
own Profession or not; if not, I advise against it—If you accept I
shall adopt him into the No. of my Friends. ⟨. . . .⟩ As I find you
are yet Mistress of your self I entirely confide in your superior
judgement that you will act the wise and prudent Part. May Heaven
direct you in that important affair.

Yrs sincerely and affectionately
A Burr
N.B. My Letter to Jesuit was wholly on Business.

As I was writing Mr Burr comes in and looked over what I had
wrote and said it was not worth while for him when he was hurried
out of his witts to write over the same things. I had said all that
was to be said—I insisted he should write somthing, so he took my
pen out of my hand and wrote what is written—If that Gentleman
was a pious man with all his other agreable quallifycations if you
had not *an intire regard for him,* it would be Preposterous to Marry
him—And as it is, and as the times go, if you can love and esteem
him I think you act quite prudently in Marrying—I can say no
more but pray for you that your thoughts and affections may be
directed.

(No 1.)

{December 1756}
Princeton Decembr [. . .]

To my Dear Fidelia

Eloquence cant paint the scenes of Confusion nay I may call it Caoss that I have passed throu since my last by Mrs Stevens—You my dear observe we are at Princeton—Notwithstanding the confusion of our affairs (which was not more then seemd nessarily to arise from the circumstances of the case) We have experienced largly of Gods goodness in our remoove—No sorrowfull accident has happened to any of our famaly—our goods came remarkably safe. I had not a China thing so much as cracked—I wrote you in my last that I was in a very poor state of helth which continued and increased till our remoove. At the time we set out several that saw me [e]xpected to hear that I was confined as soon as I got here. Indeed I expected it my self but God is kind and gracious to an unworthy Worm— for the first week after I came I was poorly, a bad fever and my Cough increasing but was directed to somthing that has helped me [*so*] much that I now injoy as good a state of helth as usual except somthing of my Cough remaining. (I have forgot both number and page of my last by Mrs Stevens which you wont wonder at considering the confusion I have been in ever since. As it is from a new place I date from, twill do to begin a new number.)

The dear little Lambs are perfectly Well—Mr Burr is very comfortable but as much crowded with business as I am with confusion— Miss Abby Camp was so kind as to come with me and assist me under my diffeculties. She has been a very great comfort to me. I hope she will tarry all Winter.[1]

Mr Thomas Foxcroft has been so kind as to call in his way to Philadelphia and take dinner with me. I had raised expectations of an Olive-Leaf when I knew him. Was disappointed. He tells me

1. Abigail Camp may have been the daughter of Nathaniel Camp of Newark, and his wife (whose name we cannot locate), who boarded numerous students at the College. If so, Abigail was the sister of Stephen Camp, who graduated from the College in 1756, and possibly the sister of Mary Camp Burnet, who married another graduate, Dr. William Burnet (see note 27, Letter No. 10, above). McLachlan, pp. 17–18, 155.

that tis two months since he le[ft] Boston but that you then exsisted whic[h] gave me some comfort, and seeing a person that came from Boston kindled anew all the flame of love I have for you[2]—and I assure you my dear I hant felt my affections so enlivend to any absent Friend I dont know the time when—I sat the whole afternoon after he was gone and Wished and Longed and Longed and Wished till I almost immagined you here—I found twas needfull that I should check myself or my desires to see you would grow two impatient— O When will the happy day come when I shall injoy again the dear Company and inlivening conversation of my dear, dear, Fidelia! God only knows—O Lord if not in this World grant that we may meet with thee, never to be seperated—never to be interrupted.

As to our situation here and of the College [. . .] impossible I should be petecular now. My present hurry of affairs will not admit but that you may know how we are fixed or rather how we are to be some time hence—I have desired Mr Foxcroft as a petecular favour to me to carry this to you himself and be ready to answer all the questions you should pleas to ask. He has been over the College and seems pleased.

{December 5, 1756}
Sabbath Eve Decm—5.

This day Mr Burr spends at Newark as that poor place is Intirely destitute—the Weather is extream cold but was out all day and am not the worse for it—We meet in the College Hall for the present. This people propose to Build a meeting House next summer.

We were entertained by Mr Ewing a very ingenious young Man, one of the Tutors—his discourses are like himself.

{December 10, 1756}
Decmbr 10.

Company flock in at all times [so] that I cant get time to say one word to you—New aquaintance and I hope new friends almost every day, *but Alas for me* I cant find a *Fidelia* amongst em all, nor need I look for it for there is not another Fidelia on the face of the Globe— and indeed my dear when I bring the case home I dont desire another.

2. We think this was Thomas Foxcroft, son of Reverend Thomas and Anna Coney Foxcroft and brother of Samuel Foxcroft (see note 1, Letter No. 10, above).

I dont want to devide my Friendship to two many—no you shall have all—But I must tell you what for neighbours I have—the Nighest is a young Lady that lately moved from Brunsweck, a prety discreet well behaved girl. She has good sense and can talk very handsomely on almost any subject, I hope a good Girl two—I will send you some peieces of poetry of her own composing that in my opinnion shew some genious that way that if proporly cultivated might be able to make no mean figure.[3]

The two pices I send you as some of the first of her composing. She is to try what she can write for me on the removal of the College to this place. When it is done you shall see it—Perhaps you have heard Mr Whitefield speak of this Capt. Grant, for he allways kept at his House when at Philadelphia, and had a very high esteem of his person and pietey. He was truly an amiable Man, and have reason to think has not left his equel in the Whole City.

{December 24, 1756}
Decmbr 24.

After a long silence I have time and strength to write—since I wrote last, much has passed, Company come and gone from all quarters. Had received many vissits and begun to return em—but last Week on Thursday was taken Ill and have been confined ever since to my Room with the Canker in my Throat and violent fever, tho' throu mercy am better. Hope soon to recover.

The Weather is very fine but everybody is taken up with the slaying. Mr Burr and Miss Abby gone from home so I am alone with my Children—I hant spirits and Life enough to write altho' tis to one that would give new Life as soon as any absent friend I have—I am greatly troubled with lowness of spirits and feel at times as if I should be meloncholy which will be a new thing with me— I can add no more at present but that I am Your Burissa

3. This was Annis Boudinot, the young poet who became one of Esther's few friends in New Jersey. Her parents were Elias and Catherine Williams Boudinot. Probably in late 1757 she married lawyer Richard Stockton, son of Abigail Phillips and John Stockton of Princeton, who is best known today as one of the signers of the Declaration of Independence. Annis published a number of her poems and other writings in colonial newspapers and magazines. Alfred Hoyt Bill, *A House Called Morven*, rev. ed. (Princeton: Princeton University Press, 1978).

{January 1, 1757}
New years day

A happy Year to you and many more at the end of it—Ill tell you a Little how the Week has been spent so that you have had none of it.

On Monday sick or at least poorly as I was, I must needs go to one of my Neighbours to dinner. A fine dinner we had, and a deal of company which if I had known should not have gone—Teusday very busy in making some prepareation for a Trustee meeting that sat here the next day and Thursday—Fryday more company to dine and spend the Eve. Saturday Mr Symmons and Wife from Brunswick to dine and drink Tea, and now they are gone to meeting. Mr Burr gives the people a sermon for a New years gift etc.

{January 2, 1757}
Sabbath Jan—2 day.

I long to begin this year with God—O for Gods presence throu this year! When I look back on the year past and take a view of the Numberless Mercies I have been the subject off, I stand amazed at Gods goodness to such an Ill deserving Hell deserving Creature [*as*] I am—Why am I thus distinguished from the greater part of the World—What obligations am I under to spend the remainder of my time for God—I dont want to live unless I can live more to the glory of God and do more good—Eve Mr Symons and Wife dined, drank Tea and spent the Eve here.

{January 3, 1757}
Monday Jan 3—a fine day.

P.M. Made a vissit at Mr Smiths the Master Builders, his Wife Lays in—she is a very clever Woman.

Eve. Came home and found my Aaron very unwell.

{January 4, 1757}

Teusday—Observe some Canker in his Mouth and fear it will prove the Throat-distemper—these cares you know nothing off my dear.

{January 5, 1757}

Wednsday. The Child is very sick but nothing worse then the common soar mouth—Last night up almost the Whole night.

{*January* 6, 1757}
Thursday. The Child no better, very Little sleep.

{*January* 7, 1757}
Fryday Night. Up the Whole Night.

{*January* 8, 1757}
Saturday. The Child is a little better.

{*January* 9, 1757}
Sabbath eve. Aaron almost well.
Out all day, Mr Burr preach very affectingly from the parrable of the Prodigal Son—some diffeculties he has meet with in the College the week past I suppose was the means of turning his thoughts on that subject—Peter Fanueil has behaved in such a scandalous manner that Mr Burr was obliged the Week past to surspend him, and accordingly he is sent to live with Mr Davenport, who lives near us—I am greived for his Mother—But indeed he is a very Wicked Boy.

{*January* 10, 1757}
Monday—Jan. 10.
I have h[ad?] a very great longing spell to see you—I would give almost any thing to see you to day.

I wonder whether you be'ant contriving a journey here next spring—I have another Wonder two, that is if you are not a going to be MARRIED and bring your HUSBAND with you—*say, ant you—I surspect and believe, and suppose, and Guss* a good many things about you.

Lets see how long since I heard from you? I believe tis half a year—hant heard whether you are in the Body or out, married or unmarried. Since we mooved to this new World, it seems as if we did not live in the same World that we did at Newark—there we used to hear from our friends, and hear publick news—but here we know not what the World, Friends or Foes, are about—I believe if the French were to take Boston we should not hear of it so soon as they would in London—The College is the greatest thing that ever the peop[le] here heard [of].

{January 11, 1757}
Teusday Jan 11.

I wonder in the name of honesty what is become of *Brother Tomy*—but since he was along I have heard that he is in bad Bread, so guss he'll not make his apearance in Boston very soon.[4]

I am heartily sorry for *Father*. It must give him a good deal of uneasiness—good Old Man.

{January 12, 1757}
Wednsday A.M.—12

This Famaly has not been well one day since we came. As soon or before one is well another is taken sick—My Wentch is very sick indeed and poor *I* hurried to Death.

P.M. Company, Mr Brainerd among the rest. Also heard from Newark as we do almost every Week—I have a very bad soar Thumb [*so*] that I can hardly hold my pen.

{January 13, 1757}
Thursday. 13.

Last night lay awake the Whole night with this Thumb. I know not what it will come to—but I cant hold my pen. It pains me excedingly, [*the*] right Thumb on the top.

{January 19, 1757}
Jan—19. Wednsday

God is threttening us but as yet the stroke is withheld—there has not one day passed in my famaly since I came from Stockbri[dge] but one or more of us ⟨ . . . ⟩ have bee[n] so Ill as to want attendance—My Wentch has been in a poor way ever since our remooval—but now is so bad as to keep her Bed. She has been under the Doctrs hands for six Weeks past but to no purpose—she is in a very uncommon way I fear poisoned, and if that is the case I dont expect she will live. The loss o[f] her will be very great. She is uncommonly good for her Colour, and I cant expect to have her place filled, but God does all Wisely and knows what is best—I desire to submit and say the Will of the Lord be done.

4. Esther was probably talking here about Thomas Foxcroft, Jr. (see note 2, Letter No. 1, above). That he was "in bad bread" may have meant that he was in a difficult situation.

{*January 21, 1757*}
Jan. 21.

I have an oppertunity to so think to commit this to fortune and hope it will reach you some time or other—I am in the utmost hast so can add only my kindest Love to all and Duty to your good parents in which Mr Burr joins as also in aboundant Love and friendship to you.

From your ever affectionate
E. Burr

P.S. Please to get for me a shade, Black, and if you think best to have any other colour intermixt, you may use your pleasure[5]—Also one Dz of Pictures of your good Minnisters—the Gentleman waits.

(No. 2.)
1757
{*January 31, 1757*}
Princeton Jan—last day

To my ever dear Friend—

When one cant hear from ones friends tis a very great sattisfaction to indulge the thoughts in what has passed—I am quite weary of looking for a Letter from you, and to comfort my self in any degree I have been entertaining my self this P.M. with a perusal of some of your former Letters, which has brought you so near me that whiles I am thinking of you am just ready to speak as if you were present— indeed my dear you are present—say ant your heart here—or at least part of it—and that is the main Chance—I woud give—I know not what I woud give to have your company only this Eve but O along, Long 350 Miles distance seperates us—Why has not art contrived some method more commodious and quick to pass such a large spot of Earth without all the buteenges [*buttings?*] of travling a long journey in a Tumbling Chaise or Troting on Horse back—Everytime the stage passes our Door I am hoping for a pacquit from my dear Fidelia but none yet—Company comes in so good night.

{*February 1, 1757*}
Teusday

Company from Trenton. It is very stormy so they will not leve us this day that is sertain.

---

5. A shade was either a lace scarf or a sunshade or parasol. *OED*.

{February 2, 1757}

Wednsday—Rain, hail, and snow with a violent Wind—my Heart achs for seamen—O what must their distress be!

{February 4, 1757}
Fryday A.M.

This morn our Trenton friends left us and also Miss Abby Camp that came here with me when we moved is gone this morn to Newark [*so*] that now our House seems quite lonesome—but tis fine slaying so I fancy it wont be long before we have company enough.

P.M. A good guss for this once—Who should come in at Teatime but Kitty and Polly with Mr Symons and Wife—I was almost overjoyed, Mr Burr quite elivated two—We had both of us got the dumps before, but now all is life, and merth.[1]

{February 5, 1757}
Saturday P.M. Feb—5.

After a good Roast Turkey and erly Tea our agreable friends left us, but seem to have left some of the same spirit that they brought— they are a couple of Charming Ladies—always the same friendly generous creatures—Kitty talked a deal about Boston, and you two. She and Mrs Donaldson retain the highest esteem for you, and speak of you with great affection and longing desires to see you in these parts once more.

{February 6, 1757}
Sabbath Eve

Very unwell with a pain in my Brest so tarried at home all day— feel dead and dull to every thing in this world and another—at times a little upon the gloom.

{February 7, 1757}
Monday Eve Feb 7.

Fine slaying so we proposed a Ride to see Mr Davenport and Wife. They live about 7 miles from hence, a fine road, the Weather very pleasant as also the Company, so returnd in much better spirits then I went.[2] Poor Faneuil is with him and with pleasure [*I*] can

1. Kitty and Polly were Kitty Bradley and Polly Banks. See notes 16 and 25, Letter No. 10, above.
2. Mrs. Davenport was Parnel Davenport. See note 9, Letter No. 18, above.

tell you that there is a very great alteration in him for the better. He seems under a good deal of concern about his soul—next Week he will be restored to College again.

Mr Cowell from Trenton comes to lodge with us—goodby.[3]

{February 8, 1757}
Teusday A.M.

Company come and go—come and go—continually it is Rap, Rap—is the President at home all this day.

Eve. We have had people from all parts of the country to day, this eve a Room full.

There is a considerable awakening in College more general then has ever been since Mr Burr has had the care of it—the sickness of Loyer Smiths Son and his concern (I think I mentioned i[t] my last that he had been at the point of Death with the Bloody flux and was under great concern for his soul which still continues.) I hope has been sanctified to the good of several very rude young fellows.[4]

{February 9, 1757}
Wednsday P.M.

A Fine day—Mr Burr walked with me to vissit at Mr Stocktons—the Old Lady is a very good Woman. I Love her company exceedingly[5]—came home and found Mr Spencer come to settle his metters as he has determined to leve the stewardship. He has a call to settle at Jamaca on Long Island in Mr Bostwicks place, and I guss he will except[6]—Mr Kittletas has a very unanimous call to settle at Elizabeth Town with the offer of 130 pound a year—but

3. David Cowell was minister of the Trenton Presbyterian church and a trustee of the College. He was the son of Joseph and Martha Fale Cowell. Apparently he never married. Twice he served as acting president of the College, first after the death of Aaron Burr, and second after the death of Jonathan Edwards. Sibley 9:139–43.

4. Lawyer Smith's son was James Smith, a member of the class of 1757 at the College. His parents were William and Mary Het Smith (see note 7, Letter No. 10, above). After he graduated he became a physician, a chemistry professor, and a writer—and the husband of a widow, Mrs. Atkinson. McLachlan, pp. 209–13.

5. The Stocktons were Abigail Phillips and John Stockton. See note 3, Letter No. 1, above.

6. Elihu Spencer (note 4, letter No. 11, above) did accept the call to the Jamaica church but did not become their regular preacher. Dexter 2:89–92.

it seems his Wife has not yet given her consent. If that can be obtained he will be Ordained very soon but she thinks tis two great a stoop in him to settle as the Minnister of a Congregation and be beholden to the people for a support—She is *LOYER SMITHS DAUGHTER* and I believe inherits some of his quallities—*Chip of the Old Block,* as say the Vulgar—Men should settle in Business, and in that follow Duty and inclination before they are incumbered with a Wife—says your E. Burr.[7]

Eve—diverted with the company of my Poetes.[8]

{February 10, 1757}
Thursday A.M.

Heard that the Governor is at the point of death which will be such a loss to this Province that we cant expect to have it made up in a Governor—things look dark—Good men one after another die, and I see none ariseng to fill their place—but this is and shall be my hope and comfort—That our God is the same Mercyfull, Wise, Powerfull, Good God that he was from Eternity, and so will continue to Eternity—altho all things Change, yet our God is what he always was.

{February 11, 1757}
Fryday fine Weather—11. [. . .]

Farther incuragement—Mr Burr tells me that yesterday a Young Man from Danbury in New England, one of his schollars, came to talk with him twice under very pressing concern for his soul—this morn came again[9]—O my dear who knows what God may do for the poor youth of this College if we pray ernestly for them! O it would be a Heaven upon Erth if he should shower down plentifully

7. Abraham Keteltas, son of Abraham and Jane Jacobs Keteltas of New York City, accepted the call to the Elizabethtown church at this time, at £130 a year. His stay was short, however; he was dismissed in 1760 after some difficulties with his parishioners. His wife, also from New York, was Sarah Smith Keteltas, daughter of William and Mary Het Smith (note 7, Letter No. 10, above). Dexter 2:289–91.

8. Annis Boudinot. See note 3, Letter No. 1, above.

9. This was Elnathan Gregory, possibly the son of Mercy Wildman and Ephraim Gregory. He later became pastor of a Congregational church in Carmel, New York. McLachlan, pp. 186–88.

of his holy spirit upon them—God is as able and willing as ever he was, if we were prepard for so great a mercy.

P.M. and eve. Thronged with company—you know tis common for people under great afflictions to apply to some good Minnister for advise and comfort. This is the case of the people we have had to day—poor unhappy Cretures! As they were calmly and pleasantly sailing (or slaying) for their diversion, there arose a sudden storm of Violent Wind and Warm Rain, that in six hours carried off all the snow not a patch as big as one of your hands left, and they cast into the Mudd, and there left to stick to their unspeakable Mortifycation! However, we found they were better able to comfort themselves then we were, and in a way that I should not have thought off—that is that there are a great many others in as bad a Box as they are—this is a sordid sort of a comfort methinks—tis not becoming the Man—nay I really think it beneath the Beasts—there is somthing of the Old Scratchum in this, ant there?

(The governor is recovered.)

{February 12, 1757}
Saturday.

Much after the old sort—one comes and another goes and the Weather very cold all of us huddling about a good large fire—I am not very well my self, somthing of a pain in my head—I dont feel disposed for writing.

{February 13, 1757}
Sabbath Eve.

Out all day altho' as cold as any we have had this Winter—We were entertained with a discourse from Revealations etc—The Key of David shuteth and no man openeth, and openeth and no Man shuteth—But I was as dead as a stone.

This eve entartained my self and my young Poetes with the perusal of some of your former favours, which always excites in me an ardent desire to be Blessed once more with your company and conversation.

{February 15, 1757}
Teusday

Writing to Stockbridge so must beg an excuse—Wednsday writing yet to one friend and another.

{February 18, 1757}
Fryday 18

The concern in College prevails and a general reformation of manners which began first before the concern—O my dear who knows what the Lord may be about to do! Nothing is beyound his power—O lets us pray ernestly for a universal rivival—I am interrupted as I often am.

{February 19, 1757}
Saturday Morn

The young Man from Danbury (Gregory by Name) we have reason to hope has found God—the temper of his mind is very Christian like. He seems to have a great sense of God and himself, and the sufficency of Christ and the safty of venturing his soul upon him, and wonders he could ever be affraid to trust his all upon him—the Concern is now become general in College—none of it in Town and several under very great distress of soul—O Help me to bless the Lord! Mr Burr is almost over joyed—for my part I am affraid that (as the Lord in Samaria) I am affraid I shall only behold it with mine eyes and not tast of these heavenly blessings.

{February 20, 1757}
Sabbath Eve.

Mr Spencer preached all day (he is much inlivened) from He that cometh to me hath life, etc. I never saw the scholars so attentive in my life. They really seemed as if they heard for their lives.

9 o'Clock—Mr Burr returnd from College, Mr Spencer with him, and glorious things they relate—Mr Burr was sent for to the College about dark, and when he came their he found above 20 young Men in one room Crying and begging to know what they should do to be saved, 4 of them under the deepest sense of thier wicked Hearts and need of Christ, Faniuel amongst the rest, and how it will rejoice his good Mothers Heart—Mr Burr praied and talked in the best Manner he could and left them and comes home greatly affected—we sat and talked till late and knew not how to lay by the glorious subject. (Mr Spencer wont lodge with us but returns to Colleg to see the salvation of the Lord.)

{February 21, 1757}
Monday Morn.

Good News my dear I have to tell you this morn—A Minnisters Son near Philadelphia hopfully received Comfort last Night in the Night. There was little sleep amongst them, some up all Night. Mr Spencer sat up till 1 o'Clock then left these poor young cretures seeking God—the Conversion of this young Treat, for that is his name, is a very dear and remarkable one. The peteculars I hant heard but Mr Burr says he thinks evidently a Work of Grace—he has been under some impressions for more then a year, but his concern has increased lately[10]—10. o'Clock—a pious young Man comes from the College, for Mr Burr. He tells me that great part of the schollars are gathered into one Room Crying in great distress, and that another has received comfort—O my Heart Exults at the thought that God is about to revive Relegion in general—May we not hope for it—My soul doth magnify the Lord for what he has done.

Eve—The Lords work goes on gloriously in the College—Mr Burr sent for Mr Tennent of Freehold to come and assist in drawing the Net ashore for it is ready to Break with the aboundance of the Fish that are Caught in it—just now he came and is gone up to the College greatly rejoiced. (This Mr Tennent is not attal like Gilbert but as prudent a Man in Conducting affairs of relegion as ever I saw in my life. He hates noise—and hates [. . .] anything that looks like judging persons safe in a hurry but says time must descover what they are.)

9 o'Clock. No work carried on here, but only to get somthing to Eat, and a little of that will suffice two—for my part I hant any creature to say one word two, and when I am ready to burst I have recourse to my pen and you—Mr Tennent is astonished, and amazed, between joy, sorrow, hope, and fear and says he dont know what passion is uppermost, but he must call it an Awfull joy that he

10. Young Treat was Joseph Treat, son of New Light preacher and College trustee, Richard Treat, and his first wife, Mary Thomas Treat. After his graduation in 1757 Joseph preached for a time in Elizabethtown, where he married Elizabeth Woodruff Bryant, the widow of Ebenezer Bryant and daughter of Elizabeth Ogden and Samuel Woodruff (see note 14, Letter No. 9, above). McLachlan, pp. 215–17.

feels, which is the case with us all—My Brother is under a great deal of concern amongst the rest—O what shall I render to the Lord for his goodness in powering [*pouring*] out his spirit in such an wonderfull degree.

{*February 22, 1757*}
Teusday P.M. 2 o'Clock

I am ready to set up my Tabernacle and say Lord it is good to be here—indeed my dear the thoughts of living hant been so comfortable to me not for years past as now—The Lord is indeed here—Mr Tennent said just now at Table (that is all the time I have with him and Mr Burr, and they begrudge one minnit from College) that he thought there was not above three or 4 in all the College but what were deeply affected—and it is not a Noisy distress but a deep concern, not a flight of fancy but their judgments are thorougly convinced, and they are deeply wounded at Heart with a sense of their sin and need of Christ. No need now of Mr Burrs sending to rooms to see if the schollars keep good hours and mind their studdies. Never was there so much studdying in College since it has had a being as now.

This wonderfull pouring out of the spirit at this time just as the College is finnished and things a little settled looks to me exactly like Gods desending into the Temple in a Cloud of Glory, there by signifying that he did except of the House for his dwelling place and would Bless it—but I fear and tremble, for fear that Sattan will get an advantage and obstruct by sowing Tares amongst the Wheat—Mr Tennent says that some will turn out for God, and some for the Divel with a Vengance—this is likely, but it looks awfull—but stay, why do I distrust God, he is as able to Carry on this work as to begin it—I will hope and pray that it may become universal—O that this might be the dawn of the glorious day! O I am transported at the thought? Come Lord Jesus come quickly! Make no tarry but come now!

Eve—Doct Shippen came in very unexpectedly—and seems rejoiced to see his son Jackey under such concern for his soul[11]—10 o'Clock a person comes to call Mr Burr and Tennent, says that Loyer

11. For John (Jackey) Shippen, see note 6, Letter No. 14, above.

Smiths Son is in great Horror, so Mr Tennent is gone[12]—My dear Brother is deeply distressed.

{February 23, 1757}
Wednsday Morn

Mr Tennent and Burr think there is no doubt but God has got possession of Smiths Heart altho' as yet hant found comfort, but I immagine Conversion and comfort to be two distinkt things—One Bawldwin of Newark has meet with somthing that looks of a saving nature[13]—another young Man from Newark that has been as stupid as a Block till today is now under great apprehensions of his undone state, out of Christ—Mr Burr and Tennent have been much concernd for fear Mr Davenport would come here upon his high Horse, and sew the seeds of inthusiasm, so they thought best to send for him and dockament him first—P.M. He comes and wants no counciling, for God has done the Work for them. O how does God do everything in this glorious affair, even before he is asked!

God has this Morn given him such an humbling sense of his former imprudences that he says he is affraid to touch the Ark of God for fear he shall give it a rong touch. He dont intend to venture up to college for fear that it may prejudice some against. Eve—had a good deal of conversation with my Brother and think him in a hopefull way—Mr Tennent says that for the World he would not venture to say that he had not Grace in his Heart now. If that be so, it will do him no hurt to be converted over again.

The company of my Poetis. She seems greatly rejoiced at the Lords Work—I hope she is a gracious person—(this day had a company of young Ladies from Trenton to dine and drink Tea—poor vain young creatures as stupid as horses. It would be casting Pirls before swine to say any thing about relegion before them.) From 7 o'Clock till 10 was happy in the Conversation of Mr Tennent, Davenport, and Spencer and Burr, all upon divine subjects—O tis a Heaven upon Erth! I long that you was here—It is truly good to

12. James Smith. See note 4, Letter No. 2, above.
13. Moses Baldwin, who graduated from the College in 1757, was the son of John and Lydia Harrison Baldwin. He later married Becca Seymour Lee and became pastor of the Palmer, Massachusetts, Presbyterian church. McLachlan, pp. 171–72.

be here—how sweet is life when God is injoied in all? I know not when I have had clearer Views of the Way of salvation—by Christ, and the excellency of it, and the safety of the souls venturing their this evening—the Lords name be praised.

{*February 24, 1757*}
Thursday Feb—24.

Mr Davenport returned home this Morn—there is a considerable awakning in his school which is further incouragement—I cant but hope that it will become universal at least in this Land—the Work goes on and prospers. Two of the Workmen at the Colleg are under deep concern, and Smith has found comfort, as also several young Men that were hopefully pious before this, but were shaken to the foundation—I assure you my dear this is a trying time—You can have no Idea of the propriety and dercrorum [*decorum*] that subsists amongst the scholars with this deep Concern. There is nothing in the Whole affair but what is desireable—and not an opposer in the College. Those few (tho' indeed I dont now know of but one but what is under some degree of concern) that are not concernd are silent—I see Company coming so must leve off.

{*February 25, 1757*}
Fryday

Last Evning Was the following peice wrote within this house by my poetis.

On hearing of the out pouring of the divine spirit in Nassau Hall Feb—24—1757 by Annis Boudanot

The joyfull The transporting news will Chear
The faithfull few, who stand unbending here
Beneath the torrents of Impetious Rage
Hurl'd on their heads by a Licentious Age
And Bravely stem the Tide and keep the Road
Which leads to Life to happiness and God.
Bear up a little longer and you'll see
The much expected day of Jubilee
Look—Even now the glorious star appears
To gild the gloom and Banish all your fears.
The day spring visits us and Jesus flys
To assert his Cause and wipe our streaming Eyes.

O Blissfull day with what a sacred Light
Dost thou appear to my Enraptured sight.
Too much Dear Lord tis such surprizing Grace
I am Overcome and would depart in peace.
Enough that I have seen one Cheerfull Ray
The Early dawn of this Triumphant Day
But be thy Intrest safe thy Cause secure
What ever future Woes I may Endure.
May Nassau Hall thy attractive Magnet be
And draw Ten Thousand precious souls to Thee.
Let not the Encumbring World again Intrude
To Mock our hopes and all our joys delude.
O! Carry on the Work thou hast begun
And spread its Influence where the vigerous sun
Begins his shining progress in the East
And hides his glory in the distant West.

Isn't it a fine thing—I wish she had more advantages for improvment—she is a good Creature I beleive—This P.M. Mr Tennent
left us, all goes on and prospers.

Saturday—Must write a letter or two to Stockbridge as I have a
very good oppertunity.

{*March 1, 1757*}

Teusday Eve March the first—whiles the company is at College.

This is the first vacant moment I have had since Saturday last—
yes every moment has been taken up with company or some nesesary
duty—When I left off last Saturday I told you I was about writing
to Stockbridge, but before I could write came Mr Gilbert Tennent
and Daughter in Law, so with great regret missed the oppertunity.
This Lady I love because she looks and walks and Talks and is like
our dear and ever to be remembered Sister Mercy—a very pious
woman tho' not equil to our departed Sister—Mr Burr has had a
difficult task of it to mannage Mr Gilbert and not affront him, for
he is mighty forward to preach and pray, and would fain preach em
to death if he could—however Mr Burr let him preach 3 times on
the Sabbath for no one thinks amiss of Preaching on the Sabbath—
as there has been no erragularities heithertwo it would be very
desireable that there might be none so long as this glorious work
lasts, [*so*] that Satan might have no handle—but he'll work, handle

or none, and does work—Yesterday Loyer Ogden of Newark sent for 3 Sons of his that were at the College. He had heard that the schollars were all Run Mad and desired his Sons might be sent home immediately, and to Day another is sent for that belongs to Brunswick—these poor young Cretures have begun well, but alass! I doubt here it will end, tho there is reason to hope that one of the Loyers Sons is savingly rought upon but he is very young and one cant be so sertain[14]—this Morn Mr Tennent and Daughter left us to go to Freehold but will return this Week—We have now 4 Minnisters here and expect more—they are coming, so good night.

{March 2, 1757}
Wednsday.

The examination is held to day, that is part of it, the Arts Siences left to an after consideration.

{March 3, 1757}

Thursday. Some of the Company gone.

{March 4, 1757}
Fryday—P.M.

This day Dined with us Mr Loyd who brought your dear kind large paquit, long looked for, come at last[15]—Altho' our House was crouded with Company, the two Mr Tennents etc, I slyly stole away and read all[16]—O what a friend have I in my Fidelia—O! for a thankfull heart for such a favour—I am heartily greived to here of Secretary Willard['s] Death.[17] It looks awfull that one good Man and Woman after another dies, and none arrising to fill their Place—

14. David Ogden's three sons were Isaac, Josiah, and Abraham Ogden. Josiah had received his degree in 1756 but had remained at the College. Young Abraham, whom Esther thought might have been converted, was still in the grammar school. None of these young Ogdens returned to Princeton after the revival was over. McLachlan, pp. 161, 238–40.

15. Possibly Byfield Lyde, son of Edward and Deborah Byfield Lyde, and husband of Jonathan Belcher's daughter, Sarah Belcher Lyde. He attended Boston's Old South Church. Sibley 7:206–14.

16. The two Tennents were Gilbert and William. See notes 8 and 32, Letter No. 10, above.

17. Josiah Willard, secretary of the province of Massachusetts, was the son of the eminent Puritan divine Samuel Willard, and husband of Hannah Appleton Clark Willard. He died on December 7, 1756. Sibley 4:425–32.

I am affraid I shant have time to write much more before Mr Loyd calls for my Letter but will do what I can.

{*March 6, 1757*}
Sabbath Eve.

I have a few moments stolen from company to talk with you— Mr Gilbert preachd all day from those words—Turn ye turn ye why will ye die O house of Israel—a very great solemnity and close attention appeared in the Congregation as well as among the students—I am soon called—good by.

{*March 7, 1757*}
Monday P.M. 5 o'Clock fine day.

All my company packt off at last, and for once I am alone again— The Relegious Concern in College still remains in its full power altho' those young Gentlemen being sent for seemed to check it for a season in some few instances where the touch was but superficial. But in general the studients seem to have a Rational, Thorough since of Eternal things, and many, I may say a great number, truly Converted to God—and some of the most Vissious.

{*March 8, 1757*}
Teusday A.M. 9. O'Clock

Yesterday I was forced to write some Letters of Complement so could not write much.

Mr Burr and I have considered our accounts and thought the matter over and conclude that you must be right about the matter, so shall leve it wholy to you to settle. If you are no looser, I am perswaded I shant be. My concern is only for you—in No. 1. which I hope you have received before now I desired you to procure for me a shade and a Dzn of Pictures of your good Minnisters. When you send them pleas to send the account that I may pay it, that we have no farther jumble about such Matters.

I wish that well conserted scheem of you coming with Mrs Stevens might be put in execution if nothing better offers—Mr Burr talks of going to Boston Next fall and tells me I must go—but I suppose it may be possible enough that I may not be in Circumstances proppor for Traveling, tho' nothing of that yet.

By the way, I am invited by Kitty to Brunswick to drink Cordale next august on account of Mrs Donaldson—this is quick work for her Child is near two Months younger than mine.[18]

I give you joy of your Matrimonial affair—Tis all for the best— My dear, God orders these things—tis he that Inclines, or disinclines our thoughts—if I can get coppied I shall send you a peice Miss Boudanot has wrote on the Removal of the College to this place— done about 3 weeks before the Revival of Relegion. I think it a good thing but capable of mending—if I have time I shall make some remarks and submit 'em to your judgment.

I take it kindly that you mention Sallys going to Boston, but shall not lay such a burthen on you as her Whole Education must be but a few years hence if We all are spared. I shall think myself happy in commiting her to your care for a season—I am affraid Sister Bettys affair will drop. Tis almost two good news to be true— Mr Burr had a hearty laugh you may easily guss at reading of it and your sprightly remarks thereon.

Brother Tomy has borrowed Money from Newyork to Philadelphia and is gone clear—poor good Mr Foxcroft, I fear it will bring his gray hairs with sorrow to the Grave—I rejoice to hear the late Miss Hubbard is so happy in her new circumstances. It gives me a pecular pleasure to hear of happiness in that Relation—for alass! how many poor creatures are like Samsons Foxes, unhappy.

Eve—I made out to write eve and one comes pop in, so it is all day and Night—We have two strangers to lodge and how long they will stay I know not.

{*March 9, 1757*}
March 9 1757
Wednsday A.M. 11 o'Clock.

Last eve 3 schollars were sent for that belong to Newyork, this by the Instigation of Loyer Ogden of Newark. He has been to Newyork on purpose—O how busy is Satan. He was drove out of College, and now stands at a distance and Barks at it like a surly Dog at the full Moon in its Glory because 'tis out of his reach— about a dzn people coming in—so lay down your pen or they will

18. Mrs. Donaldson was expecting a baby in August. Drinking cordial was part of the celebration held in a woman's chamber soon after she gave birth.

wonder what this Woman does a writing forever, for these same people have seen me at it last Night.

P.M. I had as good conclude my schralls, for perhaps Mr Loyd will call to night, and tis impossible for me to get time to say any thing. I am really drove—I dont contrive what will become of us if people drive this stroke. For my part I have been very dilligent, but for a month past hant done a shillings worth of Work, not seting work, but tis Trot, Trot, around the House, day after day, waiting upon Tom Tinker and Tom Tite.

My kindest regards to the Sisters, Duty to your honored parents and Deal out Complements as you think proper. My love to Julia in all which Mr Burr joins as also in kindest Love to you—from your most affectionate Friend—

E. Burr

(No. 3.)

{April 10, 1757}
Princeton April 10. 1757

To my Dear Friend

Sabbath Eve—(Mr Ewing preach'd all day. He is a good preacher as I have often said.)

After a very long silence I have time to say that I Love you more and more altho' I have neglected you so greatly, which I number among my greatest tryals—but must submit—my time is not my own but Gods.

Your dear agreable paquet by Mr Whitewell came safe to hand last Fryday with the sermons {and} subscriptions and Miss Bradleys Letter, which I shall se{nd} by the first oppertunity.[1]

I am surprized that you hant received a paquit from me before now. I have sent two since my remov{al} to Princeton—I fear they are lost.

My Circumstances have been pecular since I wr{ote} last {so} that it hant been possible for me to get tim{e to} write one Word—My Wentch that has been sick all Wint{er} has been gone some distance

1. Mr. Whitewell was probably William Whitwell, son of Rebecca Keen and William Whitwell of Boston. The younger William entered the College as a junior on April 8, 1757. McLachlan, pp. 253–55.

to a Doct this Month and I badly lot on it for help, besides a vast deal of Compa[ny] and sickness in the Famaly, but I'll not ware you o[ut] with a detail of my domestick troubles.

I am concernd to find you have been sick but [at] the same time would not forget to Bless God that yo[u] are recovering—I am exceding glad to hea[r] [fr]iends at Stockbridge are well. I have been much concernd about them for we hant heard one Word from them since last October but by you.

Agreable to your desire I shall not mention a sertain affair except in a private Letter to Miss Polly Crank—only that I feel a great tenderness for you, and an ernest desire for your Comfort and happyness in this life—and a disposission to pray that you may be influenced to take such steps as God shall approve off and Bless— There appears to me somthing providentiel in the [r]enewal of the affair—these things are conducted by God [h]im self, and that that is to Be, shall Be—and if we [are] faithfull in commiting the case to God and inquireing for the path of Duty, I dont in the least doubt of Gods Blessing both in Spirittuals and Temporals—I am at present under some petecular Tryals that [I] ever long to impart to you! As Mr Burr is from home I have none to unburthen myself to but God and I wish I found greater freedome in it then I do at present—In the World ye shall have Tribulation but in me ye have peace. Be of good Cheer I have [o]vercome the World, has been a comfort to me many [ti]mes of late—I shall trouble you with some [sh]ort account of my present troubles before I [en]d this, as you will see inclosed. I hoped to have had this Whole eve to my self and you but I have no more no less then s[ix] vissitors come to spend the eve, so wish you a good Nig[ht].

{April 11, 1757}
Monday A.M. 11. o'Clock—fine wea[ther]
This morn feel affected with Gods goodness to a sinf[ul] Worm of the dust. I arose erly with a violent sick Headach, kept up about an hour and was obliged to betake my self to Bed again not expecting to [be] able to rise again this day and not to recover for several days—Whiles on the bed got a little sleep and it has in a surpriszing manner almost intirely carried it off—Helth God knows I need at this time in my Famaly—I am ready to think that we loose much

of the comforts of relegion, and G[od] looses much prais, by not
remarking small mercies—as we are apt to call 'em—I dare not add
now for fear it may return the pain.

P.M. and Eve. The company of Miss Boudanot. She is a pleasant,
sociable, Friendly Creture as ever you saw—I wish you could be
acquainted with her—at her leving me she put the following peice
into my Han[d] which she wrote standing the last thing she did
before she left the house. It was done in about 10. Minutes or less—
it shews her readyness to things of this sort (a spicimen of which I
have already sen[t] you in both my Pacquets) and her overgrown
Estee[m] of me, which however absurd, will not displease [you] I
suppose—It is a humbling consideration to [think?] that any one
should have a better opinnion of one then [. . . .]

[W]hat she has wrote is as follows, altho' to repeat it to any one
but you would sertainly argue the greatest Vanity of Mind, and I
can hardly perswade my self but [it] must appear so to you—but
after all this [asside?] you shall have it look how it will.

To My Burrissa
Lovliest of Women! Could I gain
Thy Friendship, which I prize
Above the treasures of the Main
Compleat would be my joys.
Burrissa Oh my soul aspires
And clames a kin with yours
A daring Emulation Fires
My Mind and all its powers
Pardon the Bold atempt, it means
Only to Copy you
And thro' Lifes Various shiftings seenes
Will hold thee still in View
O let thy Virtue be my guide
Thy presepts I'll improve
Do thou ore all my ways preside
Reprove me and I'll Love
When first I knew thy Heavenly Mind
I felt the sacred Flame
[Of] Friendship rising in my Brest
[. . .] Darest not it proclame
But now Impatient of restraint

My Eyes Declare Its force
And Every friendly Look attests
From whence they take their siource.

{April 12, 1757}
Teusday A.M. 10. o'Clock.

I have had a smart Combat with Mr Ewing about our sex—he is
a man of good parts and Lerning but has mean thoughts of Women—
he began the dispute in this Manner. Speaking of Miss Boudanot I
said she was a sociable friendly creture. A Gentleman seting by
joined with me, but Mr Ewing says—*she and the Stocktons are full of
talk about Friendship and society and such stuff—and made up a Mouth
as if much disgusted*—I asked what he would have 'em talk about—
whether he chose they should talk about fashions and dress—*he said
things that they understood. He did not think women knew what Friendship
was. They were hardly capable of anything so cool and rational as friendship*—
(My Tongue, you know, hangs prety loose, thoughts Crouded in—
so I sputtered away for dear life.) You may Guss what a large field
this speach opened for me—I retorted several severe things upon
him before he had time to speak again. He Blushed and seemed
confused. The Gentleman seting by said little but when did speak
it was to my purpose and we carried on the dispute for an hour—
I talked him quite silent. He got up and said your servant and went
off—I dont know that ever I meet with one that was so openly and
fully in Mr Pop[e's] sordid scheam[2]—One of the last things that he
said was that he never in all his life knew or hear[d] of a woman
that had a little more lerning then [common?] but it made her proud
to such a degree that she was disgusfull [to] all her acquaintance.
P.M. Made two vissits—came home and found my Aaron very unwell
and a bad purging. The Bloudy-Flux is in Town which gives me
concern. Two Children have died of it and several more sick of it.

{April 13, 1757}
Wednsday. Mr Burr came home, brought company.

{April 14, 1757}
Thursday. Aaron better—

2. This would be the poet Alexander Pope. *DAB* 16:109–27.

{April 15, 1757}

Fryday Almost well, a good deal of Company.

{April 16, 1757}

Saturday. Exceding busy about Household affairs.

{April 17, 1757}
Sabbath Morn.

Unexpectedly Mr Spencer comes in. He preached all day and preachd Well—he is to settle at Jamaca on Long Island, Mr Bostwicks former Congregation. He is like to be settled much to his Mind and I hope will see much comfort for many years to come.

{April 18, 1757}
Monday

A day of much confusion and hurry, more company to dine, comers and goers constantly, and Lies by the Bushels and Cart Loads about our College—they think to overset it but the House is two large and strong for them—Mr Brainerd I hear has got a Son. These Boys are mighty things with the Men[3]—I am Weaning Aaron and he makes a great Noise about it so cant add.

{May 1, 1757}
Sabbath Eve, May the first

Tis almost a Fortnight sinc I have conversed with {you} but you have been the subject of many of my thoughts and remembred in my praiers—It would be two tedious for me to relate the reasons that you have been so neglected, but this you may always be sure of, that I cant pass you by one day no more then I can pass by my Food but when nesesity obliges.

The studients are generally returnd from their several Homes and I was highly delighted to observe the same solemn attention to the word, the same grave decent behaviour that appeared in them before the vacancy. It looks as if it would prove abiding—O! what a joyfull prospect does it afford. A large Class goes out into the World and almost all of them we have reason to hope truely Pious. Poor Peter Fanueil I fear will be ruined. [Half line deleted.] He was near the

---

3. John Brainerd's son, born April 11, 1757, was David Brainerd. He died September 11, 1758. Field, *Genealogy of the Brainerd Family,* pp. 285–86.

Kingdome of Heaven, [*two lines deleted.*] (This about Mr Brown Mr Burr says must not go for fear the Letter should be opened—tis the first that ever he made me scratch out—they dont stick a tall at opening private Letters.)

The College has meet with a great deal of trouble from the Enemies of jo[y] but it will turn out for the temporal as well as spiritual good of the society. This is already evident. We have lost but three and have got Ten for 'em, good exchange ant it. Some of 'em the Top of Philadelphia too.

{*May 2, 1757*}
Monday May 2

Gods judgments thretten on all hands. The oldest people we have amongst us cant remember such a changable Winter and cold backward spring—the Wheat in these parts is much hurt, some intirely ruined by the frequent heavings of the frost the Winter past. Things look dark all around but Blessed be god that any Light appears in the Middest of so great darkness—Last Week I saw a Consert for prayer published by our Reverend Fathers in Scotland, a proposal to spend an hour every Sabbath and Wednsday Morn from 7 to 8 o'Clock—It did me good to see it, and I am determined to comply as far as tis consistant with duty. I have heithertwo found assistance—I conclude you have seen the proposals—It gives great incouragement to see Gods people stired up to extreordinary prayer—Eve. A Gentleman from Philadelphia.

{*May 3, 1757*}
Teusday.

Fine Weather for the first day this spring—Company all the Morn and expecting more every minute.

{*May 4, 1757*}
Wednsday Eve 10. O'Clock

This poor Wicked missarable World! It requires mu[ch] [g]reater degrees of Grace to be Willing to Live then to Die—My paper is too short or I would add a few words altho tis late.

{*May 15, 1757*}
May 15. Sabbath Eve.

Long vacancies I am forced to make—last Week the Whole of it was filled with strangers from all parts and now I have three from

Newyork in the House—last Fryday arrived here Sister Lucy—I
need not tell you how glad I am to see her—This Week the synod
sets at about 6 miles di[s]tance, but I expect to have em most of
the time here.

{May 16, 1757}
Monday P.M.

All the Women in Princeton to see me and my Sister—hurried
a preparing for Company that is to come to morrow to the synod.

{May 17, 1757}
Teusday.

Sundry Minnisters to dine and a Whole Room full to Tea and
three to Lodge.

{May 18, 1757}
Wednsday Morn.

A Housefull to Breakfast, but all went before dinner—P.M. A
drove of Women strangers to Tea and must needs go to see the
College which I dont fancy—two to Lodge.

{May 19, 1757}
Thursday

An Army to Breakfast—I am quite sick with a pain in my Breast
Cold and bad Cough—10 O'Clock 4 Ladies and 4 Gentlemen, top
of Philadelphia call and want Mr Burr and me to go up to College
so we went and I am tired down and sick two—Mr Burr is sick
with a Cold, Sally with Worms and Lucy with the Headach so you
see what a poor pack of Crew we are as *the* Negro said.

{May 20, 1757}
Fryday Night

Last Night late came Mr Oliver and Lady which surprized us
excedingly for we did not expect em—My Sister is very sick. We
fear she has the small-pox—your dear Letters I cant get time to
read, [. . .] one sentence now and another an hour hence.

{May 22, 1757}
Sabbath Eve.

This Morn my Sister broke out very full with the small-pox—
We have removed her to a House of Mr Burrs about a mile off—it

has done her no hurt as we have reason to think. I just now heard she was very comfortable—I fear I have taken the infection. Yesterday she took a Vomit and I attended her which is said to be daingerous—O my dear, dear Friend pray for us, in petecular that Mr Burr may be preserved—I am almost sunk to the depths of Meloncholy at the possibility of Mr Burrs geting of it.

I have read all your dear kind friendly Letters but am so confused cant write anything upon them. Mr Olivers vissit is very short. They set out tomorrow morn—You need not be concernd about your Love to a sertain person for if you dont know that you Love, I know it and if he was to leve you, you would soon know it too.

Marry and be happy—God be with you and ever Bless you—perhaps this may be the last Letter you ever receive from me—But pray—pray ernestly that I may be fitted for Gods holy will and pleasure conserning me and mine and my dear Sister. I cant Write.

{May 23, 1757}

Monday morn—my Sister in a fine way.

You may get any Pictures you should like in your own House—I would have 'em glased [*glassed*]—the shade I like much and should send the mon[ey] but perhaps it may be as well to let it be until the fall when Mr Burr will sertainly go to Boston if alive, and you as sertainly come here if not Married—Mrs Oliver is a great friend of yours I assure you—she knows by somebody in Bos[ton] and of her, and your Aunt, of your diffeculties and pittys you excedingly, and says if you had a good opportunity to Marry you aught to Marry or you'll not live long but go as your Brother and Sister are gone. I cant add but my praiers and Wishes attend you always. My kindest regards to your and my friends, duty to Mr Prince in which Mr Burr joins as also to you.

From my dear friend your affectionate Friend

E. Burr

Dr. Madam

I read your proposals and your specimen of Mr Princes Psalms to the synod. All the Ministers present highly approved and did not doubt many would go off in their Congregations, tho they did not seem to incline to become subscrib[ers.] If they had come out before

Dr. Watts had been read in our Congregations, I believe they would have been almost universally read—Of this I shall say more when I come to Boston in the Fall. In mean Time let my Name be set down for ½ Doz.[4]—My hearty Thanks for Mr Princes Letter and most affectionate salutations to you all, conclude

yours most sincerely
A Burr

(No. 4th)

{May 24, 1757}
Princeton May 24. 1757

Dear Fidelia

I have sent by Mrs Oliver a heap of confused stuff. Perhaps you will with the help of your own ingenuity and good sense be able to finde out some of it—the rest had as good be buried in oblivion as not.

The Female Orator I admire excedingly. The Carracter and conduct of Emilla is truly Amiable and to be patterned after by all her sex—I cant shew it [to] Miss Boudanot for she Nurses my Sister—I could not get it coppied before Mrs Oliver left us but shall do it and send as soon as possible.

Mrs Olivers tarry was so short that I had not opportunity to talk with her so fully on the affair between Mrs Holland and you as I could wish. She had never heard anything of Mrs Holland but was astonished when I told her, and said she had thought her a good Woman but this was strange conduct—Mrs Oliver has a deep and affecting sense of your cituation. She is a quicksighted Woman and says she has seen enough her self to convince her who is to blame, and she thinks you the greatest pattern of patience and Prudence, or Matters would have been discovered to the World long ago. She could not have borne the 10 part of what you have gone throu'—She also says that your Carracter has suffered excedingly but the World begins to see and will soon know the truth. She has heard

---

4. Thomas Prince's psalms were published as *The Psalms, Hymns, and Spiritual Songs of the Old and New Testament. Faithfully Translated into English Metre. Being the New-England Psalm Book Revised and Improved. . . . With an Addition of Fifty Other Hymns* . . . (Boston, 1758).

it mentioned several times in Boston with *astonishment how they had been deceived.* They thought you had been much such an one as Mrs Holland represents but they perceive tis quite the revers—she is full with me that you aught not to tarry at home any longer. It is self Murther [*murder*], and were it not for the affair depending between you and Doctor Somebody, I should have contrived some way for your coming immediately, but I would not lay a straw in the way of your Comfortably settling your self for Life.

Mrs Oliver is of oppinnion with me *that you aught by no means to lay still and let Mrs Holland go on in her way* but talk with her and if she denies as I suppose she will, let her go (you being by) and contradict what she has said, and confess her fault to those persons to whome she has thus abused you—if she stands to what she has said (which she wont d[o]) put her upon proof, and ask her why she has never bee[n] good enough to tell you of your faults before she spread 'em behind your Back—But I need not direct you. Your own Prudence will direct you ten times better then I can—I never longed so to be with you in my Life—It appears to me I could do you some good, if not by adviseing, I might comfort and incourage and Chear you up a little. It seems to be some releaf to have one by that can only pit[y.] I cant help laughing to see you so concernd that you dont Love a sertain somebody—I can insure that part to the Gentleman.

{*May 25, 1757*}
Wednsday P.M.

Lucy yet in a fine way—Blessed be God I found More freedom at the hour of prayer then usual, and in petecular for you my dear— Your Circumstances lay heavy upon me, but this Morn found freedom to leve you with God—O my dear how able and willing is he to assist and comfort the afflicted—I must go this A.M. to vissit a Minnisters Wife that is in Town—You will wonder why she ant here but she has a Mother in Town or you may be sure she would be at our house.

{*May 28, 1757*}
Saturday.

My Sister is like to do better then we expected. Her Pock begins to turn—My Little Son very Ill.

{*June 1, 1757*}
Wednesday June 1 day.

Eve—a more Meloncholy day I carse [*scarce*] ever saw—I have reason to think Mr Burr has taken the small-pox and that in a surprizing way—O! how little signifies our care if God dont preserve.

There was a Little Dog down at the farmehouse that has lain in the room with my Sister almost constantly. Harry takes it in his Head to bring the Dog home in his arms. Mr Burr see him and plays with him, stroaking of him and made very free thinking no harm. After he had done so several times inquires whos Dog that was and how he came here. I asked the servants and found as I have told you—Is not this a strange accident—everybody says that if the infection can be carried he must have brought it—O my dear how shall I support under the distressing aprehensions of what may happen.

{*June 16, 1757*}
Thursday June 16.

Mr Burr has not taken the smallpox—O What shall I render to the Lord for this Instance of his Loving kindness and tender Mercies towards me, when I was ready to sink at the apprehension of what was only possible. How could I support under the Rod it self—O how good is our God! I hope I shall never forget this Mercy.

{*June 17, 1757*}
Fryday.

Mr Burr is going with me as far as Free[hold] to see Mr William Tennent and Lady—Good By till I come back.

{*June 19, 1757*}
Sabbath Eve Very hot.

We had a very pleasant Ride to Freehold and was much delighted with the Company of our good friends.

There has truly been a most Glorious work of God in that place, much the same Methods were used in conducting of it as here at the College. No appearance of Enthusiasm or affetation, in short, none of the imprudiences that prevailed last stir—I cant but hope God is about to vissit this Land in general. Mr Tennent thinks so.

{*June 20, 1757*}
Monday—Eve.

About 6 o'Clock P.M. We got my Sister home safe—O what a
Mercy that she was not carried in to the G[rav]e [ins]ted of being
brought home to us—[. . .] much affected with the goodness of
[God. Lucy] thinks she shall never forget the loving [kind]ness of
her God.

What an un[spea]kable Mercy that our famaly have all esc[ap]ed!
It calls for the highest gratitude and th[an]kfullness to our Good
and Mercyfull God.

{*June 21, 1757*}
Teusday Eve.

Been this P.M. to make a Wedding Vissit to a young New Married
Pair—the Woman has got a good Husband, and I hope he a good
Wife, but that I am not so sertain off—I cant help feeling a tender
Concern for new Married people, first because their Happiness much
depends on their Conduct to wards each other when first Married.
Now they begin to discouver that they are not perfect, and till now
most are apt to think that the party Beloved has no faults—It requires
some degree of prudence in a Woman that has been always used
with the greatest Complesance and as if she was absolute Monarch,
to be Gently blamed in some prety artfull Way let kn[o]w that He
is her Head and Governor—On the other hand the Husband has
need of his share of good Temper, When the Wife that he [has]
always seen in print grows Carles of her [. . .] seems more concernd
to appear decent befor[e any] body then her Husband—Each observes
the alte[rati]on. The Wife supposes His affections cooling, the Husband concludes she has more Respect for any[b]ody then him self—
and when it has gone thus far [yo]u may guss where it is like to
end.

Secondly (sermon Wise) I pitty them because most have no notion
of the new tryals that this new state must be incumbered with,
altho perhaps not so great as what they were exerscised with Whiles
single—yet they not expecting them, and not being experienced,
know not how to conduct but often grow Pevish, and gaul themselves
with the Chain which aught to be a silken Cord of Mutial Love,
and Tender sympathy and Affection.

Thirdly—The Greater part of the World have no sense of the Duties of this state, nor indeed that there is any duty in the case towards Each other—but alass how are the poor things Mistaken—All relative Duties are great, but this of the nearest and dearest Relation must sertainly be very great Indeed—God must help or we cant fulfill [a]ny one part of it—I might go on but ca[n]t add.

{June 22, 1757}

[W]ed[ns]day P.M. Vissited.

{June 23, 1757}

Th[u]rsday—a Publick fast—by order of synod.

Out all day. Hear[d] two sermons suited to the occasion of the day—but was interrupted by travillers and by an Ill turn My Sister had at Meeting.

{June 24, 1757}

Fryday. Company from Philadelphia.

{June 25, 1757}
Saturday.

A heap of folks to keep Sabbath with us, people that I never saw in my life—I dont like strangers on the Sabbath.

{June 26, 1757}
Sabbath

Out all day. Heard two sermons on the Nature and nesessity of the New Birth—*Marvil not that—I say unto you you must be Born again*—I think I never heard the subject handled so clearly.

{June 27, 1757}
Monday.

P.M. 2 o'Clock our strangers left us and at 3 o'Clock comes a Room full of new ones but only to spend the P.M. except one man that lodges with us—I cant never command my own time, tis a tryal—I am greatly concernd about your things that are here. I cant hear of any way to send them so as it will be safe to venture 'em—Mrs Oliver could not carry them on any account.

{June 28, 1757}
Teusday A.M. very busy—
P.M. Out on a Vissit and came home. Went to Bed sick.

{June 29, 1757}
Wedns-day.

Very sick so as to keep my Chamber all day.

{June 30, 1757}
Thursday.

Rode to Brunswick to see Mrs Brainerd and found the Ride of service—Mrs Brainerd is not like to recover but may continue some Months. She is in a strange way but it will lead to a Consumption in the End. Tis very affecting to see and hear her screeches.

I was at Mrs Bradleys. They are all well, Kitty in good spirits, and has heard from Mr Cary that you are going to be married to Doct Sp——, etc.[1] She is full of talk about it and wondered I had not heard of it—Mrs Donaldson is very large. She will not keep up long—Doct Cummings and Wife are just as before. She is very friendly.

{July 1, 1757}

Fryday. Came home and feel almost well.

{July 2, 1757}

Saturday. Very busy.

{July 3, 1757}
Sabbath P.M.

Mr Burr preached against Whoredom and never did a people need it more then this.

{July 11, 1757}
July 11.

Received a Letter from you dated July 4 by Post, full of affection and friendly concern—It was very refreshing to us indeed. I am sorry we hant wrote before that you might know of Gods goodness to us sinfull Worms of the dust, and rejoice with us, and help to bless and praise God for such distinguishing favours.

---

1. Mr. Cary was probably widower Richard Cary of Charlestown, Massachusetts. See note 2, Letter No. 13, above.

{ July 13–16, 1757}

Wednsday, Thursday, Fryday and Saturday, Busy a quilting. Mr Burr answered your Letter at the College and would not let me put in one Word because he Was affraid I should say two much, and I was so vexed that I had a good mind to have wrote a Whol[e] Letter my self and sent two.

{ July 17, 1757}
Sabbath

A.M. An Evangellical sermon—P.M.—against the sin of Drunkness which is also a crying abomination of this wicked place— Whoredom and Wine and new Wine take away the Heart—were the words of the Text.

{ July 18, 1757}
Monday P.M.

Made a *set, starched stiff Lazy Trifeling Wedding Vissit—did no good nor got any.* Come home more tired by half then if I had been hard at Work the Whole day—O the Nonsense of this World!

{ July 19, 1757}
Teusday—Budge and Budge.

{ July 20, 1757}
Wednsday.

Prepareing for examination which is next Week.

{ July 21, 1757}
Thursday July 21.

Good News, upon good news. I Congratulate you on the sucsess of the King of Prussia—O that we might be truly thankfull—I am interrupted.

{ July 25, 1757}
Monday July 25.

Mr Peter Smith and Lady from Newyork to keep examination with us—all in a bustle.

{ July 26, 1757}
Teusday A.M.

Comes Mr Tennent of Freehold and Wife, so you may think I cant write much—.

{ July 27, 1757}
Eve Wednsday.

A great Number of Gentlemen here, the schollars stood their examination Well. Two very handsome Orations delivered, etc.

{ July 28, 1757}
Thursday Morn.

Mr Smith and Wife set out for home—all our company gone or going except Mr Tennent and Wife—I am quite sick worried out of my life, and in a poor state of helth.

{ July 29, 1757}
Fryday Morn.

Mr Tennent left us and we are by our selves again.

P.M. 3 o'Clock. My Sister with Miss Sueky Shippen and some Ladies of the Town set out in the stage for Philadelphia.

{ July 30, 1757}
Saturday Morn 6 O'Clock.

Mr Burr and my Brother set out for Stockbridge and now I am perfectly alone and quite sick—How full of changes is the World. This Week past shews just what the World is, every day some remarkable change. 3 days ago my Famaly consisted of about 30. persons, so sudden is the transsison—I am alone in this great House. Every step I take sounds like a Bell. In short I am almost affraid to Walk for fear of disturbing this still house.

{ July 31, 1757}
Sabbath

The oldest Tutor preached well but not so well as I have heard him—after Publick exercises, the time I spent alone was comfortable.

{August 1, 1757}

Monday. Rode with a friend to see an New aquaintance about 3 miles off. Found 'em very pleasant agreable openhearted honest Farmers (I hope relegious two.) Such are some of the best people that the World raises.

{*August 2, 1757*}

Teusday P.M. Somme Quakers to vissit me that did not seem very stif but prety pleasant—had a Letter from my Sister. She is much pleased with Philadelphia, intends to tarry a fortnight.

{*August 3, 1757*}

Wednsday P.M. Company and I but poorly. Had a pleasant season alone this mor[n.]

{*August 4, 1757*}

Thursday. I am of the Mind that a journey will be nesessary for my helth. If so you may depend on seeing me in Boston. P.M. Received a Letter [pr?] Post Written by Mr Prince with his own hand. Mr Pembertons and Foxcrofts Names to it desireing a Minnister from these parts for Groten—who Mr Burr can send I know not—I was much disappointed that I had not one Word from you— I expect that you will be Married before you can receive this scraul.

{*August 5, 1757*}

Fryday—A Letter from Mr Peter Oliver. He says your affairs are concluded upon—May the Wise disposer of all events order that affair in Mercy is the continual desire and prayer of your ever affectionate E. Burr.

{*August 6, 1757*}

Saturday. Very exceding busy.

{*August 7, 1757*}
Sabbath.

Out all day but so dull in Body and soul that I could not give close attention which troubled me some but not enough.

{*August 8, 1757*}
Monday August 8.

A.M. A paquit from Stockbridge. They are all well and have heard of my Sisters recovery—My Father confirms the news that Mr Oliver wrote that your affairs only waited the last Ceremony.

P.M. A deal of company.

{August 9, 1757}
Teusday

A.M. Bad news from our Forts, but no worse then I have been
expecting for many weeks past[2]—tis a comfort that we are in the
hands of a just God who will order all right.

P.M. Rode out with a friend, made a vissit, came home tired and
long to see a Dear ———— , you know who. It seems to me he has
been gone a Month, and not two weeks yet by 3 days, but no more
of this. I know tis disagreable to you, so Ill think the rest to my
self—for I have none to speak to—goodnight.

{August 10, 1757}
Wednsday

I am almost distressed about my friends at Stockbridge—if the
Forts are taken they must quit all, and what will become of them
God only knows! All I can do at present is to pray for them—I am
glad Mr Burr is there to advise them in this time of distress.

P.M. A deal of company. I am but poorly—received two Letters
from Lucy. She wants to come home, begins to be weary of the
Town and longs to be at Princeton.

{August 11, 1757}
Thursday

I think to get a little Box made for your Gound and send it by
Cap Gibs, Rhode Island. I dont know what better to contrive. I
feel quite uneasy abut it.

{August 12, 1757}
Fryday P.M.

About Noon I was surprized by Mr Burrs coming home—My
friends are all well but under dreadfull apprehentions of the Enemy.
O that God would protect 'em and direct 'em. Mr Burr says they
heard the fireing at the Fort very plain. I feel quit sunk. It seems
as if this whole Land would be laid waist.

2. Esther had just heard about the siege of Fort William Henry on Lake George.
General Montcalm and his forces took the fort on the day Esther wrote this letter.

{August 14, 1757}
Sabbath

I think I never saw Mr Burr so sunk in my life as now. He preach'd all day suitable to the Meloncholy times. People were much affected—O that it might work some good amongst us.

I fully expect that this land is to tast of Persecution before the Glorious days begin and perhaps soon but I hope it will not last long before the Lord desends and takes the Kingdom into his own hands.

Satturday my Sister and Miss Suky returnd.

{August 15, 1757}
Monday

I wonder that you hant answered Mr Burrs Letters by the Post but perhaps you have and It has miscarried. Posts are very carless—P.M. Well our fort is given up as I expected but upon what terms there is no knowing. There is so many stories and now what hinders the French from driving down to Albany. Fort Edward is very Weak. It will be but play for the French to take that in their way to Albany—this is all my comfort that God Rules in the Armies of Heaven and amongst the inhabitence of the Earth.

{August 16, 1757}
Teusday. Not very well.

{August 20, 1757}
Saturday

Wednsday Thursday and Fryday very dull Weather. I not well, low spirited—P.M. Mr Symons come to keep Sabbath with us. My Sally is very sick with the Throat distemper and Worms. I am affraid she will not live.

{August 21, 1757}
Sabbath.

Sally is better but still a good deal of Fever—tis a very sickly time in this place. The inhabitance say the like was never known here.

{August 22, 1757}
Monday Mr Burr gone to Philadelphia with Mr Symmons—Sally better.

{*August 23, 1757*}
Teusday

Lucy has got an Humble servant come to see her, a young Minnister. How it will go I cant tell—P.M. 3 o'Clock Mrs Cummings two daughters came to tarry a day or two—4 O'Clock Vissited sick people until Night. Eve Miss Annis Boudanot very sick so Lucy is gone to tarry with her until she gets better.

{*August 31, 1757*}
Wednsday August 31. P.M. 4 O'Clock

Just now I received a Letter with a Black Seal but contained Blacker news. Governor Belcher is dead, died this Morn—the Righteous are taken away from the Evil to come—This is such a loss that we cant expect to have made up in a Governor—I feel quite sunk with this and other bad news. His Lordship is returning to Newyork and then Hallifax will be taken no doubt.

Eve—Mr Burr not returnd. Heavy news the Governors death will be to him.

{*September 1, 1757*}
Thursday Eve. Sept 1. 1757.

A.M. Mr Burr returnd in helth—O how good is God in preserving him in his goings out and his comings in. These mercies aught not to be forgotten by me.

Mr Burr is sent for to Preach the Governors Funeral Sermon—P.M. A deal of company.

{*September 2, 1757*}
Fryday morn Sept. 2 1757.

Just now heard that the Eastward scholars are going home so am set down to scratch a little more and Indeed I hant much to say only that I wish I cou[ld] seal my self up in this Letter and go to Boston wit[h]out any fuss and Noise about it—We seem ye[t] undetermined about Boston. If we do go we shall be at your House by the 2 Week in October, if n[ot] there by that time, shant go— I wish I knew whea[ther] you was Married or not but that I cant know so I had as good be easy.

Now about Sally and Aaron.

Sally has got prety hearty again, is not much of a Baby, affects to be thought a Wom[an]. Nothing she scorns more then to be told she is a Baby or Child. We are about sending her to school, but Mr Burr is expecting that she will pr[ove] a Numbhead, but for my part I think her abo[ut] Middling on all accounts—she grows thinner, [. . .] more shapeable. I have taken her to Meeting and s[he] behaves very well and can give a good account w[hat] Papa does there—she can say some of Doct Wa[tts] verses by heart and the Lords prayer and some other pr[ayers] but she is not over apt about the matter etc.

Aaron is a little dirty Noisy Boy, very different from Sally almost in every thing. He begins to talk a little, is very sly and mischevious. He has more spri[ghtliness] then Sally and most say he is handsomer, but not so good tempered. He is very resolute and requires a good Governor to bring him to terms—My Love to Miss Jenny. I hope she will not complain that I hant said no more about the Children.

I wish I could say somthing sert[ain] about Boston but Mr Burr is so very Meloncholy at the loss of our excellent Governor that he say he can[t th]ink one word about whether he shall go or not [b]ut tis my opinnion that we shall—I cant exp[ect] a better *Vacancy* nor indeed desire a better, for tis a good time of the year—perhaps next year this time I may be in *Circumstances,* etc.

Miss Lucy is gone to Newark, Miss Shippen I have with [me]— if you are not Married I depend on your com[ing] here before Winter. If we go, with us, if we dont per[haps y]ou would be willing to come with Mr Stockton who [w]ill be at Boston this fall for his helth—Mr Burr [w]rote to you by the Post and desired you would answer [by] the Post [*so*] that we might be better able to contrive o[ur] matters to advantage for we propose either to go or re[turn] [. . .] by Water as far as Road Island and perhaps it wo[uld] suit your circumstances better to return by Wat[er]—at present I am inclined to think that we sha[ll] go by Water and return by North-ampton, unless w[ord] from you to the contrary, so pray my d[ear] send word by the first Post after you receiv[e . . .] whether you are your own or at your own d[is]posal or have chose a Lord and Master to disp[ose] of you—I am concernd about the Female [. . . .] I asked my Brother for it but he forgot to give it, as I suppose, and he is not returnd with Mr Burr [*so* that] I cant get it till Commencement.

I think I hant told you that Mr Donaldson has [a] Daughter. They are much pleased with it I assure [you.]

Kitty told me when I was in Brunswick las[t] that Mr Cary had wrote her word that your affair Had droped throu, but I think it cant be true so tis [hard]ly worth mentioning.

I could add and add if I had time but am forced to [stop?] several Letters of busyness to Newyork and Philadel[phi]a to send this day.

Mr Burr joins me in Duty to your Honored par[ents] and Love to the Sisterhood as if petecularly mentioned. Love Miss Jenny and you aboundantly—I am [and] ever shall be your sincere Friend.

E. Burr

Related Correspondence

The following thirteen documents are letters written to, by, or about Esther Edwards Burr. The first several were written before Esther began her journal, the last one shortly after her death. We have included these letters, most of which are familial, because each adds something to our understanding of the daily life and spiritual concerns of this latter-day Puritan woman. The location of individual letters is indicated at the end of each headnote.

This first letter comes from Aaron Burr's Newark letterbook and is addressed to Sarah Prince in Boston. Eighteenth-century women and men sometimes kept drafts of letters in letterbooks and copied them over to send them. The actual letter has been lost. Because it is a draft and therefore difficult to read, we have expanded abbreviations and conjectured more frequently than elsewhere in this text. Aaron probably wrote at such length here because Esther was too sick to continue her journal for Sarah. (AND)

{February 8, 1753}

Mrs Sally our much esteemed and dear Friend

Your dear Burrissa, my best beloved—has been confind with a lingring Fever for about 2 Months—It intermits but seldom if ever goes clear off—We have been apprehensive of an Hectick—And am not yet without Fears it may issue in that—You may guess the Anxiety I often feel on her acct.—The Thoughts of parting with so dear a Companion are distressing beyond What I can express—I find it a hard Thing to be wholy resigned—We have of late taken Encouragement from the Advice of a very skillfull Phisician in these Parts—but have but just begun to use his Means—God is mixing Mercy with Affliction—she is in better spirits than usual in Illness and is very comfortable to her Friends and in some good Measure to her self—sets up the bigger Part and sometimes all Day—looks [. . .] pleasant and is cheerfull—but is not able to write—I do therefore in her Name with much gratitude acknowledge your obliging Favor of Dec. 9 ie. (No. 2) which meet with an hearty Wellcome

and was very refreshing—It has given us a good Deal of agreable
[. . . .]

The Imprint was especialy edyfying—To spill the spleen, to raise
the spirits and invigorate animal Nature—it exceeds the Prescriptions of the best Phisicians.

However we humbly conceive you made a small slip of the
Pen in the 2d Inference—and for *Maid* we read *married,* as it best
[. . .] up the [. . .] with the forgoing Inference and makes the
sense more clear and intelligible. It will then read thus, never let
me infer that Widows are [never easy?] (much less maids). 2: Therefore tis better to be married. This makes it read much better—We
therefore humbly propose that it may stand so corrected in all future
Editions—and That to make your Imprint compleat you would be
pleased to add a [Word] of [example] and [exhortation] to those
that are not married and a Word of Warning against the Danger
of Old-Maidism—As to your 4. Inference: about Women's loosing
their Brains upon marrying, we are willing it should stand as it is.
But it [. . .] a Word of Encouragement to those Ladies that cant
find Gentlemen of equal Brains to themselves to marry however, in
Hopes there will be a Ballance afterward.

As to the last Query—Whether Men's increase in Proportion to
the Decrease of the Women's I beg leave to reply—That if the
Gentleman that marries you don't find his to increase Twill be a
plain Evidence he had none before.

We shall be much better able to write you News after you have
made a visit [which] we shall still request and plead [. . .] with
the Hopes of.

Gov. Belcher is well—The College is fixed at Princeton—They
have secured the Trustees 200 Acres of Wood land. [10?] Acres for
College and President's House and £1000 [promised?]—But
[whether?] we shall get money sufficient to build with is uncertain.

All Communication between us and Stockbridge is cut off this
winter—we expect Sister Lucy in Jan.

I need not tell you how much My Wife values your Friendship
and Correspondence: how earnestly she desires you to write every
Opportunity and how desirous she is to answer your Letters tho
unable—Be assured that the more frequent and longer your Letters
are the more obliging—And I doubt not your generous Disposition

will give you a Pleasure in communicating where you have no Hopes of equal Returns.

We reject your Excuse for not visiting as insufficient—And insist upon it—That it belongs to you to begin and lead in a Conversation that will be improving—God has qualified you for it and you ought not to let your Talents lie hid in a Napkin.

Your fruitfull Invention and good sense will furnish you with suitable Matter for profitable Discourse and ability to Manage it in such Manner as will be engaging and edifying to all that hear you.

Who shall begin a Reformation in these degenerate Times; What young Lady could [appear?] in it with so good a Grace as you whose [. . .] for Duty and good sense is so universaly establisht—how happy might you be [. . .] improving the young Ladies of your Acquaintance with a Tast for a Conversation that would both instruct and delight—And making them ashamed of wasting [. . .] they might no longer wast away their precious Moments in such Frights as [*not*] only [enamour?] the Fancy but distract and corrupt the Heart—The kind Influences of this might reach far and wide, even to Generations yet unborn. [Dare?] to be singularly, I will add, publickly good.

Accept of our best Regards and good Wishes and present the same with all Gratitude and Respect to Mr. Prince and Madam.

I am, Dear Mrs Sally, your much obliged Friend and affectionate [. . .] servant.

This is Sarah Prince's response to Aaron Burr's letter of February 8, 1753. Like Aaron, Sarah was primarily concerned with Esther's lingering illness, but she also used the opportunity Aaron provided to discuss what seems to have been an essay she had printed for circulation among her acquaintances. (Yale)

Boston the 27. of March 1753.
Reverend and Honored etc., etc., etc., Sir.

You have so highly obliged me by your very agreable favour of February 8—I account my self bound to return you my thanks in a more imediate manner than ever before; and you may be assured I shall aim to do it in the best manner I am capable; my powers will be stretch'd to the utmost, and you will see the farthest reach of that invention you have pass'd so pretty a compliment on.

The account you have given me of the Languishing Illness of one of the dearest and the lovelyest of friends is very melancholly tho' not surprizing to me; tis what I have presaged [. . .] her last visit, a *presage partly* founded on what with the tenderest Concern I observed then; *partly* on an observation I have often *seen* verified and may add *thrice have felt* viz,

All more than common menaces an End.
A Blaze betokens brevity of Life.
                                        Young[1]

Indeed Dear Sir I feel a painfull simpathy with you and wou'd fain strive with you in ardent suplications to the *Father of Mercies* that this dear Enjoyment may yet be continued to you, to me, to all, that know how to value her. Oh! that kind heav'n wou'd spare this one comfort to me is the sincerest language of my heart. The news come's the more heavily *now* as the season is just revolv'd when *My dearest delight* was first confined by her last sickness: the circumstances of that distressing time are brought afresh to mind, and my heart is even now bleeding at the remembrance.[2]

That I have a real affection for your dear Lady I doubt not you are fully sensible, what the Qualities are which have engaged it I am not able to describe;

Was I possest of that fine art,
Which chaste Urania does impart;
I wou'd in gentle numbers tell,
What graces in Burrisa dwell.

But oh! my genius is not form'd,
In pleasing lines by friendship warm'd;
For while I strive her worth to paint,
My thoughts prove low my language faint.

And to you who know her it wou'd be superfluous to attempt it.
    If I am guilty of a mistake in the peice you mention I am willing

1. Most likely British poet Edward Young (see note 5, Letter No. 13, above). The three deaths Sarah was alluding to here were those of her siblings (see note 16, Letter No. 9, above).
    2. Sarah was referring here specifically to her sister Mercy Prince, who died in 1752.

to stand corrected by any of my Friends, more especially by so masterly a pen as Mr Burr's. But under favour I honestly think you have rather *Marr'd* than *Mended* my performance, and asking your pardon, I shou'd think you a very indifferant Preacher did you manage every subject as you have done this. I can by no means consent to the alterations proposed nor can I see [. . .] propriety in them for the Inferances were deduced from a Matter of Fact relating to a *Widow* not a *Maid;* but to convince you of the defferance I pay your judgement, I have made an edition and enclose a coppy of the 2nd Edition. They are so well aprov'd of here that there are but a few to be had, and you must allow the people in the *court end* of this polite town to be good judges.

That part of your letter in which you have given a *faint* scetch of my character is really fine—and since you have discovered what I never knew before; that I have an assemblage of excellent qualities I don't know but I shall alter my conduct, and go about to reform the World, and teach the Ignorant Ladies of Boston things they never heard of—but I must postpone this till I have printed your Letter for if they ⟨ . . . ⟩ don't see it attested by you they will never believe it tho' I tell them ever so often—for you have the happiness to be the first and the only person that know it—I will venture to affirm there is not a single person in Boston that has penetration enough to think as you do.

Mr Dummer has perused the Charter and has one of the peices you sent.[3] I am glad to hear of any thing done in favour of your Society. I wish with all my heart I had a thousand pound or two to give it, but you know wishes are easier form'd than gratuities bestow'd.

I am now so far recovered that I have been down stairs once and my Father and Mother have ventured to leave me *alone* while they are attending the Ordination of Mr Badger which is now solemnizing in *our Church.* He is to be minister of the English and Indian Church at Natick—a Gentleman much approv'd of by good judges—such

3. Possibly William Dummer, son of Jeremiah and Ann (or Hannah) Atwater Dummer, and widower of Catherine Dudley Dummer. Although he had formerly served as both lieutenant governor and acting governor of Massachusetts, William was semiretired from public life. He did, however, still hold a seat on the Provincial Council. Raimo, *Biographical Directory,* pp. 138–39.

as Dr Sewall, Mr Secretary, Mr Cary etc. I have no knowledge of him myself, but it gives me joy when I hear of a faithfull Labourer going to Work in My Lords Vineyard[4]—Mr Adams, a Gentleman of a Good Character has a Unanimous Call at Roxbury[5]—Mr Moody of York died last week.[6]

My Father and Mother have charged me with their Cordial Salutations to your whole self tenderly resenting the affliction you are call'd to bear—Miss Jenny is well, and I have the pleasure to say grows in knowledge and judgement—I have not seen her these 5 days, her Grandmamma lies at the point of Death which obliges her to be there.

You are quite right in saying I take a pleasure in communicating. I have a generous soul which prompts me to endeavor your improvement in hopes you will answer the pains I have bestowed on you—now my Invention fails—my stock is quite exhausted and I must rest a twelvemonth in order to get recruited. And you will need an anodyne to compose your tired spirits: after which it will be a part of your Litany "from such Letters Good etc." May I be

4. Stephen Badger, son of Mary Noseitor and Stephen Badger of Charlestown, was ordained at Boston's Old South Church the day Sarah wrote this letter. He had been preaching to the Natick Indians since 1751. In September 1753 he married Abigail Hill, daughter of Prudence Hancock and Abraham Hill of Cambridge. Many years after his death, Harriet Beecher Stowe drew on his life for the character Parson Lothrop in *Old Town Folks.* Joseph Sewall was Sarah's father's colleague at Old South Church. He was the son of the well-known diarist Samuel Sewall and Hannah Hull Sewall. Joseph's spouse was Elizabeth Walley Sewall, daughter of John and Bethiah Eyre Walley. For Richard Cary, see note 2, Letter No. 13, above. Sibley 12:104–08; 5:376–93.

5. Amos Adams, son of Jemima Morse and Henry Adams, was called to Roxbury's First Parish church in February 1753 and accepted the position in May. Sarah's father took part in his ordination four months later. In October 1753 Amos married Elizabeth Prentice, daughter of Henry and Elizabeth Rand Prentice of Cambridge. Sibley 8:178–86.

6. Minister Joseph Moody of York, Maine, died on March 19 or 20, 1753. Since the death of his wife, Lucy White Moody, in the late 1730s, many of his neighbors had considered him mentally unbalanced. He continued to preach occasionally in his father's former church, however, and counted among his friends several prominent New England ministers, including Jonathan Edwards. He was the son of the Reverend Samuel and Hannah Moody. Sibley 6:259–62.

allow'd after all this to add, that

> I am very respectfully your most humble
> servant
>
> Fidelia

If there shou'd be a remarkable alteration for the worse, I earnestly beg you to write me by the post. I shall account the charge a very triffle. If she remains Ill till May I shall use my utmost endeavors to be with her. But if you have a hopefull prospect of her recovery pray let me know it by the first opportunity; and dispense with my coming this spring. My extream Illness prevented my sending for the Picture—and now Mr Walley sends me word he must ship it.[7] It is grievous to [. . .] that I have not seen it since October.

Jonathan Edwards, who was also deeply concerned about Esther at this time, wrote the following letter to advise his daughter on both her spiritual and physical health. His postscript contains Sarah Edwards's remedies for her daughter's illness. (BPL)

Stockbridge March 28. 1753.

Dear Child,

We are glad to hear that you are in any respect better but concerned at your remaining great Weakness. I am glad to see some of the Contents of your Letter to your Mother; and particularly that you have been enabled to make a Free-will-offering of your self to God's service, and that you have experienced some inward divine Consolations under your affliction, by the extream weakness and distressing Pains, you have been the subject of. For these you ought to be thankful, and also for that unwearied kindness and tender Care of your Companion, which you speak of. I would not have you think that any strange Thing has happen'd to you in this affliction: 'Tis according to the Course of Things in this World, that after the worlds smiles, some great affliction soon comes. God has now given

---

7. We think Mr. Walley was John Walley, brother of Elizabeth Walley Sewall (see note 4, Sarah Prince to Aaron Burr, above) and spouse of Elizabeth Appleton Walley. Since 1747 he had been a minister in the South Church in Ipswich, Massachusetts. Sibley 9:450–60.

you early and seasonable warning, not at all to depend on worldly Prosperity. Therefore I would advise, ⟨ . . . ⟩ if it pleases God to restore you, to lot upon no Happiness here. Labour while you live, to serve God and do what Good you can, and endeavour to improve every dispensation to God's Glory and your own spiritual good, and be content to do and bear all that God calls you to in this wilderness, and never expect to find this world any thing better than a wilderness. Lay your Account to travel through it in weariness, Painfulness, and Trouble, and wait for your Rest and your Prosperity 'till hereafter where they that die in the Lord rest from their Labours, and enter into the joy of their Lord. You are like to spend the rest of your Life (if you should get over this Illness) at a great distance from your Parents; but care not much for that. If you lived near us, yet our Breath and yours would soon go forth, and we should return to our dust, whither we are all hastening. 'Tis of infinitely more Importance to have the Presence of an heavenly Father, and to make Progress towards an heavenly Home. Let us all take care that we may meet there at last.

As to means for your Health, we have procured one Rattle-snake, which is all we could get. It is a medicine that has been very serviceable to you heretofore, and I would have you trie it still. If your stomach is very weak and will bear but little, you must take it in smaller Quantities. We have sent you some Ginseng. I should think it best for you to make Trial of that various ways: trie stewing it in water, and take it in strength and Quantity as you find suits your stomach best. You may also try steeping it in wine, in good madera or Claret; or if these wines are too harsh, then in some good white wine. And whether you stew or steep it, you had best to slice it very thin, or bruise it in an Iron mortar. And for a Cordial take some spices steep'd in some generous Wine that suits your Taste, and stomach. And above all the Rest, use riding in pleasant weather; and when you can bear it, Riding on Horse-back; but never so as to fatigue you. And be very careful to avoid taking Cold. And I should think it best pretty much to throw by doctors, and be your own Physician, ⟨ . . . ⟩ hearkening to them that are used to your Constitution.

I desire that Mr. Burr and you would be frequent in counselling Timmy as to his soul-Concerns.

0 ve

0 ve

0 ve

0 ve.

Commending you to God, before whom we daily remember you in our Prayers, I am

your affectionate Father
Jonathan Edwards.

P.S.
Your mother would have you use a conserve of Raisins; A Pound of good sugar to a Pound of Raisins, after they are ston'd. Mix with it, nutmeg, mace, Cinnamon, Cloves, ground in a spicemill, with some orange-Pill; one Nutmeg to half a Pound of Conserve, and the other spices in the same Quantity. Take a little as suits your stomach, in the morning, and an Hour before dinner, and in the after-noon. ⟨ . . . ⟩ The same spices and orange Pill to be put into your spiced wine. But when you take this, you must omit taking the wine. The only danger we apprehend in these things is that possibly the heat of 'em may raise a Fever; therefore you must observe the operation of them as to that. And when you drink your spiced Wine you may mix some water with it to abate the Heat of it—Your mother has also an Inclination that you should sometimes try a Tea made of the Leaves of Robins Plantain, If it be known at Newark by that name; she says she has found it very strengthening and comfortable to her in her weakness.

The Family all unites in their Love to you.

———————

This letter was written later that year by the recovered Esther Burr to her nineteen-year-old sister, Mary Dwight, who lived in Northampton with her husband, Timothy, and infant son, Timothy, Jr. Esther's opening remarks suggest some of the tension that existed between her and the Dwights. (AND)

———————

Newark Decembr the 2. 1753.

Dear Sister
I much wonder that we never have any Letters from you. I am sure you have some oppertunities if you were desposed to improve them—if it is but one line just to tell whether you are dead or alive, it would be much better than nothing. But perhaps you dont think any thing abot us—tho I cant think so of you in earnest—I am throu the goodness of God in avery comforttable state of helth—I suppose more Fleshey an Fresh than ever you saw me in your life.

Tho just now I have a very bad cold and cough[1]—You dont know nor cant think how much I want to see you—do pray send me word whether you dont think of coming into the Jersys next spring—I want to hear what you are adoing at Northhampton—I hear you are about to settle Mr Hooker, but I dont know how true it is.[2] I wonder you cant send abody word what you are about—you might go to England and back again before we should hear one word of it—I wonder if your House is finished, and a hundred other shuch things. Mrs Sarah Prince is come to winter with me, tho no[w] she is in Newyork—they are in a sad jumble there. I suppose you have heard before this time that Mr Commins is dismised and Mr Pemberton is like to leve them for Boston—I have not much news to tell you but I tell all I can think of—Mrs Brainerd has got a fine Daughter[3]—I have been to Princeton this fall and am much pleased with the place—I wish Mr Dwight had a good settlement there insted of Northampton—O I had like to have forgot it—I hear Mr Dwight is made Colonel—I wish him joy[4]—Mr Burr is well, joyns with me in Affectionate regards to you and Brother, and Humble service to Colo' Dwight and his Wife—Wishing you all the comforts of this Life, and the blessings of another I remain your ever affectionate and Loving Sister.

Esther Burr

PS Lucy and Timo' send their Love. Pleas to give my service to Mr Mather and to all other friends that enquire after me[5]—Adieu— E B.

1. Esther was in a "Fleshey" way at this time because she was pregnant with her daughter Sally, who was born five months later on May 3, 1754.

2. John Hooker succeeded Jonathan Edwards as minister of the Northampton church on December 5, 1753. He was the son of John and Mary Hart Hooker and, after 1755, the husband of Sarah Worthington Hooker. Apparently the new minister and his family got on well with the Northampton congregation, for they lived for many years in the King Street parsonage vacated by the Edwardses in 1752. Dexter 2:254–56.

3. Mrs. Brainerd's daughter was Sophia Brainerd. See note 13, Letter No. 11, above.

4. This Mr. Dwight was Mary Dwight's father-in-law, Timothy. See note 25, Letter No. 9, above.

5. Probably Dr. Samuel Mather, son of Dr. Samuel and Abigail Grant Mather, and husband of Martha Holcomb Mather. Samuel had been a physician in Northampton for many years and had been a loyal supporter of Jonathan Edwards during his prolonged dispute with his congregation. Dexter 1:330.

Lucy Edwards's letter from Stockbridge to Mary Dwight in Northampton in August 1754 reveals more about Esther's and Mary's relationship. Seventeen-year-old Lucy spent much of her time in one or the other of her sisters' households. (AND)

{August 20, 1754}

Dear Sister

Your kind Letter I receiv'd by my Brother Parsons, which was very acceptable to me.[1] It is true I did think it somthing hard that you wrote so seldom, and I began to think that I was quite burdensome to you with my Letters. But since you let me know they are not so you may be sure of having them very often as heretofore.

We none of us tho't that you would willingly be the cause of uneasiness betwen Sister Burr and any of us, but we did'nt know but you might ignorantly by not knowing how Little able she was to bear to have any body say any thing as tho they did'nt like her way of marrying. You know she never could bear pestering very well, but I think she grows worse about it if that be possible than ever, so we must take care what we say.

We never till last week heard of your Circumstances, which is that you are like to increase your family.[2] As to my coming to Northampton this winter, my mother says she shall leave it to your choice (as she concludes you will want some of us this winter) whether she comes or I. She says that you know she cant stay a great while if she should come, for my father will not be willing, and she says if I go I shall be with you as long before hand as you please and sometime afterward. Now my mother says if you choose she should come under these Circumstances rather than I, she will come, for she knows father will be willing she should go if she dont stay too long. Mother would be Glad if you would send word as soon as you can which of us you would have come, and how long before you think you shall want any of us.

---

1. Brother Parsons was Elihu Parsons, a native of Northampton who married Esther's sister, Sarah Edwards, in 1750. The couple followed Sarah and Jonathan Edwards to Stockbridge in 1752. Jones, *Stockbridge,* pp. 152–53.

2. Mary Dwight was pregnant with Sereno Edwards Dwight. See note 4, Letter No. 12, above.

You desire to know who Sister Burrs Child looks like. My mother says she never was a judge who babies look like when they are so young, but people at Newark she says some of them said that it looked one part of the face like the father and tother part like the mother and some that it look'd very much like me. Mother says she believes it will have black eyes for it had such Coloured eyes as her Children us'd to have when so young. She says also that it was not handsome when it was born but began to gro[w] handsomer before she came away. I intend the next time that I write to Sister Burr to ask her all about her little Sally and then I will tell you. We are all thro' the goodness of God moving about tho my mother is not quite so well as Common, And father has not had any fit of the feaver and ague since I wrote to you last, but is quite weak yet and gains strength very slowly.

Sister Parsons's Little Esther is better tho' she is very weak yet.[3] We are very sorry to hear of your being so troubled with the teeth ach and other Difficulties as you say you have been. Mr Searls is gone from us and has been for above a fortnight and is going upon Long Island for his health.[4]

I hope you will write by the bearer of this if you have any time to write a few lines if no more.

My Father and mother and all of us join in Love to Mr Dwight and your self.

From you affection[ate]
Sister
Lucy Edwards
Stockbridge Augt the 20th 1754.

PS Mother says she would not have you be discouraged, but hope in a good God who is able to carry you thro' all that is before you.

3. Two-year-old Esther was the daughter of Esther's sister, Sarah Parsons, and Elihu Parsons. Young Esther recovered from this illness but died when she was about twenty-two. See note 1, Lucy Edwards to Mary Dwight, above.

4. This was minister John Searle, a frequent guest in the Edwards household. The son of James and Mary Searle, he spent his early years in Northampton and probably studied theology with Jonathan Edwards. His health was a recurrent problem, and he was at this time without a church. In 1759 he became pastor of a Stoneham, Massachusetts, congregation, where he also worked on the posthumous publication of some of Jonathan Edwards's writings. His spouse was Hephzibah Dunbar Searle from Stoughton, Massachusetts. Dexter 2:53–55.

My parents send their regard[s] to the Col and his wife.

L.E.

Here Esther Burr shared news with her sister Lucy about family, friends, and the garden, along with her chagrin that her brother Timothy, then a student at the College, had decided not to lodge with her. Esther's daughter Sally was six months old at the time. (Princeton)

(No 6)
Newark Novbr, 4. 1754.

Dear Lucy

I received yours No 8 by Mr Burr. I am very glad you are with Sister Dwight at this time (I think more glad than if you had come here, which I had some hopes of when I heard of the rupture at Stockbridge)[1] for I realy believe she wants you more than I do tho' I have nobody with me nor have had since Commencement, tho' throu mercy I have my helth as well as ever I had in my life or I could not possibly get a long in any shape. But you know there is nobody to have. *Girls* are very scarce for all are *Ladys* now a days.

I wrote you a letter whiles Mr Burr was gon which I suppose you have not yet received. I enclosed it in one to my Mother and sent it to Stockbridge, and when I wrote it I had forgot that I had wrote by Mr Badger, and I beleive the bigger part of it is for substance the same with that Mr Badger carried.[2] Only this I remember, I wrote somthing about the Chince which I have not yet got for the reasons there mentioned, but I shall get it soon, that it may be ready to go by Pomroy. Mr Murry could not carry it if I had it.

I wish you would send me word whether you have received all my No [*numbers*] or not. Timo' went to Princeton last week, he will write you about it I suppose. He is going out of the house I this Morn perceive, tho he has said nothing about it to me, but only in general when Mr Burr was gon, what if he should, what should I think of it, should I be displeased, and so on. I hope he has a good desighn in it and wish it may be for his good, but indeed *tiss very hard*. I can hardly bare it, but I must for I promised my Mother when she was here that I would not oppose it if he desired it again.

----

1. For the "rupture at Stockbridge," see note 20, Letter No. 9, above.
2. Probably Jonathan Badger. See note 22, Letter No. 9, above.

She said she thought twas best I should not. But only think of it, *No Brother! No Sister! but he* not here and he not ⟨ . . . ⟩ live with me, is it not hard! I beleive I should not consent if I had not given my word. I expect it will set all the Town a talking. Tis a pety, for now they are prety still.

It is for no dislike he says to anybody, or anything, but purely for his own advantage. He proposes to live with Mr Duffield at Justis Ogdens. You will not wonder if you see many blunders for I write Rocking the Cradle. By the way people say Sally looks much like you, dont you want to see her?

I have no news to tell you, I think. O yes I have! Miss Elizabeth Eaton is like to be married at RoadIsland, ant you glad? Now I think of another pice of News. Joseph Woodruffs Wife has got a fine Son.[3] One thing brings another, I thought I had no news. Mrs Sergent is like to have a Child, pray what do you think of this? I know you will laugh.

Now I write with Sally in my arms for I am resolved to write. Loyer Ogdens Wife lately Layin with Twins, two Daughters and lost em both.

Perhaps you may loose that Letter I sent by the way of Stockbridge so I will tell you what Mrs Cuming said about the Chince. She says the Brown Chinces wash all out in a little time. Kittys and Pollys did so and they were sorry they got such.[4] Now if I could hear from you before I get it I should feel easyer.

I am exceding glad to hear that Pinty and Betty are at Northampton. I hope they will not go to Stockbridge till the dainger is quite over. I wish I had some of em here with me. Give my very kind love to em, tell em I think a great deal about them, and long to see them.[5]

3. Anne Hunloke, who married Joseph Woodruff, son of Elizabeth Ogden and Samuel Woodruff (see note 14, Letter No. 9, above) earlier that year, gave birth to Hunloke Woodruff on October 23, 1754. In 1757 Anne died, and her husband's death followed twelve years later. Their son became a physician, after graduating from the College of New Jersey in 1772. McLachlan, pp. 89–90.

4. Kitty Bradley and Polly Banks. See notes 16 and 25, Letter No. 10, above.

5. For Esther's youngest sister Betty, see note 5, Letter No. 14, and note 5, Letter No. 19, above. Pinty was Esther's youngest brother, four-year-old Pierpont. Two years after the death of his parents in 1758, Pierpont was living in the household of his brother Timothy and Rhoda Ogden Edwards, where he was raised with Esther's children, Sally and Aaron, Jr. Pierpont became a Connecticut lawyer and politician. He married Frances Ogden of Elizabethtown in 1769. McLachlan, pp. 637–42.

I can add no more, but my very kind regards to all enquiring friends, and a deal of Love to your self.

From very dear Sister, your most affectionate,

Esther Burr

I find you are still of the mind not to come to see us till we get to Princeton. In my Letter by Stockbridge I tell you not to shew my Letters to Mr Dwight, and you must tell me that you will not.

As soon as Sister Dwight is abed contrive I should know it for I feel much concernd about it. I hope Mother will be with her.

We have had a very warm fall. We had string Beans till the middle of last week and of the same vines that were planted last May. A few days ago I had six sorts of flours in the garden and court-yard [so] that it looked like sumer. And in two days more should have pinks blown [bloom] the second time. The bigest part of people go to meeting without their Clokes yet.

Why did not you write to me by Murry. You cant write two often, nor two long.

Sir Hait is got a preaching.[6] You dont know how smart Timo' looks with his gound and New Coat. I think there is not one in College looks so smart and genteel.

The following is an extract from a letter, now lost, written by Esther Burr to her mother, Sarah Edwards, after Aaron Burr's death. It was dated October 7, 1757, and has been reprinted in Dwight, *Edwards*, pp. 566–67.

No doubt, dear madam, it will be some comfort to you to hear, that God has not utterly forsaken, although he has cast down. I would speak it to the glory of God's name, that I think he has, in an uncommon degree, discovered himself to be an all-sufficient God, a full fountain of all good. Although all streams were cut off, yet the fountain is left full. I think I have been enabled to cast my care upon him, and have found great peace and calmness in my mind, such as this world cannot give nor take. I have had uncommon freedom, and nearness to the throne of grace. God has seemed

---

6. Benjamin Hait (see note 15, Letter No. 10, above) had just graduated from the College and had been assigned to preach at the Forks of the Delaware.

sensibly near, in such a supporting and comfortable manner, that I think I have never experienced the like. God has helped me to review my past and present mercies, with some heart-affecting degree of thankfulness.

I think God has given me such a sense of the vanity of the world, and uncertainty of all sublunary enjoyments, as I never had before. The world vanishes out of my sight! Heavenly and eternal things appear much more real and important, than ever before. I feel myself to be under much greater obligations to be the Lord's than before this sore affliction. The way of salvation, by faith in Jesus Christ, has appeared more clear and excellent; and I have been constrained to venture my all upon him; and have found great peace of soul, in what I hope have been the actings of faith. Some parts of the Psalms have been very comforting and refreshing to my soul. I hope God has helped me to eye his hand, in this awful dispensation; and to see the infinite right he has to his own, and to dispose of them as he pleases.

Thus, dear madam, I have given you some broken hints of the exercises and supports of my mind, since the death of him, whose memory and example will ever be precious to me as my own life. O, dear madam! I doubt not but I have your, and my honoured father's prayers, daily, for me; but, give me leave to entreat you both, to request earnestly of the Lord, that I may never despise his chastenings, nor faint under this his severe stroke; of which I am sensible there is great danger, if God should only deny me the supports, that he has hitherto graciously granted.

O, I am afraid I shall conduct myself so, as to bring dishonour on my God, and the religion which I profess! No, rather let me die this moment, than be left to bring dishonour on God's holy name. I am overcome—I must conclude, with once more begging, that, as my dear parents remember themselves, they would not forget their greatly afflicted daughter, (now a lonely widow,) nor her fatherless children. My duty to my ever dear and honoured parents, and love to my brothers and sisters.

From, dear madam,
Your dutiful and affectionate daughter,
Esther Burr.

After her husband's death, Esther Burr also wrote this letter to her father, Jonathan Edwards. (AND)

To my Ever Honored Father—

Princeton Novr 2. 1757.

Honored Sir

Your most Affectionate comforting Letter by my Brother Parsons was excedingly refreshing to me, altho' I was somthing damped by hearing that I should not see you untill spring; but tis my comfort in this disappointment as well as under all my afflictions that God knows what is best for me and for his own glory—perhaps I lotted two much on the Company and conversation of such a near and dear affectionate Father and Guide—I cant doubt but all is for the best and I am sattisfied that God should order the affair of your removal as shall be for his Glory what ever comes of me.

Since I wrote my Mothers Letter God has carried me throu new tryals and given new supports—My little Son has been sick with [the] slow Fever ever since my Brother left us, and has been brought to the Brink of the Grave but I hope in mercy God is bringing off him back again—I was innabled to Resighn the Ch[ild] (after a severe strugle with Nature) with the gre[at]est freedom—God shewed me that the Child w[as] not my own but His, and that he had a right to recall what he had lent when ever he thought fit, and I had no reason to complain or say God was hard with me. This silenced me. But O how good is God! He not only kept me from complaining but comforted me by ennabling me to offer up the Child by Faith, I think if ever I acted Faith. I saw the fullness there was in Christ for little Infants, and his willingness to accept of such as were offered to him—suffer little Children to come unto me and forbid them not, were comforting words—God also shewed me in such a lively manner the fullness there was in himself of all spiritual Blessings, that I said altho all streams were cut off yet so long as my God lives I have enough—He enabled me to say that altho' thou slay me yet will I trust in thee—In this time of tryal I was lead to enter into a renewed and explissit Covenant [wi]th ⟨ . . . ⟩ God ⟨ . . . ⟩ in a more solemn manner then ever before with the greatest freedom and delight, after much self examminnation and prayer I did give my self and Children to God with my whole Heart—never untill now had I a sense of the privilage we are allowed in love—[starting?] with God—This act of soul left my mind [with] a great calm and steady trust in God—a few days after this one Eve in talking of the glorious state my dear departed Husband must be in, my soul was carried out in such longing desires after this glorious state that I was forced to retire from the Famaly to conceal my joy. When alone I was so transported and my soul carried out in such Eager desires after Perfection and the full injoyment of God and to serve him uninterruptedly that I think my Nature could not have borne much more—I think dear Sir I had that Night a foretaste of Heaven—this frame continued in some good degree the whole Night. I slept but little, and when I did my Dreams were all of Heavenly and divine things—Frequently [since] I have felt the same in kind tho' not in degree. This was about the time that God called me to give up my Child—Thus a kind and gracious God h[as] been with me in six Troubles and in seven.

But O Sir what cause of deep Humiliation [and] abasement of soul have I on account of remaining Corruption which I see working continually, especually Pride—O how many shapes does Pride Cloak it self in—Satan is also bang shoting hi[s] Dar[ts]. [B]ut blessed be God those temptations of his that used to overthro' me, as yet hant touched me—I will just hint at one or two if I ant two Tedious in length. When I was about to renew my Covenant with God it seemed as if one spoak it to me and said tis better that you should not renew it then to Break it when you have. What a dreadfull thing will it be if you dont keep it—My reply was I did not do it in my own strength. Then the temptation would return, how do you know that God will help you keep it—but it did not shake me in the least—O to be delivered from the power of Satan as well as sin! I cant help hopeing the time is near—God is sertainly fiting me for himself, and when I think it will be soon that I shall be called hence the thought is transporting.

I am affraid I have tired out your patience and will begge leve only to add my need of the ernest praires of my Dear and Honored parents and all good people that I may [n]ot at last be a castaway, but that God would con[st]antly grant me new supplies of divine grace—I am Tenderly concernd for my dear Brother Timo' but I hope his sickness will not be unto Death but for the Glory [o]f God—Pleas to give my duty to my Honored Mother.

Love to all my Brothers and Sisters.

I am Honored and dear Sir with the greatest respect your affectionate and Dutifull Daughter—E. Burr

---

Jonathan Edwards's warm response to his daughter's letter of November 2, 1757, followed quickly. In it Jonathan also referred to the College trustees' request that he replace Aaron Burr as the College's president and the deliberations of a ministerial council that winter to consider whether he should be relieved of his Stockbridge responsibilities. The original of this letter is located in the Congregational Library of the American Congregational Association, Boston.

Stockbridge Novem. 20. 1757.

Dear Daughter,

I thank you for your most comfortable Letter; but more especially would I thank God that has granted you such things to write. How good and kind is your heavenly Father! How do the Bowels of his tender Love and Compassion appear, while he is correcting you by so great a shake of his Head! Indeed, he is a faithful God; he will remember his Covenant forever; and never will fail them that trust in him. But don't be surprized, or think some strange thing has happen'd to you, if after this Light, Clouds of Darkness should return. Perpetual sunshine is not usual in this World, even to Gods true saints. But I hope, if God should hide his Face in some Respect, even this will be in Faithfulness to you, purify you, and fit you for yet further and better Light.

As to removing to Princeton, to take on me the office of President I have agreed with the Church here to refer it to a Council of ministers, to sit here Decem. 21, to determine whether it be my duty. Mr. Tennent can inform you more of the matter. I with this, inclose a Letter to him, which I desire may be delivered to him as soon as possible. I have wrote more particularly about the Council in my Letter to the Trustees, directed to Mr. Stockton; which Mr. Tennent will see.[1] I know I cant live at Princeton, as a President

1. William Tennent II and Richard Stockton (see note 8, Letter No. 10, and note 3, Letter No. 1, above) were both trustees of the College at this time.

must, on the salary they offer—yet I have left that matter to their Generosity—I shall have no money wherewith to furnish the House. I hope Mr. Tennent will exert himself to get a full Trustees meeting, to settle College affairs. I shall not be willing to come thither, till that is well done. If the Trustees don't sent me an Account of their doings immediately by the Post to Claverack, I wish you would do it and direct your Letter to be left with Capt. Jeremiah Hoghoboom. I should be glad, on some Account, to have the Letter before the Council. What the Council will do, I cant tell. I shall endeavour as fairly and justly as possible to lay the Matter before 'em, with every material Circumstance. Deacon Woodbridge is a cunning man, and an eloquent speaker; he will strive to his utmost to influence the Council by his Representations, and perhaps by influencing the Indians to make such Representations before the Council as will tend to perswade them that its best for me to stay. And their judgment must determine the matter. Not only has Mr. Woodbridge and others a Friendship for me, and liking to my Ministry, but it is greatly against their temporal Interest for me to leave them.[2]

As to Lucy's coming Home, her mother will greatly need her, especially if we remove in the spring. But yet, whether your circumstances don't much more loudly call for her continuance there, must be left with you and her. She must judge whether she can come consistently with her Health and comfort at such a season of the year. If she comes, let her buy me a staff, and ask advice, and get a good one, or none. Mr. Effelsteen has promised her a good Horse and side saddle, and his son to wait on her to Stockbridge. And I suppose Mr. Fonda can let her have a Horse and side saddle to Mr. Effelsteen's.

If you think of selling Harry your mother desires you not to sell him, without letting her know it.

Timmy is considerably better, tho' yet very weak. We all unite

2. Timothy Woodbridge, son of Jemima Eliot and Timothy Woodbridge, was deacon of the Stockbridge church and Superintendent of Indian Affairs. He was the brother of Joseph Woodbridge (see note 3, Letter No. 22, above) and the husband of Abigail Day Woodbridge. Jones, *Stockbridge*, pp. 134–37.

in Love to you, Lucy and your Children. Your mother is very willing to leave Lucy's coming away wholly to you and her,

I am
your most tender and affectionate Father
Jonathan Edwards.

Esther Burr wrote this letter to William Hogg, a Scottish benefactor of the College. Here again, her main concern is her husband's death. (AND)

Decr. 22. 1757.

Honored Sir

I flatter my self I shall not be thought impertinent by a gentleman of your Carracter if I acknowledge in a few lines the receipt of your Letter dated in August to my late dear Husband which fell into my hands near three months after he was beyound the reach of all mortal things. The affectionate regard you express for one that was dearer to me then my own life was extreamly affecting ⟨ . . . ⟩, nor can I forgive my self if I neglect to acknowledge it in terms of the greatest respect—You Sir had a large share with me in the dear good Mans Heart which he often expressed with the warmest affection—I thought it might not be improper to lay your Letter before the Trustees as they were then convened and it cheifly concerned the College and then I sent to my Honored Father the Revd Mr Edwards who is Chosen to succed my dear companion which I hope will be gratefull to the friends of this College in Scotland—I here inclose you Sir the last attempt my dear Husband made to serve God in publick and do good to his fellow Creatures, a sermon that he preached at the funeral of our late Excellent Governor[1]—[you] will not think strang of its imperfections when I tell you that all he wrote on the subject was done one afternoon and eve when he had a fit of the Intermiting Fever on him and the whole night after was irrational.

Give me leve to beg an interst in your praires at the throne of Grace for a poor disconsolate Widdow and two fatherless Orphans— Pleas to Present with great respect my kindest regard to your Lady and Daughters.

1. Aaron Burr, *A Servant of God dismissed from Labour to Rest. A Funeral Sermon . . . Preached at the Interment of his late Excellency Jonathan Belcher, Esq.; Governor of New-Jersey, who died at Elizabeth-Town on August 31, 1757* (New York, 1757).

I am Honored Sir with the highest Esteem in terms of the greatest respect.

Your most obliged
Humble servant
E. Burr

P.S. Pleas to present one of the sermons with one of Mr Livingstons Elogiums to Mr. Erskine with my most respectfull Compliments.[2] I hope he will remember the Widdow and Fatherless.

In a letter to an unidentified recipient, Esther Burr described her attainment of a degree of resignation concerning her husband's death. (AND)

Princeton Jan 2. 1758.

Sir

Your most agreable Letter of Condolence came safe to hand for which I return my most hearty thanks—it gave me inexpressable pleasure and at the same time afresh set open all the avenues of Greif and again Probs the deep Wound Death has given me—My loss—shall I attempt to say how great my loss is! God only can know and to him would I carry my Complaint! Indeed Sir I have lost all that was or could be desireable in a Creature! I have lost all that ever I sat my Heart on in this World! I need not inlarge on ⟨ . . . ⟩ the innumurable amiable quallities of my late dear to one that was so well acquainted with him as you was, however pleasing it is to me to dwell on them.

Had not God have supported me by these considerations first by shewing the right he has to his own Creatures and to dispose of them when and in what manner he pleases and secondly by innabling me to follow him beyound the Grave into the Eternal World and there viewing of him in unspeakable glory and happyness freed from all sin and sorrow, I should long before this have been sunk amongst the dead and covered with the Clods of the vally. God has wise ends

---

2. William Livingston's eulogy was entitled *A Funeral Elogium on the Rev. Mr. Aaron Burr, Late President of the College of New-Jersey* (New York, 1757). John Erskine of Edinburgh, Scotland, was a benefactor of the College of New Jersey. A Presbyterian minister, he filled a number of small pulpits near Edinburgh before becoming pastor of New Greyfriars in Edinburgh in 1758. *DNB* 6:850–51.

in all that he doth. These things dont [come] by chance. [I] rejoice that I am in the hands of such a God.

My Brother is not here but I have sent your Sons Chest to Mr ———— with a line to desire him to take petecular care of it and here inclose your Sons accts since May 7 last. Most of these accts I had received and paid before I received your Letter as I had been informed he was not to return—it gives me great pleasure that I have it in my power to do the least service for you—if you would pleas to deliver the money to Miss Prince who will come here soon in the spring I shall be further obliged to you—I hear inclose you a sermon preached at Governor Belchers Funeral, the last attempt that ever my dear Husband made to serve God and do good to his fellow Mortals—I need not apoligize for its imperfections when you have read the prefeas and especually when I tell you that all that was wrote was part of one afternoon when he had a violent fever on him. Also an elogium, your acceptance of which will greatly oblige me.

In this letter of April 3, 1758, to her widowed daughter Esther, Sarah Edwards shared her grief at the death of Jonathan Edwards. Seventeen-year-old Susanna Edwards added her own note, which described Jonathan Edwards's leave-taking from Stockbridge that winter when he went to Princeton to assume the College presidency. As Esther died on April 7, she probably never read this letter. (AND)

O my very Dear Child

What shall I say. A holy and Good God heas cover'd us with Dark Cloud. O that we may all kiss the rod and Lay our hands on our mouthes. The Lord heas Done it. He heas made me adore his goodness that we had him so Long. But my God Lives and he heas my heart. O what A Legacy my Husband and your Father heas Left us. We are all given to God and their I am and Love to be.

                                                              Sarah Edwards

Dear Sister

My Mother wrote this with a great deal of pain in her neek [*neck*] which disennbled [*disenabled*] her from writeing any more. She thoughtt you would be glad of these few lines from her own hand.

O Sister how many Calls have we won [*one*] uppon the back of annother. O I beg your Praiers that we that are yong in this fammely might be awokend and stir up to Call more ernest uppon God that he would be our father and frind forever.

My father took leve of all his people and fammely as affectionately as if he knew he should not com again. He preached from those words We have no Continnuing City therefore let us seke own [*one*] to com. The Chapter that [*he*] red was Acts the 20. O how proper. What could he don more—When he had got out of dooers he tirn'd about. I commit you all to god said he. I doubt not but god will tak a farherly [*fatherly*] Care of us if we dont forfit it.

So I rest your ever Affecttionate and simpethiseing
Sister
Susanna Edwards

Stockbridge Aprel 3d 1758

Sarah Edwards Parsons wrote the following letter to Mary Dwight. In it she struggled to resign herself to the deaths of her father on March 22 and her sister Esther on April 7. (AND)

Stockbridge April 18th 1758

Dr Sister

I received your kind Letter by my Husband for which return you my hearty thanks—but what or how to write or speak I know not. Last Saturday we had another Expre[ss] from Princeton which brought us the sorrowful Tidings that Dear Sister Burr was dead and buried yesterday week and no doubt have join'd the Company of our dear dear Friends lately deceased ⟨ . . . ⟩ who have all got safe home to their heavenly Fathers House, are *come to the New Jerusalem the City of the living God and to innummerable Company of Angels, and to Jesus the Mediator of the new Covenant and to God the judge of all, and to the spirits of just Men made perfect*—O how loud the call to us that survive ⟨ . . . ⟩ of this Family, be ye also ready. How much does it concern [*us*] to be as servants with their Loins girt and their Lamps trimmed and burning waiting for the coming of their Lord, now we are so plainly taught not only in Gods word but by his Providence, that we know not what hour our Lord will come—God is now Chastizing us. May he not only Correct but teach us what he would have [*us*] to do. We are now loudly called upon to search our hearts and try our ways and turn our feet into God['s] testimonies—Sister I hope you are in a much better [way] under these tryals than I am. I find I'm far from being in such a tender Humble frame as I ought to be in—It is what has lain with great weight on my Heart and has ever since the Moment I heard of my Fathers death that Gods dealings might be sanctified. Oh! my heart [trem]bles at the thought of disposing [these Chastizings] of the Lord. God grant these Corrections may be in Covenant love and faithfullness.

The residue of the spirit is with God. May we all cry mightily that his gracious Presence and [. . .] may not be buried with our Friends, but that he would grant that a double portion of the spirit of Christ that was in them might rest on us but in order to [do] this as you observe we had need to [Give] our selves to every duty.

My Brother Timo' set out this Day from here to go to Princeton. I cant but feel much Concerned about him but twas judg[ed] by all his call was clear—poor Lucy, Im grievd for her. May she get much spiritual liquor in this Furnace of affliction—and oh the Dear Little babes, my heart overflows with Pity and Compassion towards them. Timo expects to bring them up with him but is not Certain. Sister Burr made a Will but we dont know the Contents as to that Matter fully—Mr Cummins was to Preach her Funeral Sermon upon her desire—she died of an acute Feavour, by Lucys account was much like the Feavour that Carried my Sister Jerusha out of the World, lived but just a Week after she was taken, apprehended she should die from her being first taken. Her illness appeared not at all threatening till Tuesday (she was taken on Friday Night). She was then taken with a violent Headake and soon delirious and so remained till she died on Friday the 7 Instant—Oh how fast has she been ripening for that world she is now gone. What amercy that God should take those out of [. . .] that were ready to die and is warning us hereby and yet giving further opportunity to prepare. May we have hearts to improve the same.

My Mother and Sisters and Brothers join with me in kind [love] to you and Brother and your Little ones.

From your very affectionate and Sympathizing
Sister
Sarah Parsons

P.S. Should be very glad if you'd get me at Hez Wrights 3 yards and ½ of good Cypress and ⟨ . . . ⟩ a scain of black silk. There was an unhappy Mistake about the silk that was carried down. Please to send them by the first safe conveyance. I return you thanks for the Apples you sent me.

Your [. . .] S.P.

Sarah Prince's Eulogy
to Esther Burr

This last document is Sarah Prince's April 21, 1758, entry in her private book of meditations. She wrote these words, which expressed her deepest feelings for her friend, shortly after she heard of Esther's death. (BPL)

April 21. 1758

"GOD will have no Rival in the heart which he sanctifies for himself "

God in Holy but awfull severity has Again struck at one of My Principle springs of Earthly Comfort. In taking from me the Beloved of my heart, my dearest Friend Mrs Burr—This is the heaviest Affliction next to the Death of My dear Sister *Mercy* I ever met with. My whole Prospects in this World are now Changed. My whole dependance for Comfort in this World gone: she was dear to me as the Apple of my Eye—she knew and felt all my Griefs. She laid out herself for my good and was ever assidously studying it. The God of Nature had furnished her with all that I desir'd in a Friend— her Natural Powers were superior to most Women, her knowledge was extensive of Men and Things, her Accomplishments fine—her Prudence forethought and sagacity wonderfull—her Modesty rare— In Friendly Quallity none Exceeded her—she was made for a Refin'd Friend. How Faithfull? how sincere? how Open hearted? how Tender how carefull how disinterested—And *she was mine!* O the tenderness which tied our hearts!—O the Comfort I have Enjoy'd in her for allmost 7. years[!] O the Pleasant days and nights we have spent in opening our whole souls and pouring them into Each others breasts! O the dear Prudent Advice she gave me under all my difficulties— O the Pleasure of seeing hearing loving Writing Conversing thinking we took in Each other. O the Lovely Pattern she set me—The Grace appearing in her Exalted her above all—a bright Example of Personal and Relative social and Divine Duties—A Dutifull Affectionate Respectfull Obedient Tender Daughter and Wife—The Tender yet discreet and wise Mother and Mistress—The every way loving and lovely Sister and Friend—A Pattern of Meekness Patience and sub-mission under heavy trials—The Mortified Humble self denied lively

307

Christian—Generous Affable Courteous and Kind to all—But—she is gone! Fled this World forever. Tired, she longed for rest—dead to this world, she Prayed and panted and Agonised for a Better and with her went allmost *the All* in which I had sum'd up my Earthly Good! O Painfull seperation! O Desolate World, how Barren art thou *now to me!* A Land of Darkness and a vale of Tears and no ⟨ . . . ⟩ lightsome ray is left me—My Earthly joy is gone! Not only so but My God hides his Face! Can't see Love in this dispensation! All seems anger yea Wrath to me! What shall I do. Whither shall I turn, Not to Creatures for there is none to comfort me! And I do not find Comfort from God—O Wretched Me. God Points his Arrows at me and I'm ready to say My Way is hid from the Lord. My judgement is passed over from My God and that he has set me as a Mark for his Arrows! I'm ready to sink and I cant find my wonted Comfort! O how shall I drag thro' Life—If God supports not, I shall inevitably sink. ⟨ . . . ⟩ [A] Great part of my atachment to this World is gone. O! were I ready I wou'd gladly wellcome the kind summons to follow my dear Beloved into the Valley of DEATH. Had I the Evidence I want of a title to Glory, joyfully wou'd quit Earth and all that Earthly minds admire. I want to lay low at the Foot of God and resign to him. I chuse to live at loose from the World, and live only on him and have done with Idols and get prepared for Heaven and get more intimate and [Dare?] Acquaintance with Him, the all *in all*. Lord Grant these Mercies for thy Sons sake. AMEN.

INDEX

Academies, female, 31
Adams, Amos, 284 and *n*
Alexander, James, 193 and *n*, 218*n*
Allen, Timothy, 72 and *n*, 76
Anglicans, 186*n*
Apprenticeship, 30–31, 67*n*, 120*n*, 182
Army training, 55, 107

Badger, Jonathan, 57 and *n*, 100, 198, 204, 291 and *n*
Badger, Stephen, 283, 284*n*
Baldwin, Moses, 248 and *n*
Banks, James, 82*n*, 110
Banks, Mary Ogden, 77*n*, 82*n*, 110
Banks, Mary (Polly), 82 and *n*, 129, 241 and *n*, 292 and *n*
Bartlet, Phebe, 21 and *n*
Belcher, Abigail Allen, 177*n*, 202 and *n*
Belcher, Jonathan, 17, 52*n*, 55 and *n*, 72, 105, 106*n*, 110, 120, 139, 144, 152, 176 and *n*, 179, 180, 280; death of, 139*n*, 273, 274, 299 and *n*
Belcher, Jonathan, Jr., 176*n*, 179, 202*n*
Belcher, Mary Louisa Teal, 52 and *n*, 72, 110, 113, 139, 144, 150, 152, 176, 179, 180, 181, 198, 205, 230
Bellamy, Joseph, 63 and *n*, 74, 126, 132, 143 and *n*
Boat travel, 75, 101, 225, 226, 227–28; Newark-New York City, 73 and *n*, 75, 126, 217–18. *See also* Travel
Boston, 47, 66 and *n*, 85, 88, 101, 120, 213
Bostwick, David, 132 and *n*, 141, 143

and *n*, 154, 157, 163, 164, 174, 209, 242
Boudinot, Annis, 17, 36, 38 and *n*, 236 and *n*, 243 and *n*, 248, 249–50, 256–57, 273
Bourgeois values: growth of, 31 and *n*, 41–42
Braddock, Major General Edward, 136 and *n*, 137, 140, 141, 142 and *n*, 152–53*n*
Bradley, Kitty, 75 and *n*, 109, 126, 196, 241 and *n*, 267, 292
Bradstreet, Anne, 21, 23, 35*n*
Brainerd, David, 54*n*, 258 and *n*
Brainerd, Experience Lyon, 17, 54*n*, 127 and *n*, 129, 134, 135 and *n*, 142, 165–66, 179, 185, 267, 288 and *n*
Brainerd, John, 54 and *n*, 99, 100, 122, 127, 135*n*, 172–73, 185, 207,208–09, 258 and *n*; ministerial duties of, 100, 124–25, 128, 131, 133, 137, 139, 145, 148–49, 163, 166–67, 198, 208–09
Brainerd, Mary, 135 and *n*
Brainerd, Sophia, 99 and *n*, 288 and *n*
Breastfeeding, 192; weaning, 29, 258; wet-nursing, 25, 214 and *n*. *See also* Child care and raising
Breeze, Elizabeth Anderson, 74, 75 and *n*, 83
Bromfield, Abigail Coney, 209–10 and *n*
Browne, — , 58 and *n*, 92, 101, 124, 125, 159, 183, 194, 201, 212
Browne, Isaac, 58*n*, 72, 92, 125, 134, 159, 183, 212

13, 106, 288 and *n;* French and Indian War in, 56 and *n*
Noyes, Abigail Pierpont, 140 and *n*
Nursing the sick, 14, 28, 51, 52, 53,
95, 144, 146; children, 106, 107,
114, 130 and *n,* 133, 162, 228–29,
237–38, 272; visiting the sick, 28,
51, 52, 53, 57, 111, 129, 143, 179,
208, 267. *See also* Illness and injury

Ogden, Abigail, 66*n,* 78 and *n,* 79
Ogden, Abraham, 251 and *n*
Ogden, Catharine, 85*n,* 91 and *n*
Ogden, Colonel Josiah, 77 and *n,* 82*n,*
85*n,* 91 and *n,* 100
Ogden, David, 66*n,* 77*n,* 85*n,* 91 and
n, 108 and *n,* 172, 186 and *n,* 251
and *n*
Ogden, Elizabeth Charlotte Thébaut,
85 and *n*
Ogden, Gertrude Gouverneur, 91*n,* 177,
186 and *n,* 188
Ogden, Hannah Sayer, 66 and *n,* 78 and
n, 85 and *n*
Ogden, Isaac, 251 and *n*
Ogden, John, 66*n,* 78*n,* 79
Ogden, Josiah, 251 and *n*
Ogden, Mary Banks, 77*n,* 85 and *n*
Old South Church, Boston, 15, 54*n,*
90*n,* 106*n,* 211*n,* 251*n,* 284 and *n*
Oliver, Andrew, 106 and *n,* 107, 110,
144 and *n,* 149–50, 199*n,* 260
Oliver, Mary Sanford, 106*n,* 144 and
n, 149–50, 260, 262
Oliver, Peter, 199 and *n,* 270
Osborne, Elizabeth (Betty) Burr. *See*
Burr, Elizabeth (Betty)
Overwork, 11, 17, 24; religious sig-
nificance of, 32–33

Parsons, Elihu, 289 and *n*
Parsons, Esther, 290 and *n*
Parsons, Sarah Edwards, 25, 289*n;* cor-
respondence with Mary Edwards
Dwight, 302–04

Pemberton, Catharine, 47 and *n*
Pemberton, Ebenezer, 47 and *n,* 64*n,*
69, 153, 154, 156, 271
Philadelphia, 18, 85, 88 and *n,* 117,
119–22, 187
Philadelphia Synod, 14, 154
Physicians, 105 and *n,* 133 and *n,* 279,
286
Pierpont, James, 7
Pierson, John, 56 and *n*
Plays, 83, 121
Poetry, women's, 62 and *n,* 73*n,* 80 and
n, 113, 128–29, 236 and *n,* 249–50,
256–57. *See also names of poets*
Pomeroy, Benjamin, 127 and *n*
Pope, Alexander, 257 and *n; Pastorals,*
121 and *n*
Porter, Ezekiel, 133 and *n*
Potter, Hannah, 192 and *n,* 201, 204
and *n*
Potter, Nathaniel, 192 and *n,* 201, 204,
205–06, 207–08
Powels, "Cousen Jonne," 126, 194
Pownall, Thomas, 183 and *n,* 213
and *n*
Prayer groups, 36, 90*n*
Pregnancy, 14, 29, 37, 166 and *n,* 175
and *n,* 180 and *n,* 181 and *n,* 287–
88 and *n. See also* Childbirth; Lying-
in
Prentice, Thomas, 109 and *n,* 190 and
n
Presbyterian Church, First of New York,
46*n,* 47*n,* 71*n,* 74*n,* 90*n,* 117*n,* 132*n,*
139*n;* internal disputes, *see*
Presbyterianism
Presbyterianism: Middle Colonies
schism, 14 and *n;* New York disputes, 63–64 and *n,* 132*n,* 143 and
n—"women popes," 74, 75 and *n*
Prince, Deborah Denny, 54*n,* 102 and
n
Prince, Mercy, 54*n,* 282 and *n*
Prince, Sarah, 3 and *n,* 13, 54*n;* correspondence with Aaron Burr, 279–

172n; funds, 86 and n, 96 and n; Lake George battles, 151 and n, 168, 271n, 272; Massachusetts, 56 and n, 59, 60–61, 134, 135, 142, 172n, 220–21, 271; New Jersey, 172n, 174, 177; New York, 16, 151 and n, 168, 172n, 271n, 272; Pennsylvania, 16, 172n; 1755 defeat of Braddock's army, 136 and n, 137, 140, 141, 151n; 1756 capture of Oswego forts, 220 and n, 222; reluctant local support for, 86 and n, 171–72 and n. See also Indians, Northampton, Stockbridge

Sewall, Joseph, 284 and n

Shippen, John (Jackey), 120n, 247 and n

Shippen, Susannah (Sukey), 27, 30, 61n, 120n, 139 and n, 170, 177 and n, 182, 186, 191, 274

Shippen, Susannah Harrison, 120n

Shippen, William, 7n, 18, 120 and n, 170, 193, 247

Shirley, William, 86n, 142 and n, 183 and n, 184, 213 and n

Sick: nursing of. See Nursing the sick

Sickness. See Illness and injury

Sisterhood, 33–40, 62–63, 184; death and, 53–54, 110, 118, 129, 307–08; dependence on, 118, 307; equal intellectual exchange in, 37, 39, 41; honesty in, 59; male criticism of, 257; secrecy in, 50–51, 167–68 and n; spiritual significance of, 34–38, 41, 50–51, 92, 112, 124, 129, 235, 308

Slaves or servants, 5, 25, 27, 104, 109, 192, 213. See also names of slaves or servants

Smith, Ann (Nancy), 74 and n, 75, 126. See also Hait, Ann Smith

Smith, Caleb, 50n, 53 and n, 54, 77n, 82, 93, 99, 109, 150

Smith, James, 242 and n, 248 and n

Smith, John, 71 and n, 76

Smith, Martha Dickinson, 17, 50 and

n, 52n, 55, 135, 154, 164 and n, 210

Smith, Mary Bryant, 139n, 157, 161, 214, 215, 268

Smith, Mary Harrison, 120 and n

Smith, Robert, 91 and n, 120n

Smith, Samuel, 120 and n

Smith, William Peartree (Peter), 139 and n, 153, 157, 161, 174, 214, 269

Social duties and issues, 3n, 5, 24, 27–28, 31; as recreation, 28, 71; religious attitudes in, 10–12, 17, 20 and n, 28, 31–38, 41–42, 57, 61, 79, 101, 104–05, 138, 143, 244; resentment toward, 32–33, 34, 37, 40, 59, 61, 68, 70, 91–92, 93, 95, 155, 180, 192, 214, 216, 268. See also Entertaining; Frolics; Visits, visiting

Spencer, Elihu, 91 and n, 99, 102 and n, 113, 115, 116–17, 122, 130, 139, 172, 242 and n, 246, 258

Spencer, Joanna Eaton, 91n, 102 and n, 114, 130 and n, 137

Sproat, James, 77 and n, 78

Standley, Susannah Chevalier, 121 and n

Stockbridge, 18, 134, 200n, 201 and n, 291 and n, 298 and n; Edwards family in, 13, 16, 18, 106; Indian mission in, 49n, 298; Seven Years' War, 16, 56 and n, 59, 60–61, 134, 135, 142, 222, 271

Stockton, Abigail Phillips, 236n, 242 and n

Stockton, John, 236n, 242 and n, 274

Stockton, Richard, 236n, 297 and n

Stoddard, Esther Warham Mather, 6

Stoddard, Solomon, 6

Stowe, Harriet Beecher, 23, 284n

Sukey (Sue) — (slave or servant), 27, 61 and n, 76, 114, 138 and n

Tennent, Catharine Van Brugh, 71 and n, 72

318 Index